GOD USES THE
FOOLISH TO
CONFUSE THE WISE

Reverend Dr. Eugene Edwards

Publisher's Name: Reverend Eugene Edwards

ISBN: 978-1-968442-44-6

God Uses the Foolish to Confuse the Wise *By Reverend Dr. Eugene Edwards*

God's greatest works often come through the most unexpected people.

This bold and timely book reveals how, throughout history, God has used the weak, the outcast, and the unlikely to fulfill His purpose and shake nations. From biblical heroes to modern-day movements, what the world calls foolish, God uses to display His power.

In these last days, *God Uses the Foolish to Confuse the Wise* challenges the Church to rise, repent, and trust God's higher wisdom. If you have ever felt unqualified or overlooked, this message is for you.

Cover Design Note:

The cover image, featuring an ancient scroll resting on rugged stone, was carefully chosen to reflect the central message of this book: that God's wisdom is often revealed in the most unexpected places and through the most unlikely people. The rocky terrain represents the harsh realities and challenges of life, while the scroll symbolizes divine truth, purpose, and eternal wisdom.

This design was chosen by my daughter, **Mrs. Kelysha Christians**, after carefully reviewing several options. Her discerning eye and spiritual insight captured the essence of this message beautifully: *God uses the foolish things of the world to confound the wise.*

Cover Design by: Mrs. Kelysha Christians

Memoir Dedication

In Loving Memory of My Spiritual Mentors and Trailblazers of the Faith

"Remember your leaders, those who spoke to you the word of God. Consider the outcome of their way of life and imitate their faith."
—Hebrews 13:7 (ESV)

 Reverend Dr. Rosa E. Lee

Former District Superintendent, Leeward/Virgin Islands Church of the Nazarene, Pastor, Beacon-Light Church of the Nazarene, Antigua, West Indies

Rev. Dr. Rosa E. Lee

With a voice full of wisdom and a heart anchored in holiness, Reverend Dr. Rosa E. Lee stood as a beacon of light not just to Antigua and the Caribbean but to every life she encountered. A spiritual mother, mentor, and visionary, she poured deeply into my life and walk with Christ.

Her prayers lifted me through valleys. Her counsel sharpened my calling. Her unwavering belief in God's power to transform lives helped shape the very foundation of *Love from a Distance* and *God.*

Uses the Foolish to Confuse the Wise. Her life was the gospel in action—she lived what she preached.

To her memory, I owe gratitude that cannot be measured. I carry forward her legacy with every word I write and every truth I speak in Jesus' name.

"God uses those who love deeply, serve humbly, and pray without ceasing." – Rev. Dr. Rosa E. Lee.

Reverend Joseph Bentham

Former District Superintendent, New Zealand Church of the Nazarene, Pastor, Clapham Junction Church of the Nazarene, London

 Rev. Joseph Bentham

Rev. Joseph Bentham was a man of profound humility, Spirit-filled wisdom, and apostolic vision. As a spiritual father to me, his teachings grounded my theology while his life example inspired me to remain faithful in seasons of testing and triumph.

He spoke truth with boldness and walked in deep compassion—both a preacher of righteousness and a champion of grace. From the bustling streets of London to the mission fields abroad, his commitment to seeing the Church restored and revived never wavered.

His life planted seeds in my heart that God watered through the pages of these books. *God Uses the Foolish to Confuse the Wise* is

Especially born from the lessons he imparted, reminding me that God's power is made perfect in weakness, and His wisdom often flows through the unexpected.

"If you want to see God's glory, follow the narrow road—even when you're walking alone." –

Rev. Joseph Bentham.

Their Legacy Lives On

To Rev. Dr. Rosa E. Lee and Rev. Joseph Bentham:
You were more than mentors—you were living epistles. You carried the fire of revival in your bones and the wisdom of heaven in your speech. Thank you for not just teaching me, but for modeling a life surrendered to God.

These books are dedicated to your memory.
Your impact lives on through every reader, every page, and every soul that encounters the love and truth of Jesus Christ through these writings.

I pray that I and those who come after me may continue the work you began with integrity, faith, and courage.

With eternal gratitude and love,
Rev. Dr. Eugene Edwards
Author of Love from a Distance
And God Uses the Foolish to Confuse the Wise

Author's Note

Thank you for picking up this book. I hope that as you read these pages, you will be encouraged and challenged to see the times we live in through God's eyes—eyes that look beyond the surface and into the heart of history and humanity. This book was born out of a desire to understand how God works through unexpected leaders and events, especially in our contemporary political and spiritual landscape.

I do not write to promote any political agenda or endorse any individual, but to point readers toward a deeper spiritual perspective: that God is sovereign over all things, even when the world seems chaotic or confusing. He uses what appears foolish or broken to fulfill His divine purposes and to awaken his church to repentance, unity, and faithful witness.

My prayer is that this book will strengthen your faith, expand your spiritual discernment, and inspire you to live with hope and wisdom as we await the return of our Lord Jesus Christ.

May God bless you richly on this journey.

— Reverend Dr. Eugene Edwards

Preface – God Uses the Foolish to Confuse the Wise

This book was born out of a burden placed on my heart by the Spirit of God during a time of great shaking in the world and within the Church. It was not written to display human wisdom or clever theology, but to echo the words of 1 Corinthians 1:27 (NLT): "Instead, God chose things the world considers foolish to shame those who think they are wise. And he chose things that are powerless to shame those who are powerful."

The last few years have been marked by unprecedented political and cultural upheaval. Leaders have risen and fallen with surprising speed. Nations have been shaken by division, fear, and uncertainty. Amid this storm, many believers have asked: "What is God doing? Why is this happening now?"

What you are about to read is not just a collection of biblical stories or modern insights—it is a prophetic cry to a generation that has wandered too far from truth, too confident in self, and too distracted by worldly noise to recognize God's voice. Yet through weak vessels and unexpected messengers, God still speaks.

God Uses the Foolish to Confuse the Wise seeks to answer these questions by returning to scripture's timeless truths about God's sovereignty and His ways of working through the unlikely and the flawed. History reveals that God often raises leaders who shock the world, not as an endorsement of their character but as a divine wake-up call to His people.

In these pages, you will see how God used stammering prophets, flawed leaders, unlikely women, and even animals to carry his

Message. You will learn that God does not need polished perfection to display His power. Instead, He delights in those who are willing, even when the world calls them foolish.

This book is a wake-up call to the Body of Christ and challenges readers to look past personalities and political ideologies and instead focus on the spiritual message behind the moment. It calls the Church to repentance, unity, and Kingdom-minded engagement, reminding us that no election, no leader, and no earthly power escapes God's sovereign plan. The days grow darker; we must understand that God is still using what the world rejects to prepare the Church for Christ's return. I pray that as you read, you will not just gain knowledge, but experience conviction, repentance, and renewal.

Let every page remind you: if God could use a donkey, a shepherd boy, a fisherman, or a widow's last coin, He can use you. His power is made perfect in weakness. May you never again despise your flaws—only surrender them. As you read, my prayer is that you will gain clarity, peace, and purpose. May you be equipped to navigate these challenging times with spiritual wisdom and courage, ready to be a faithful witness to God's truth and love.

Welcome to the journey of awakening.

— Reverend Dr. Eugene Edwards

Dedication and Acknowledgments

Dedication
I dedicate this book to my precious grandchildren. Though they are still in their toddler years and may not yet grasp its message, this book is meant to serve as a spiritual compass, guiding them as they grow, helping them understand the world around them, and anchoring them in the truth of God's Word.

It is my prayer that as they journey through life, they will not be swayed by the deceptive lessons of the world but will walk in the paths of righteousness laid down by their grandparents— paths ordered by God Himself. I passionately believe this book will play a meaningful role in their spiritual development. With the support and love of their parents, who are committed to raising them in the fear and knowledge of the Lord, I trust they will grow up grounded in strong biblical principles and unwavering faith.

Acknowledgements

Primarily, I give all glory and honor to my Heavenly Father, who planted the vision for this book deep within my spirit. In a time when many live in fear and confusion about the direction of the world, God revealed a truth that often goes unnoticed—His divine work continues, even in the silence of spiritual leaders. He led me to 1 Corinthians 1:27 (NLT):

"Instead, God chose things the world considers foolish to shame those who think they are wise.

And He chose things that are powerless to shame those who are powerful. " This Scripture became the foundation for this work and the message I have been called to share.

Thank you, Jesus, for Your sacrifice on the cross and for being my constant reminder of redemption. Thank you to the Holy Spirit, my Comforter and Guide, who leads me into all truth and equips me to speak boldly in these uncertain times.

I also want to express deep gratitude to those who encouraged me and helped bring this book to life through proofreading, wise counsel, and unwavering support. A special thank-you to co-Pastor Latisha Henderson, who graciously wrote the Foreword, and to Pastor Larry Henderson, her husband and my steadfast supporter and pastoral friend.

To my beloved daughter, thank you for designing the cover of both my books and for standing by me, even when you think I am juggling too many things at once. Your creative support and love mean more than words can express. I was especially honored to collaborate with you on an eBook designed to help new believers navigate their spiritual journey, another meaningful project that reflects our shared calling.

To all who walked alongside me on this journey, thank you. Your prayers, encouragement, and faith have helped birth something that I believe will touch lives for generations to come.

About the Author

Reverend Dr. Eugene C. Edwards is a pastor, educator, and spiritual leader with a lifelong passion for inspiring transformation through faith, service, and education. Born on the twin Caribbean islands of Antigua and Barbuda, he is the youngest of four children raised during a time of deep economic hardship and strong communal values. Like many families of that era, he was raised not only by his parents but also with the support of grandparents who played a vital role in his early formation.

From a young age, Dr. Edwards dreamed of becoming a schoolteacher dream fueled by admiration for the discipline, care, and influence of his educators. That passion for teaching never left him, and it later became one of the foundational pillars of his ministry and writing.

At the age of sixteen, a life-changing invitation to a church service introduced him to the life-giving message of Jesus Christ. Captivated by the grace and mercy of God, he surrendered his life to Christ and was soon baptized, marking the beginning of a lifelong journey of faith. At 22, he received the call to full-time ministry—a call he initially wrestled with but ultimately embraced, enrolling in Bible College in Trinidad. There, his calling as a teacher and preacher merged in powerful ways.

Dr. Edwards spent over 32 years in the classroom, shaping the lives of young men and women, many of whom would go on to become lawyers, doctors, teachers, pastors, and community leaders. His impact extended globally through his pastoral work across several countries. In the United Kingdom, he served in the National Health Service (NHS), held a leadership position on a Board of Governors, and co-pastored the Clapham Junction Church of the Nazarene in London.

After migrating to the United States, he joined Duane Dean Behavioral Health Center in Illinois, initially as an Outreach Specialist. He quickly rose to the role of Program Coordinator for the Greater Illinois Violence Prevention Coordinating Council—now known as the Community Response & Engagement Workgroup— where he leads mental health and community healing efforts.

A devoted father and grandfather, Dr. Edwards delights in seeing his two adult children actively engaged in ministry, as well as nurturing the next generation of believers through his family legacy.

About This Book

God Uses the Foolish to Confuse the Wise is a bold and prophetic call to the Church in a time of global upheaval, political unrest, and spiritual apathy. Drawing inspiration from 1 Corinthians 1:27, Dr. Edwards exposes the silence of today's Church and confronts its complacency in the face of injustice, moral decline, and cultural compromise.

This book was written with a deep burden—to awaken the Body of Christ and remind believers that God often uses unexpected voices and ordinary vessels to carry out His extraordinary plans. From biblical prophets to modern messengers, God has always chosen what the world deems foolish to disrupt the wise and bring forth His purposes.

Through enthusiastic teaching, biblical insight, and real-world relevance, Dr. Edwards challenges readers—especially spiritual leaders—to reject religiosity, abandon political idolatry, and rise as authentic witnesses of Jesus Christ. In these pages, the reader will find not only a warning but a divine commission: to reclaim the prophetic voice of the Church, to live out the Gospel with boldness and love, and to prepare for the return of Christ.

This is more than a book; it is a trumpet call to awaken, repent, and respond. In a world desperately in need of hope and truth, God is still speaking through the "foolish" to reveal His wisdom and draw His people back to Himself. This book is also a tribute to his beloved mother, **Doraine Browne**, who, at 92 years old, has lived as a testimony of faith, resilience, and prayer. Her example remains a shining light, reminding us that a godly life leaves an eternal legacy.

Reverend Dr. Eugene C. Edwards,
Servant. Shepherd. Messenger of Hope

Foreword

by Pastor Latisha Henderson, Co-Pastor of Total Deliverance Church of the Nazarene, Aroma Park, IL

In a world that increasingly celebrates human wisdom, power, and self-sufficiency, the message of this book is both a divine interruption and a necessary awakening. *God Uses the Foolish to Confuse the Wise* is not just a collection of biblical reflections—it is a prophetic trumpet sounding in a time of spiritual complacency, political deception, and cultural distraction.

Reverend Dr. Eugene Edwards has penned a timely message birthed in prayer, Scripture, and prophetic insight. With humility and clarity, he reminds us that God has always chosen the unlikely, the overlooked, and even the rejected to accomplish His greatest works. From Noah to Rahab, from David to Mary, from flawed political leaders to stammering prophets—God shows us again and again that He is not limited by human expectations or worldly qualifications.

This book confronts the reader with a sobering truth: everything in this life is temporary. Whether you are a president, a preacher, a parent, or a student, your life is but a vapor. Titles, talents, and treasures will all pass away. What remains is your response to God's call, your readiness for Christ's return, and your willingness to be used—even in your weakness—for His glory.

Each chapter draws on powerful biblical narratives and modern-day parallels, urging us to live with eternity in view. It challenges political leaders to walk in truth, church leaders to remain faithful to the gospel, and everyday believers to surrender fully to God's will. With deep reverence for Scripture and a passion for the

Coming of the Lord, this book invites readers to stop leaning on human understanding and start trusting the divine strategy of God.

Reverend Dr. Edwards does not just inform—he equips. He prepares the Bride of Christ to awaken, to repent, to rise, and to shine in a world drowning in deception. This is not just a book; it is a wake-up call. May every reader who turns its pages be stirred to action, convicted in heart, and transformed by the wisdom of heaven that often appears foolish to the world.

As you read these chapters, may you see yourself in the stories, sense the urgency of the times, and fall deeper in love with the God who still chooses the foolish to confound the wise. For His return is near. May you be found ready.

Co-Pastor Latisha Henderson
Total Deliverance Church of the Nazarene, Kankakee, IL

Commissioning **Prayer for** *God Uses the Foolish to Confuse the Wise*

Righteous Father,

You are the God of unexpected strategies, divine reversals, and holy disruptions. Thank you for the prophetic voice you have given to Reverend Eugene Edwards in *God Uses the Foolish to Confuse the Wise*. This is not a comfortable message, but a convicting one—sent to awaken nations, leaders, churches, and hearts in these final hours.

We pray that this book becomes a trumpet in the hands of the Spirit. Let it break the pride of man, expose deception, and reveal the foolishness of this world compared to the wisdom of God. May it reach political figures, church leaders, and ordinary believers alike, calling each to repentance, readiness, and realignment with Your truth.

Empower Reverend Edwards to remain bold, unshaken, and yielded to Your will. Let this book spark revival, reformation, and reverence for Your sovereignty. May it shake foundations and prepare the Bride for the return of the King.

In Jesus' name, Amen.

Table of Contents

Introduction
A brief overview of how God uses unexpected leaders and
events.
To fulfill His sovereign plan and awaken His Church in the last

Chapter 1: Sovereignty Over Thrones
An exploration of God's supreme authority over all rulers and
kingdoms, reminding believers to trust His control in every political

Chapter 2: The Foolish Vessel, the Divine Message
God often delivers His greatest messages through the most unlikely people.
This chapter highlights how "foolish" vessels—despised, overlooked, or
Underestimated—are entrusted with life-changing revelations. It reminds
Readers that God does not look at outward qualifications but at the

Chapter 3: Pharaoh's Hardened Heart and Heaven's Glory
The Pharaoh's resistance to God's command became a stage for
divine power. This chapter shows how God can use hardened
hearts to display His glory and fulfill His plans. It urges readers

Introduction: When God Shouts Instead of Whispers

"He changes times and seasons; he removes kings and sets up kings." — Daniel 2:21 (ESV)

There comes a moment in history when God ceases to whisper. He moves mountains. He shakes thrones. He speaks so loudly that the entire world stands still—and listens. Today, we find ourselves in such a moment.

When the U.S. President rose to power, some celebrated; others recoiled in shock or outrage. Headlines blazed across every screen, social media erupted in praise or protest, and nations watched, stunned. But beneath the political rhetoric and cultural division lies a deeper reality: this was never merely about the man in the Oval Office. It was—and remains—about the message God is shouting through this season.

The Bible makes clear that no ruler ascends or falls outside God's sovereign purposes. In Daniel's day, King Nebuchadnezzar's heart was hardened so that God's glory might be revealed (Daniel 3). Pharaoh's obstinacy set the stage for Israel's deliverance (Exodus 7–14). Cyrus, a pagan Persian king, became God's chosen instrument to rebuild the Temple in Jerusalem (Ezra 1). Each demonstrates a timeless truth: **God uses the most unlikely, the most flawed, and** sometimes the most frightening vessels to accomplish His will.

A Spiritual Wake-Up Call

When God allows a controversial leader to rise, He is doing more than orchestrating election results. He is shining a light into the darkest corners of our hearts and our communities. He is exposing our idols—political allegiances, cultural comforts, and personal agendas—that we might repent and refocus our trust on Him alone.

- Are we entrusting our security to a candidate or the King of kings?
- Have we mistaken policy victories for spiritual breakthroughs?
- Do we hear Heaven's alarm bell, or have we grown deaf to the still, small voice?

This is not a call to endorse or condemn any person, party, or platform. It is an invitation to ask: **"Lord, what are You saying in this hour?"** When our eyes fix on a man, we miss the providence behind his rise. When our hearts incline to prayer and discernment, we glimpse Heaven's agenda.

Divine Sovereignty in Every Era

The same God who spoke through Nebuchadnezzar and Cyrus is speaking today. He is the One "who removes kings and sets up kings," the Architect of history and the Author of redemption. His wisdom often appears foolish to the world:

"But God has chosen what is foolish in the world to shame the wise… so that no human being might boast in the presence of God." — 1 Corinthians 1:27 29 (ESV)

What looks like chaos is often divine clarity. What looks like folly is often heavenly strategy. As we navigate national upheaval, let us remember:

1. **No public figure catches Heaven off guard.** Every election, every scandal, every sweeping change unfolds under God's watchful eye.

2. **God's voice is heard in two ways: through prophetic warnings and the silence of complacency.** When he shouts, we must listen.
3. Our greatest question isn't "Do I like this leader?" but "What is God doing through this season?"

How to Read This Book

Over the coming chapters, we will:

- **Trace biblical precedents** of flawed leaders used by God for His glory.
- **Unpack the spiritual messages** behind national and cultural shake-ups.
- **Challenge our loyalties**, uprooting political idolatry and false security.
- **Equip you to discern** the voice of Heaven amid the clamor of public opinion.

Each chapter closes with a **Reflection** and a **Prayer**, inviting you to apply these truths, seek God's heart, and stand firm in the wisdom of His upside-down Kingdom.

Reflection

1. Recall a time when a public event or leader shook your world. What did God teach you through that season?
2. In what ways have you allowed politics to shape your identity more than Christ?
3. How can you cultivate ears to hear Heaven's warnings today?

Prayer

Sovereign Lord,
You sit enthroned above every ruler and reign. Forgive me for placing my trust in fallen flesh instead of in Your unshakable throne. Open my eyes to see Your hand at work in this moment.

Give me the courage to speak Your truth, the wisdom to discern Your voice, and the faith to walk in Your Kingdom, regardless of who holds power in Washington.

In Jesus' name, Amen.

Chapter 1: Sovereignty Over Thrones

"He changes times and seasons; He removes kings and sets up kings."
— Daniel 2:21

God often speaks to nations not just through prophets or preachers, but through leaders, righteous or corrupt. The character and direction of national leadership reflect the spiritual state of the

people. Just as Pharaoh's hardness revealed Egypt's pride, and Nebuchadnezzar's fall showed Babylon's arrogance, today's political leaders serve as divine signals. When ungodly rulers rise, it is not always a sign of God's absence, but of His warning. He allows flawed leadership to expose societal idols and awaken His people. This chapter challenges us to stop cursing the leadership and start discerning the message: God is calling the Church to repent, to pray, and to rise as voices of truth in a deceived generation.

In an age intoxicated by human intellect, influence, and innovation, God's wisdom remains scandalously simple—and often misunderstood. As society celebrates the "wise" of this world, the Lord intentionally reveals His truth through means that seem foolish to the proud. This chapter opens with a divine confrontation between man's arrogance and God's eternal wisdom. We see how God confounds the wise with what appears weak or absurd, shaking the very foundations of worldly systems. Church leaders, believers, and skeptics alike are called to lay down their intellectual pride and receive the truth not from a podium of popularity, but from a cross of sacrifice.

God often uses leaders—not just pastors or prophets—to send His warnings to the world. When bad leaders take power or good leaders fall, it's often a sign that something deeper is happening in the spiritual realm. Think of it like a red flag in your life telling you to pay attention. Today, we see leaders making choices that confuse, frighten, or cause division. This is not random chaos— it is a wake-up call. God wants us to notice what is happening, to pray, and to examine our hearts and lives. Are we listening to His warnings or ignoring them?

For teenagers growing up in a world full of mixed messages and broken examples, understanding God's voice amid political noise can be hard. This chapter helps young people see that God's wisdom often comes through imperfect people, so they should not wait for "perfect" leaders or feel helpless. Instead, God invites them to be part of the solution by standing for truth and living with courage and faith in their schools, families, and communities.

Adults, too often, feel overwhelmed or disillusioned by leadership failures. This chapter encourages them to see beyond the surface of politics and to engage with God's bigger picture. Leadership changes can be tools for God to purify the Church, expose hidden sins, and prepare His people for revival. No matter who is in power, God is still faithful—and He wants His Church to be faithful in prayer, repentance, and witness.

For teenagers growing up in a world full of mixed messages and broken examples, understanding God's voice amid political noise can be hard. This chapter helps young people see that God's wisdom often comes through imperfect people, so they should not wait for "perfect" leaders or feel helpless. Instead, God invites them to be part of the solution by standing for truth and living with courage and faith in their schools, families, and communities.

Adults, too often, feel overwhelmed or disillusioned by leadership failures. This chapter encourages them to see beyond the surface of politics and to engage with God's bigger picture. Leadership changes can be tools for God to purify the Church, expose hidden sins, and prepare His people for revival. No matter who is in power, God is still faithful—and He wants His Church to be faithful in prayer, repentance, and witness.

God is Never Surprised

When the world is shaken by the rise of an unexpected leader, many question the process, the politics, or the power. But in Heaven, no one panics. God does not react — He reigns. Every leader, good or evil, righteous, or corrupt, rises under the sovereign eye of God.

Daniel made this clear when he stood before the most powerful man of his time, Nebuchadnezzar, and declared that it is **God** who sets up and removes kings. This is not just a historical truth — it is a divine pattern. It means no election, coup, appointment, or rise to fame happens apart from His permission.

We may see a man's personality or policy; God sees purpose. He uses both righteous kings and pagan rulers to accomplish His will — for correction, for exposure, or fulfillment of prophecy. Whether it is **Pharaoh's pride**, **Cyrus' decree**, or **Nebuchadnezzar's humiliation**, God's hand is always working.

America's Awakening

When the U.S. President rose to power, it wasn't about a man winning an office — it was about Heaven sounding an alarm. For some, he became a hero. For others, a villain. But the deeper question was not, "Do we like him?" It was, **"What is God saying through this leader?"**

We live in a time when God is speaking louder than before. His whispers have become shouts. The shaking of nations is a trumpet blast for the Church to wake up. Political chaos is often a **spiritual wake-up call**. What we interpret as instability, God uses as an invitation to return to Him.

In the last days, God is not silent. He is warning, exposing, and revealing hearts, not to destroy, but to give people a chance to repent.

Prophets of Warning

- Before judgment comes, God always sends a warning:
- Noah preached for 120 years before the flood (Genesis 6–7).
- Jonah warned Nineveh, and the people repented (Jonah 3).
- John the Baptist cried out in the wilderness before Christ came (Matthew 3:13).
- Jesus Himself warned that before His return, there would be deception, division, and a great falling away (Matthew 24; 2 Thessalonians 2:1-4).

God never brings judgment without mercy. His warnings are not born from anger, but from love, to stir repentance before the return of Christ.

Shaking for Salvation

Could it be that the political upheaval, division, and exposure we are seeing in America and across the world are not signs of God's absence, but of His presence? Could the shaking be His hand moving to awaken the Church and call the world to repentance?

God often uses flawed figures to reveal the flaws in us. He uses leaders to stir sleeping people. He uses nations to bring nations to their knees.

Scripture Focus

- **Daniel 2:21** – "He changes times and seasons; he removes kings and sets up kings…"
- **Romans 13:1** – "For there is no authority except from God, and those that exist have been instituted by God."
- **Isaiah 45:17** – God calls Cyrus His "anointed," even though he did not know Him.
- **Amos 3:7** – "Surely the Sovereign Lord does nothing without revealing His plan to His servants the prophets."

Matthew 24:6-12 – Signs of the end: wars, rumors of wars, deception, and betrayal

Can you discern God's hand even when He uses the unqualified? Are you more loyal to a party or the Kingdom of God?

The election of a U.S. President who does not conform to traditional moral or political expectations is not merely coincidental; it represents a divine orchestration. Similar to historical figures such as Nebuchadnezzar of Babylon, Pharaoh of Egypt, and Cyrus of Persia, God employs world leaders—even those deemed ungodly—to fulfill His prophetic purposes. The contentious ascent and influence of American leadership serve as a reflection of how God utilizes what may be perceived as foolish (as articulated in 1 Corinthians 1:27) to bring low the proud and to awaken the indifferent.

When leadership appears morally or spiritually deficient, it is often indicative of God allowing a reflection of the nation's spiritual state. The church is urged not to idolize politicians or to condemn them indiscriminately. Instead, it is imperative to pose the question: "What is God conveying through this leader's rise, conduct, and influence?"

The occurrence of wars, border crises, national unrest, and global disruptions under this administration highlights a spiritual pattern: God is disrupting complacency to call His people back to Him. Throughout history, figures such as Jesus were mocked and misunderstood, much like the prophets were in their time. That which may appear foolish could be delivering a critical spiritual warning. The unrest in the White House parallels a deeper turmoil within the church; are we heeding God's warning, or are we too preoccupied with political discourse?

Chapter 2: The Foolish Vessel, the Divine Message

"But God chose the foolish things of the world to shame the wise; God chose the weak things of the world to shame the strong." — 1 Corinthians 1:27 (NIV)

Nations may plan, governments may legislate, but the Lord sits enthroned above them all. In this chapter, we explore how every nation, from ancient Israel to modern empires, ultimately bows to God's sovereignty. He raises kings and brings them low. He orchestrates global events not by accident, but by divine design. Even in times of war, economic collapse, or political chaos, God is not shaken—He is shifting. The world stage is being set for the fulfillment of prophecy.

Through current events, God is reminding us that He alone rules history. The Church must stop reacting in fear and start recognizing God's supreme hand in the affairs of men.

Noah's obedience stood in stark contrast to a world drunk with sin and self. While others laughed at the absurdity of a man building an ark in the sunshine, God was issuing His final warning before judgment. This chapter parallels Noah's generation with our modern one, full of mocking, moral confusion, and spiritual deafness. But God, in His mercy, is once again preparing a "remnant ark"—a safe place in Christ— while scoffers continue to party on the edge of disaster. The Spirit is urgently calling today's Church to wake up, take heed, and warn others before the rain begins to fall again.

No matter how powerful a country or leader seems, nothing escapes God's control. He is the King over kings and Lord over lords. This means every decision made on the world stage happens under His watchful eye and within His plan. When nations rise and fall, it's not chaos— it's part of a divine story unfolding according to God's perfect timing. Understanding this helps us trust God even when things seem uncertain or scary around us.

For teenagers, who may feel small and powerless in the big world, this truth offers great comfort. It means their lives and actions matter because they are part of God's bigger plan. God isn't distant or disinterested; He is actively working through history, and He invites young people to join Him in prayer, kindness, and standing for justice in their schools and friendships. This chapter encourages them to remember that God's sovereignty means hope, no matter how dark things look.

Adults often worry about the future because of political instability, wars, or social unrest. But this chapter challenges them to see these events through God's lens. It calls them to stop fearing leaders or systems and to focus on God's unchanging power. The Church is called to pray for leaders, seek God's will for the nation, and be salt and light amid confusion. Recognizing God's sovereignty also fuels boldness because the outcome is already in His hands— victory belongs to the Lord.

God's Choice Offends Human Logic

God has a history of choosing people who confuse everyone around them. If man were to choose a vessel for leadership, revival, or deliverance, he would choose someone with pedigree, charisma, and polish. But God often chooses the rejected, the rough-edged, the flawed — the ones who offend our sensibilities.

Why? Because **when the vessel is weak, the message is strong**. When the person seems unworthy, the glory goes to God.

We are reminded in 1 Samuel 16 that while man looks on the outward appearance, **God looks at the heart**. David was overlooked even by his father, yet God anointed him king. In the same way, when flawed modern leaders rise to power, we must ask not, "Why him?" but "What is God doing?"

Samson: Power and Weakness in One Man

One of the clearest examples of a foolish vessel used by God is **Samson**. A Nazarite from birth, he was chosen to begin the deliverance of Israel from the Philistines (Judges 13:5). But Samson's life was a contradiction — strong yet impulsive, chosen yet careless, victorious yet bound by his desires.

Despite his weaknesses, God still used him. Even in Samson's final moment, **blind and broken**, God granted him strength to defeat more Philistines in his death than in his life (Judges 16:30). This was not about Samson's greatness — it was about **God's purpose prevailing** despite Samson's flaws.

Balaam: A Prophet for Hire

In Numbers 22–24, we see another strange vessel: **Balaam**, a pagan prophet hired to curse Israel. Yet God intervened — even speaking through a donkey to get Balaam's attention. And instead of cursing, Balaam ended up blessing Israel repeatedly. Though Balaam's motives were corrupt, **God still used his voice to deliver truth**.

If God can use a donkey and a corrupt prophet, He can use anyone — even a political figure whose character is questionable, whose words offend, or whose past is controversial. **It is not about the worthiness of the vessel; it's about the sovereignty of the Sender.**

The Modern Parallel: The U.S. President

Many were confused by the rise of the U.S. President, not because of his policies alone, but because of his personality. He was loud, divisive, controversial, and unorthodox. Yet in the spiritual realm, his rise exposed deep things in the heart of the Church and the nation:

- False allegiances
- Political idolatry
- Fear, racism, ambition, and apathy
- The hidden divisions among believers

Like Samson or Balaam, his leadership was not about perfection, but **provocation**. God used him as a **mirror** to show us what lies beneath the surface. What we call foolish, **God may have appointed as a megaphone of truth.**

Don't Miss the Message Because of the Messenger

The danger for many believers is that they reject the message because they do not like the messenger. But throughout Scripture, God has used prostitutes, murderers, foreigners, outcasts, and even enemies to accomplish His will.

If you're only looking for polished prophets, you'll miss the raw voices crying in the **wilderness.**

This is why discernment is essential in the last days. We must ask: **"God, are You speaking — even through someone I don't understand or agree with?" "Am I too offended to hear what you are saying?"**

Scripture Focus

- **1 Corinthians 1:27-29** – God uses the foolish, weak, and lowly to shame the wise and strong.
- **Judges 13–16** – Samson's flawed leadership and ultimate purpose
- **Numbers 22–24** – Balaam, the donkey, and prophetic warnings
- **1 Samuel 16:7** – "The Lord does not look at the things people look at… the Lord looks at the heart."
- **John 7:24** – "Stop judging by mere appearances but instead judge correctly."

Will you respond with panic when global systems collapse, or will you engage in prayer, repentance, and discernment? Will you place your trust in that which cannot be shaken?

The current global landscape is undergoing significant upheaval, as economic, governmental, and institutional structures are being challenged to reveal misplaced confidence and redirect hearts toward a higher purpose. Historically, extensive reliance has been placed on political frameworks, financial institutions, and human strategies; however, these systems are being dismantled to illustrate their inability to provide true salvation. Much like the plagues that led to the collapse of Egypt's power (Exodus 7–12), contemporary events such as natural disasters, economic instability, and public distrust signal a similar disruption in today's world.

The COVID-19 pandemic has underscored the vulnerabilities of nations, including the United States, which has often been perceived as invulnerable. Fear, mortality, and uncertainty have laid bare the limitations of medical science and governmental authority.

Scriptural teachings inform us that all that can be shaken will indeed be shaken (Hebrews 12:26- 27). This process of shaking is not intended for destruction but rather serves to realign our dependence on a higher power. The idolization of wealth has been significantly challenged.

Issues such as inflation, food shortages, housing crises, and the spiraling of national debt underscore the fragility of currency and the illusion of economic control. The biblical instance of Babylon, a once-proud empire characterized by wealth and arrogance (Daniel 4), serves as a cautionary tale, as it was humbled in a single night. This prompts the question: Is modern America charting a similar course?

The church, too, has not been spared from this period of upheaval. Mega-ministries, celebrity pastors, and the doctrine of prosperity are being scrutinized, paralleling the divine exposure of false prophets in the Old Testament. This crisis extends beyond politics; it is inherently spiritual. The current challenges catalyze God to call His people back to the foundational principles of His Word and His Spirit. Many individuals are reassessing their confidence in media, political entities, and religious institutions. This is not merely a loss; it represents a divine invitation to reevaluate and renew one's confidence in Christ alone.

Reflection

1. Have I ever dismissed someone because I did not like their style or past?
2. Can I recognize when God is speaking, even if it comes from an unexpected source?
3. What flaws in me might God still want to use for His purpose?

Prayer

Lord of Wisdom,
I confess that I sometimes judge too quickly — by appearance, by tone, or by personal comfort. Open my ears to Your voice, even when it comes in unexpected ways. Teach me not to idolize vessels, but to seek Your Spirit. Raise whomever you choose to bring revival, correction, and repentance — even if it offends my pride. I want to hear from you clearly in these last days.

In Jesus' name, Amen.

Chapter 3: Pharaoh's Hardened Heart and Heaven's Glory

"But I will harden Pharaoh's heart, and though I multiply my signs and wonders in Egypt, he will not listen to you." — Exodus 7:34 (NIV)

God's greatest works often come through the least likely people. From Cyrus, a Persian king who funded the rebuilding of Jerusalem, to the US President, whose presidency stirred spiritual awakening and division alike—God has a way of using outsiders and imperfect vessels for His glory. This chapter examines how divine purpose is never bound by human approval. When the Church prays for revival, God may answer through someone we would not choose. He uses the foolish to confound the wise. We must learn to look past the packaging and discern the purpose. It is time for the Body of Christ to stop rejecting the instruments God is using to fulfill His end-time plan.

Against all odds, a teenage shepherd steps forward—not with armor or strength, but with a sling, a stone, and supernatural faith. David's confrontation with Goliath reveals how God bypasses man's expectations to accomplish His will. In this chapter, God is calling a new generation of "Davids" to rise—those who are dismissed, underestimated, and seen as foolish. As nations tremble under the threats of giants—violence, immorality, corruption—God reminds His Church that victory still comes through those who carry a bold, childlike trust in Him. It is time to stop trembling before giants and start walking in the authority of God's anointing.

God often chooses leaders who seem unlikely or unexpected to carry out His plans. From the Bible's history of unlikely heroes—like Cyrus the Persian king or King David as a young shepherd—to modern examples, God shows that He does not look at the usual qualifications. Instead, He looks at the heart and purpose. When the world rejects or mocks these leaders, God is often using that very rejection to confuse the wise and accomplish His will. This chapter reminds us that God's ways are higher than ours and that He can raise anyone to fulfill His divine purposes.

For teenagers, this can be encouraging because it means you do not have to be the most popular or perfect to be used by God. Even if you feel overlooked or underestimated at school or in your community, God can use your unique gifts and your faithfulness to have an influence. It is a reminder to stay humble and open to God's calling, even if it looks unconventional. God values obedience and trust more than status or ability.

Adults can also be inspired to see that God's leadership isn't based on human approval or strength. This chapter challenges believers to stop limiting God by their expectations and instead pray for God to use whoever He chooses, including people outside the Church or society's norms. It calls Church leaders to be more open and discerning, recognizing that God may be working through people they least expect to bring revival and change in these turbulent times.

God Uses Resistance to Reveal Glory

One of the most astonishing truths in Scripture is that God not only works through cooperative vessels—He also works through resistance. God told Moses in advance that Pharaoh would not listen. God Himself hardened Pharaoh's heart. This was not divine cruelty; it was divine strategy.

God allowed Pharaoh's stubbornness to create the stage for His greatest signs and wonders. It was through resistance that the plagues came. It was through defiance that deliverance was birthed. God's power was put on full display in a land that refused to acknowledge Him.

Hardened for a Holy Purpose

In the eyes of Egypt, the Pharaoh was a god. He held total political and spiritual authority. But God exposed him as a man. By allowing Pharaoh's pride to build to its peak, God orchestrated a dramatic confrontation between Heaven's power and human arrogance.

"But I have raised you for this very purpose, that I might show you my power and that my name might be proclaimed in all the earth." — Exodus 9:16 (NIV)

God raised Pharaoh, not to exalt him, but to expose him.

The Pattern Repeats: Political Arrogance vs. Divine Authority

Pharaoh is not just a historical figure. He is a symbol of what happens when human leaders exalt themselves above God. Throughout history, we have seen this pattern repeated:

- Kings who wage war without wisdom
- Leaders who pass laws contrary to God's Word
- Rulers who demand allegiance while rejecting righteousness

But each time, **God has the final word**.

In the modern age, when a political leader seems to rise in pride, provoke division, or harden hearts, it is tempting to respond with fear or outrage. But Heaven sees further. Could it be that God is allowing arrogance to peak again, not to destroy the Church, but to **deliver it?** Not to exalt a man, but to reveal His glory through the confrontation?

The U.S. President: A Modern Pharaoh?

While some may find it uncomfortable to draw parallels, the principle remains: **God will allow hearts to harden and leaders to rise when it serves His eternal plan.**

The former U.S. President may not be a Pharaoh in the literal sense, but his rise ignited confrontation:

- Confrontation with moral compromise
- Exposure of racism, nationalism, and pride
- The testing of where the Church's allegiance truly lies.

Some hearts grew softer during this time, pressing into prayer, humility, and repentance. Others grew harder, doubling down on political identity over Kingdom values.

As in Egypt, the plague was not just outside the palace — it was also inside the hearts of the people.

The Danger of Misreading the Moment

Pharaoh misread the moment. He saw Moses as a political nuisance rather than a prophetic voice. Many today do the same, dismissing prophetic warnings such as extremism or distraction. But God always sends voices before He sends judgment.

Do not be like Pharaoh. Do not wait until the Red Sea crashes into you to recognize that **God is not to be ignored.** Discern the season. The resistance you see may be **the very means God is using to deliver His people and proclaim His name.**

Scripture Focus
- **Exodus 5–14** – The full account of Pharaoh's resistance and God's judgment
- **Exodus 9:12** – "The Lord hardened Pharaoh's heart..."
- **Romans 9:17 18** – "I raised you... that I might display My power in you..."
- **Psalm 2:1 4** – "Why do the nations rage and the peoples plot in vain?... The One enthroned in Heaven laughs."
- **Isaiah 14:27** – "For the Lord Almighty has purposed, and who can thwart him?"

Are you listening to polished preachers or pierced prophets? Are you more impressed by a stage presence or a Spirit-filled message? Are you one of the hidden ones God is calling?

God raises unlikely messengers from hidden places, not from stages, to warn, prepare, and call the Church to repentance. Throughout history, during periods of spiritual decline, God has raised voices from obscurity—not the religious elite or the political elite—but from the wilderness, the cave, the prison, or the marketplace. Elijah wore camel hair, not a king's robe. John the Baptist preached in the desert, not in the synagogue. Amos was a shepherd, not a scholar (Amos 7:14- 15).

In today's world, true prophets are not always found on social media or behind pulpits. They may be rejected, overlooked, or dismissed by mainstream church culture. God is not seeking popularity; He desires purity. The prophetic voices in this generation will often be seen as foolish by the world and even by the church. The decline of established religious platforms has created space for authentic messengers—those who pray with urgency, fast in secret, and cry out with trembling voices. The U.S. has tended to celebrate motivational speakers more than messengers of God. This message highlights the danger of replacing repentance with inspiration. Today's prophets are warning about judgment, repentance, and the return of Christ, not the promise of prosperity without holiness or grace without truth.

Like Jeremiah's time, false prophets proclaim peace when turmoil is approaching. However, God is raising a remnant who will cry out with tears and trembling: "Return to the Lord!" Church leaders must humble themselves and make room for these voices, as spiritual pride has silenced many whom God has called to speak.

Reflection
- Have I been responding to national resistance with fear or with faith?
- Do I trust that God can use even hard-hearted leaders for His glory?
- Is there a Pharaoh-like spirit in my own heart — a resistance to God's voice or correction?

Prayer
Righteous Judge,

I acknowledge that you alone rule over kings, presidents, and powers. When pride rises in a nation, it helps not to despair but to discern. Let my heart never grow hard in times of testing. Use what the enemy means for evil to reveal your power and deliver your people. Give me eyes to see and ears to hear You clearly in these last days.

In Jesus' name, Amen.

Chapter 4: Cyrus the Persian and Divine Rebuilding

"This is what the Lord says to His anointed, to Cyrus, whose right hand I take hold of... though you do not acknowledge me."
— Isaiah 45:1, 4 (NIV)

Just as the sons of Issachar understood the times, today's believers must interpret political seasons through spiritual eyes. Elections are more than ballots; they are mirrors. Each cycle reflects the heart of a nation and reveals the maturity of the Church. In this chapter, we will explore how political seasons bring exposure, refinement, and divine testing. Some seasons bring blessings; others bring judgment. But all serve God's redemptive plan. The Church must not simply vote—it must intercede. Political shifts often signify spiritual thresholds. Are we crossing into deeper compromise—or a moment of revival?

When God reduced Gideon's army from 32,000 to 300, He was making a bold statement: deliverance is not by numbers, but by obedience. In a time when many churches measure success by size and popularity, God is trimming down His army, not to weaken it, but to purify it. This chapter challenges both leaders and members to embrace divine strategy over human logic.

Through pruning, God strengthens. Through weakness, He wins. The Church is being called to shed every worldly dependency and walk boldly with fewer, purer vessels prepared to conduct His mission.

Political seasons—such as elections and major government changes—are not just about policies or power struggles. They are spiritual indicators, revealing the heart of a nation and the readiness of the Church. Just as the sons of Issachar in the Bible understood their times and knew what to do, believers today must learn to interpret these seasons with spiritual insight. This chapter explores how political shifts reflect deeper spiritual battles and how God uses these seasons to test, refine, and prepare His people for what is coming.

For teenagers, this chapter helps make sense of confusing headlines and political debates by showing that these events are part of a bigger spiritual story. It encourages young people to pay attention, pray, and not just be passive observers. They learn that their voices, votes, and prayers have power and that God wants to use them to influence their communities positively. This helps young people feel empowered rather than overwhelmed by political chaos.

Adults are challenged to move beyond partisan division and to seek God's wisdom above all. The chapter calls for mature faith, where prayer and discernment guide actions more than political loyalty. It reminds adults that every political season offers an opportunity for revival if the Church will humble itself and intercede. The spiritual significance behind political seasons should awaken believers to a higher calling, standing firm in faith while navigating the storms of culture and government.

A Pagan King, a Divine Assignment

In Isaiah 45, God calls **Cyrus**, the king of Persia, **His anointed**. That word — *anointed* — is usually reserved for prophets, priests, and kings who know and walk with God. But Cyrus was a **pagan ruler**, a Gentile conqueror with no covenant relationship with Yahweh. Yet God says of him:

"I summon you by name and bestow on you a title of honor, though you do not acknowledge me." (Isaiah 45:4)

God used Cyrus to release the Jewish people from Babylonian captivity and commission the rebuilding of the Temple in Jerusalem (Ezra 1:1-4). Cyrus did not know the God of Israel, but the God of Israel certainly knew him. His rise was **foretold by name** over a hundred years before his birth. That is how intentional God is about fulfilling His purposes.

God's Use of Outsiders

This is the mystery and majesty of God's sovereignty: **He can use people who do not know Him to fulfill His perfect will.** He does not need someone's permission to use them as a tool in His hand. That includes kings, presidents, and public officials. Cyrus was not "holy," but he was **chosen.**

God has always used **unlikely instruments**:
- Rahab the prostitute (Joshua 2)
- Nebuchadnezzar, the Babylonian king (Daniel 4)
- Balaam the false prophet (Numbers 22–24)
- Even a talking donkey!

So why should it shock us when God uses a president, politician, or world leader today— someone not known for humility or godliness— to provoke revival, reset the Church, or fulfill prophetic patterns?

America and the Modern Cyrus

Many believers have wondered if the U.S. President could be a "Cyrus" figure. While not righteous in the traditional sense, his leadership aligned with some of the biblical values — pro-life policies, religious liberty, and protection of Israel — even while his character raised concerns.

Whether or not one accepts that title, the *Cyrus pattern* still applies: **God can use a national leader who does not fully acknowledge Him to fulfill divine purposes for His people.**

The lesson isn't about endorsing a man. The lesson is about recognizing the movement of God **through** the man.

"I will go before you and will level the mountains… so that you may know that I am the Lord, the God of Israel, who summons you by name."
— Isaiah 45:2–3

Rebuilding in a Time of Political Shift

Just as Cyrus released God's people to **rebuild the Temple**, we may be in a season where God is releasing His people to **rebuild the Church**, not the structure, but the **spiritual altar**. Many believers have been in spiritual captivity — asleep, distracted, or disengaged. The political shaking of recent years may be **permission to return** and restore:

- The broken walls of worship
- The neglected disciplines of prayer and holiness
- The disunified Body of Christ

This is a **Cyrus moment** — a divine opportunity to reset and rebuild what matters to God.

Scripture Focus
- **Isaiah 44:28, 45:7** – God's call of Cyrus to rebuild Jerusalem.
- **Ezra 1:1-4** – Cyrus issues a decree to rebuild the Temple.
- **Proverbs 21:1** – "The king's heart is in the hand of the Lord… He directs it like a watercourse."
- **Romans 13:1** – All authority comes from God.
- **Acts 17:26** – God determines the times and boundaries of nations.

If you are a leader, are you guiding others out of fear of God or fear of man? If you are a believer, are you listening to voices that merely entertain or those that touch the heart? Are you ready to witness God shake His Church into holiness?

God is purifying the Church, exposing compromised leadership, and calling pastors and ministers to return to truth, repentance, and Spirit-led guidance. The Church is not exempt from this shaking; in fact, judgment begins in the house of God (1 Peter 4:17). Before God addresses nations, He cleanses His sanctuary. Many pulpits have exchanged conviction for comfort, trading biblical truth for cultural relevance. This isn't a new phenomenon—Israel's priests once offered strange fire (Leviticus 10), and Jesus drove the money changers out of the temple (Matthew 21:12-13).

Currently, God is allowing public exposures, moral failures, and leadership scandals to bring hidden issues to light. This is not for destruction but for healing. The rise of entertainment-driven worship, personality cults, and diluted sermons has weakened the Church's spiritual authority.

This shaking is calling pastors to repentance and renewal. True revival begins when the pulpit is restored—not through better marketing or larger crowds, but with a return to the altar. God is searching for shepherds after His own heart (Jeremiah 3:15).

The prophetic role of pastors has often been stifled in pursuit of popularity, but God is reigniting that boldness. Like the Apostle Paul, modern-day leaders must be willing to speak difficult truths in love (Galatians 1:10). Church divisions over politics, race, money, and doctrine have distracted us from the mission of the Gospel. This shaking is separating those who build kingdoms for themselves from those who build for Christ.

God is shifting the pulpit from performance to purity—from branding to brokenness. He is removing Saul-type leaders and raising Davids: flawed but surrendered and repentant. This is a moment of mercy. The Church still has time to return, rebuild, and realign with God's heart, but the window is narrowing.

The Spiritual Significance of Political Seasons

Just as God used Cyrus to rebuild what had been destroyed in Jerusalem, we, too, are in desperate need of divine rebuilding today. Our churches in the U.S. are fractured—doctrinally, morally, and spiritually—leaving many believers confused about where their leaders truly stand with God. Likewise, our political system is in disarray. There is division in the rule of law, confusion over the U.S. Constitution, and a growing gap between righteousness and rebellion. This spirit of confusion has spread globally, infiltrating both church and government. But the Word of God reminds us: "A house divided against itself cannot stand" (Mark 3:25), and "God is not the author of confusion but of peace" (1 Corinthians 14:33). If God could use a Persian king to restore what was broken in Israel, surely, He can raise modern-day voices—unlikely and even foolish by the world's standards—to bring clarity, unity, and divine order in our time.

The divisions we witness in the political realm are often a mirror of the spiritual disunity in the Church. Just as churches are divided over doctrine, leadership, and cultural compromise, our national leadership is fractured over the Constitution, laws, and morality. These divisions are no coincidence; they are spiritual battles manifesting in earthly systems. The enemy thrives in confusion, but Scripture reminds us that "God is not the author of confusion but of peace." As long as the Church and nation remain divided, we stand vulnerable to collapse.

Reflection
- Have I dismissed someone as unusable by God because of their background or beliefs?
- Am I paying attention to how God might be using political shifts to open spiritual doors?
- What in my life or ministry needs to be rebuilt right now

Prayer
Sovereign Lord,
You are not limited by men's beliefs, character, or background.
You are God, and You use whom You choose. Help me to recognize Your hand in unexpected places. Give me wisdom to see not just politics, but prophecy. Let this be a season of rebuilding in my heart and Your Church. Use every Cyrus You appoint for Your glory. In Jesus' name, Amen.

"The Most High is sovereign over all kingdoms on earth and gives them to anyone he wishes."
— Daniel 4:32 (NIV)

In the last days, God is not silent—He is shouting through prophecy, warning, and revelation. Like watchmen on the wall, prophetic voices are sounding alarms about coming judgment, deception, and the need for repentance. Yet many in the Church have grown dull to the sound. This chapter unpacks the urgency of listening to God's prophetic messengers. Whether through dreams, divine insight, or bold proclamation, God is speaking louder than ever. Just as Nineveh repented at Jonah's cry, there is still time for nations and individuals to turn. But that window is closing. The question is: Will we listen before it's too late?

Who would have thought that a woman with a stained past would become part of the lineage of Christ? Rahab's story is a radical testament to redemption. In a world that labels people based on past failures, God identifies them by future purpose. This chapter is an invitation to sinners, backsliders, and those who have been counted out—even by the Church. God is raising Rahabs: people whose messy stories are about to display His mercy and power. He is reminding us that no one is too dirty to be delivered, and no past is too broken for God's plan.

In the last days, God is speaking loudly through prophecy and warnings, urging His people and the nations to wake up before it is too late. Prophets and messengers, both ancient and modern, have long been God's watchmen—sent to sound alarms about coming judgment and the need for repentance. This chapter reveals how prophecy is not meant to scare but to prepare and protect. It shows that God's heart is full of mercy, giving people chances to turn back to Him even in dark times.

For teenagers, this chapter clarifies that prophecy is not just mysterious or scary talk, but a call to live with purpose and awareness. It teaches young believers to listen carefully for God's voice and understand that warnings are a sign of God's love. God desires to rescue everyone before the final day of judgment. This helps teens see their role in sharing hope and truth with their peers and families.

Adults are encouraged to take prophecy seriously, not dismissing warnings as negativity or fear-mongering. The chapter challenges the Church to embrace prophetic voices and to pray fervently for revival and repentance on a national and personal level. It reminds believers that God's warnings are an invitation to salvation, and that the Church must be a vessel of truth, mercy, and urgent prayer in the face of coming judgment.

When Kings Think They're Gods

Nebuchadnezzar was the most powerful ruler of his time. His military victories, architectural achievements, and political dominance made Babylon the jewel of the ancient world. But his pride was just as towering as his palace.

After God gave him multiple dreams and prophetic warnings through Daniel, Nebuchadnezzar still refused to acknowledge the Most High as the true ruler. One day, he looked over Babylon and said:

"Is not this the great Babylon I have built as the royal residence, by my mighty power and for the glory of my majesty?"
— Daniel 4:30

That moment triggered divine judgment. God stripped him of his sanity and authority, and he lived like a beast in the wilderness for seven years—until he lifted his eyes to Heaven.

God Humbles to Heal

Nebuchadnezzar's fall was not about destruction; it was about correction. **God humbles leaders not to shame them, but to show them—and their people—that He alone is Lord.** The king's restoration did not come through politics or military might. It came through brokenness, surrender, and worship.

"At the end of that time, I… raised my eyes toward heaven, and my sanity was restored… Then I praised the Most High." — Daniel 4:34

His testimony became one of the most powerful declarations in Scripture:

"His dominion is an eternal dominion; his kingdom endures from generation to generation… all the peoples of the earth are regarded as nothing."
— Daniel 4:34 35

National Pride, Global Consequences

Like ancient Babylon, modern nations often exalt themselves, boasting about their power, technology, wealth, or military. Leaders may believe their rise is due to their greatness. But God is still sovereign. And when pride rises to the heavens, **God responds with humility**:

- Economic crashes
- Political division
- Natural disasters
- Scandals and public exposure
- Spiritual drought

These are not coincidences. They are warnings. **God still humbles nations today, just as He did with Nebuchadnezzar.**

America's Warning

The United States has often seen itself as a modern Babylon — a beacon of freedom, prosperity, and power. But in recent years, it has also seen:

- Increased polarization and hostility
- Moral confusion and compromise
- A decline in reverence for God's Word
- Leaders exalting themselves rather than God.

This is not just political — it is prophetic.

Could God be humbling America, not to destroy it, but to **draw it back to Him**? Could instability be a divine invitation to repentance and spiritual restoration?

Just as Nebuchadnezzar was reduced to nothing so that he might recognize God as everything, God may be shaking nations today so that the Church and the world return to Him.

God Rules… Always

Even when rulers forget Him, **God never abdicates His throne.**
Even when people rebel, God's sovereignty remains.

As Daniel reminded King Belshazzar later:

"You did not honor the God who holds in his hand your life and
all your ways."
— Daniel 5:23

It is time for leaders — and the people they serve — to **look up
to** God before they fall.

Scripture Focus
- **Daniel 4** – Nebuchadnezzar's dream, fall, and restoration.
- **Daniel 5:23** – God holds our lives and our ways.
- **Proverbs 16:18** – "Pride goes before destruction…"
- **Isaiah 2:11-12** – "The eyes of the arrogant will be humbled…"
- **Psalm 33:10-12** – The Lord brings the plans of nations to nothing.

Are you seeking a peace that keeps you comfortable or one that
draws you closer to Christ? Can you discern when a message
sounds appealing but lacks the Spirit of God?

The world advocates for peace without requiring repentance, but
Scripture warns that such peace is deceptive. God allows conflict to
reveal spiritual lies and provoke awakening. In many countries—

including the U.S.—leaders, politicians, and even some church voices proclaim messages of peace while ignoring the deeper spiritual decay beneath the surface. The Bible cautions against this: "They dress the wound of my people as though it were not serious. 'Peace, peace,' they say, when there is no peace" (Jeremiah 6:14).

While cries for unity, prosperity, and coexistence may sound good, they are empty slogans without repentance and righteousness. True peace comes only through reconciliation with God.

World leaders may sign peace agreements, yet wars and threats continue to escalate. Why is this? Because sin, injustice, and rebellion against God still exist. Just like in ancient Israel, today's prophets must speak out when peace is proclaimed without a call for repentance; otherwise, people risk being lulled into a false sense of security.

The current political climate reflects this tension: people desire calm but resist conviction. They want comfort but shy away from confronting sin. Often, God allows the disruption of false peace to lead to genuine spiritual awakening. This mirrors Noah's day—people were eating and drinking until the flood came (Matthew 24:37-39).

Church leaders must be cautious not to emulate the prophets and political leaders who told Ahab only what he wanted to hear. Micaiah stood alone but spoke the truth, even at great personal cost (1 Kings 22). The call to peace must always be grounded in truth. Jesus Himself stated, "I did not come to bring peace, but a sword" (Matthew 10:34)— indicating that His message divides truth from falsehood.

Reflection
1. What forms of pride have I seen rising in national or church leadership?
2. Have I ever ignored a warning from God until I was humbled?
3. How can I help call my community or nation back to humility and repentance?

Prayer

Most High God,
You are sovereign over every throne and every nation. Forgive us for our pride. Forgive us for thinking our power or plans can succeed without You. Humble our hearts before You, must humble our nation. Let us return before we are ruined. Help us see your warnings as mercy, not wrath.
May we exalt You as King before the world reminds us, we are dust.
In Jesus' name, Amen.

Chapter 6: When God Exposes Through Elevation

"For there is nothing hidden that will not be disclosed, and nothing concealed that will not be known or brought out into the open." — Luke 8:17 (NIV)

When political systems shake, the Church must not scatter in fear or divide in anger. This chapter explores how God is using political upheaval to purify and reposition His Church. Are we clinging to parties or His presence? Are we echoing partisan outrage or declaring eternal truth?

When early believers faced persecution from Rome, they didn't retaliate—they rose in power. Today, God is calling His people to respond not with panic, but with purpose. Political storms are creating a divine opportunity to shine with truth, compassion, and prophetic authority. The Church's greatest hour will come—not in peace—but in pressure.

Political upheaval—times when governments or societies seem unstable—can feel frightening and confusing. But God is not caught off guard by these storms. This chapter teaches that the Church is called not to panic or divide during these times, but to rise as a steady and holy presence. The Church has a divine role to pray, encourage, and offer solutions rooted in God's truth, not in fear or anger. Political upheaval often exposes hidden sins and injustices, giving the Church a chance to repent and lead the way toward healing.

For teenagers, this chapter guides how to stay grounded and hopeful when they see conflict around them, whether in their communities, schools, or families. It encourages them to be peacemakers, to stand for justice, and to pray for leaders and nations. Young people are reminded that God can use their faithfulness to bring peace amid chaos, and that their voices matter even when grown-ups seem divided.

Adults are called to lead by example, showing calm faith and unwavering commitment to God's kingdom regardless of political turmoil. This chapter challenges Church leaders and members to avoid getting trapped in partisan fights or worldly anger, and instead focuses on prayer, unity, and serving those in need. The Church's response during upheaval will either confirm God's faithfulness or cause many to stumble, making this moment crucial for spiritual leadership and courage.

Not Every Promotion Is a Blessing

In the eyes of the world, rising to power is often seen as success, favor, or divine approval. But Scripture paints a different picture. Sometimes, God elevates individuals not to **reward** them, but to **reveal** something far deeper — and far more sobering.

God may allow a person to rise in leadership, influence, or attention **so that what is hidden beneath the surface becomes known**. The elevation becomes a platform, not for pride, but for exposure. The higher the platform, the clearer the view.

The Rise of Saul: A Cautionary Example

Israel begged for a king. Though God warned them what kingship would cost, He allowed it — and **gave them Saul**, a man who looked the part but lacked the heart.

At first, Saul's reign seemed strong. He was tall, handsome, and charismatic. But his disobedience, insecurity, and pride slowly unraveled before the people. God did not remove Saul immediately instead, He let him rule, while the consequences of his character flaws played out publicly.

"Because you have rejected the word of the Lord, he has rejected you as king."
— 1 Samuel 15:23

Saul's elevation was not to celebrate him — it was to **expose Israel's desire for a king like the nations**, and to reveal how far the people's hearts had drifted from dependence on God.

Exposure by Leadership Today

We often assume that when someone rises to power — especially in politics, religion, or media that it's a sign of God's favor. But the Bible teaches us to think deeper. Exposure does not always happen through scandals or failures. It happens through testing.

God allows flawed leaders to ascend so:
- The **hearts of the people** can be assessed.
- The **idols of the Church** can be revealed.
- The **true state of the nation** can be exposed.

This is especially true when leaders are elevated who speak boldly, divide opinions, or polarize the culture. The question becomes: **What is God showing us through this leader's presence and influence?**

A Mirror for the Church and the Nation

When the U.S. President was elected, people had strong, emotional reactions. Many praised him as a savior of morality and tradition. Others condemned him as a threat to unity and peace. But the real issue was not who the man was — it was **what his rise revealed**:

- **Which voices did the Church listen to?**
- **What values do Christians truly prioritize?**
- **Where we placed our identity — in the Kingdom or culture.**

His presence did not just shake the political world; it revealed the **fault lines already inside the Body of Christ.** And in that exposure, God was speaking loudly.

"Judgment must begin at the house of God…"
— 1 Peter 4:17

God is more concerned with our hearts than our headlines. He is more focused on our repentance than our comfort. When He elevates someone who stirs division, He may be showing us what we have ignored for too long.

Exposure Is an Act of Mercy

It's easy to view exposure as punishment, but from Heaven's perspective, exposure is often **mercy**. God reveals so He can **heal**. He shines light so darkness loses its power.

If God did not love us, He would allow us to stay comfortable, asleep, and deceived. But because He loves us, He elevates, shakes, and exposes — not to destroy us, but to wake us up.

Scripture Focus
- **Luke 8:17** – Nothing hidden will remain concealed.
- **1 Samuel 8–15** – The rise and fall of King Saul
- **1 Peter 4:17** – Judgment begins in the house of God.
- **Deuteronomy 8:2** – God tests us to know what's in our hearts.
- **2 Chronicles 16:9** – God searches hearts to show Himself strong.

Are you troubled by what you see, or are you turning it into prayer? Are you reading headlines or interpreting prophecy? Are you preparing your heart for the return of the King?

Global unrest and conflict are not random; they are prophetic signs that God has permitted to awaken the Church and prepare the world for Christ's return. Jesus warned plainly: "You will hear of wars and rumors of wars... but the end is not yet" (Matthew 24:6). These events are not the conclusion; they are the contractions before the birth of a new era. What we are witnessing today—war in Ukraine, tensions in the Middle East, civil conflicts, and nuclear threats—is all part of a divine narrative unfolding in real time.

God has allowed these tumultuous events to remind a distracted world that no nation is exempt from judgment or disruption, not even the most powerful ones. Just as God used Assyria, Babylon, and Persia to discipline Israel, He may be using modern-day global powers to discipline and realign His people.

Every war has spiritual roots. The war in heaven (Revelation 12), the conflict between Cain and Abel, and countless biblical battles all stemmed from spiritual rebellion and divine intervention. These present-day wars reveal the spiritual condition of nations: greed, pride, deception, injustice, and the rejection of God's authority.

The Church must not be a passive observer of political news. We need to be discerning intercessors, asking not only what is happening but also why it is happening. Like Daniel, we must seek understanding during times of national conflict. God gave Daniel dreams and visions because he humbled himself in prayer and fasting (Daniel 10:12). The world interprets war as a failure of diplomacy, but the Word interprets it as both a warning and an act of mercy, a last call to repent before greater judgment.

Reflection

1. What recent leadership rise (in church or government) has exposed something to me or my community?
2. Have I placed my hope in a person instead of God?
3. What might God be revealing through the leaders I admire or fear?

Prayer

Father of Light, You expose what is hidden not to harm us, but to heal us. Forgive me for judging by appearance rather than asking what you are revealing. Help me discern the message you are speaking through every leader, movement, or shift. Let my heart be open to correction.

Keep me humble and awake.

In Jesus' name, Amen.

Chapter 7: Divisive Leaders and Divided Hearts

"If a house is divided against itself, that house cannot stand."
— Mark 3:25 (NIV)

Divisive leaders are not merely the cause of division—they are often the revelation of it. God allows polarizing figures to rise to expose what is hidden in the hearts of the people. Just as Korah rebelled against Moses and split the camp, or Saul's reign exposed Israel's demand for a human king, modern leaders reflect the spiritual fractures within both the Church and society.

This chapter uncovers how God uses division not to destroy, but to divide the pure from the polluted, the sincere from the superficial. It's time for self-examination. Are we truly united in Christ, or have we been divided by culture, politics, and personal idols?

Divisive leaders often reflect deeper divisions within society and even within the Church. When leaders sow discord, it reveals the fractured state of our hearts and communities. This chapter explores how God uses such times to expose hidden bitterness, pride, and selfishness, calling His people to repentance and unity. It challenges believers to look inward and ask: Are we part of the problem or part of the solution? True healing begins when hearts are united in Christ rather than divided by politics, race, or ideology.

For teenagers, this chapter helps make sense of the arguments and fights they see among adults and peers. It encourages young people to be agents of peace, understanding that the Church's unity is a powerful witness to a watching world. It reminds them that their friendships, conversations, and choices can either build walls or build bridges, and God calls them to be bridge-builders who reflect His love.

Adults are urged to move beyond political loyalty and personal preferences toward genuine reconciliation. This chapter exposes the dangers of allowing political divisions to fracture the Body of Christ. It calls Church leaders and members alike to promote forgiveness, humility, and grace. Only through such spiritual maturity can the Church stand as a unified witness in a polarized world and demonstrate God's transforming power.

Division Exposes What Is Hidden

Division is often painful and feared. But God sometimes allows divisive leaders to rise not to create new splits but to **expose existing fractures** in the hearts of a people. Like a surgeon's scalpel, division reveals what has been festering beneath the surface—pride, fear, idolatry, and unforgiveness.

Jesus warned that the truth would cause division (Luke 12:51-53), and history shows that leaders who provoke strong reactions often serve as catalysts, forcing communities and nations to confront uncomfortable truths.

Biblical Examples of Division
- **Jeremiah's Prophetic Ministry:** Jeremiah was hated because he spoke God's judgment, exposing both Judah's sin and their false security. His message divided families and communities, but it was necessary for repentance.

- **Paul and the Early Church:** The Apostle Paul's teachings caused division as some embraced the Gospel and others resisted, revealing the true state of hearts (Acts 15).
- **Jesus Himself:** Jesus was the ultimate divisive figure, exposing sin and calling for repentance, which split the crowds and even His followers.

The Role of Divisive Leaders Today

In modern politics and church life, leaders who polarize often reveal underlying divisions:

- **Political allegiances** that overshadow the Kingdom's identity
- **Cultural and racial tensions** were previously ignored.
- **Moral and ethical conflicts** within the Church
- **Spiritual complacency or legalism** in communities

The rise of such leaders is a call to examine ourselves: **What is dividing us? What is causing our hearts to harden?**

Across America, churches are split, not just in denomination but in truth. People are left questioning where their leaders truly stand with God. The same pattern of confusion exists in politics. There are divisions over the Constitution, the law, and moral responsibility. These parallel fractures—religious and governmental—are not isolated events. Globally, we are witnessing the same spiritual decay. A divided house, whether church or nation, cannot stand. When leaders fear men more than they fear God, confusion reigns. And we know, biblically, confusion does not come from God.

The Danger of Division Without Repentance

Division itself is not God's ultimate goal. When division leads to bitterness, hatred, or violence, it becomes destructive. God desires that division should lead to:

- **Repentance** — turning back to God and His ways.
- **Healing** — restoration of relationships and communities
- **Renewed unity** — based on truth and love.

If division only hardens hearts, it can signal judgment, but if it leads to confession and change, it can signal revival.

Scripture Focus
- **Mark 3:24-26** – A house divided cannot stand.
- **Jeremiah 20:7-10** – Jeremiah's struggle with rejection
- **Acts 15** – Division and resolution in the early Church.
- **John 7:43** – Division over Jesus' message
- **Ephesians 4:3** – "Make every effort to keep the unity of the Spirit…"

Where have you placed your trust? If the government fails, will your faith remain strong? Are you more politically engaged than spiritually aligned?

No human government, political party, or national system can redeem the soul of a nation. Only God's rule brings true deliverance. Nations rise and fall, but God's kingdom is everlasting (Daniel 2:44). America, though blessed and influential, is not eternal, and it cannot save itself from spiritual decline. Many place their hope in presidents, policies, and elections, believing that the right party or leader will fix what is broken? But Scripture reminds us, "Do not put your trust in princes" (Psalm 146:3).

The Israelites begged for a king like other nations (1 Samuel 8), thinking that human rule would bring security. God granted their request but warned them that a man's rule would lead to oppression. Like then, today's obsession with political saviors reveals a spiritual void. We look to Washington for answers that only the cross can provide.

Whether liberal or conservative, every administration has fallen short because the heart of man is flawed. Even the best laws cannot change the human heart. During crises—such as pandemics, wars, school shootings, and economic collapse—we cry out for government aid. But the answer must begin at the altar, not in the Oval Office. God uses political leaders to carry out His will—sometimes as a blessing, other times as judgment. Nebuchadnezzar ruled by God's permission, but also to humble and shake Babylon.

The Church must detach its identity from nationalism. We are citizens of heaven first (Philippians 3:20), and our allegiance must reflect that priority. As the government fails to meet deep needs, the Church is called back to its original role—to be a refuge, a light, a voice of truth, and a house of healing.

Reflection

1. What divisions have recent leaders revealed in my community or church?
2. How have I contributed to division or unity?
3. What steps can I take toward healing and repentance?

Prayer

God of Unity, You see our divisions, and You desire healing. Forgive us for hardening our hearts and turning away from one another. Help us to respond to division with repentance and love. Let us be agents of peace and restoration in a fractured world. Use every leader and every event to bring your truth to light and your people to yourself. In Jesus' name, Amen.

Chapter 8: God's Warning Through Unlikely Messengers

"The Lord does not look at the things people look at. People look at the outward appearance, but the Lord looks at the heart." — 1 Samuel 16:7 (NIV)

God once used a donkey to warn a prophet. He used fishermen to launch a global Church. He used a Samaritan woman to preach in her city. This chapter reminds us that God's warnings often come through the mouths we least expect. Today, He may speak through the broken, the outcast, or even a controversial leader— not to confuse, but to confront. The religious may scoff, but the humble will hear. The Church must be cautious not to reject truth just because it comes from a source we dislike. God is sounding the alarm—but will we recognize His voice, even when it comes wrapped in the unexpected?

Throughout history, God has chosen unexpected people to deliver His messages—people society often overlooks or dismisses. From a talking donkey in the Old Testament to fishermen and tax collectors in the New Testament, God reminds us that His voice can come from surprising places.

This chapter explores how God's warnings and calls to repentance today might come through people or circumstances we would not expect. The challenge is to stay open and discerning, listening for God's truth no matter where it comes from.

For teenagers, this idea is empowering because it shows that God can use anyone—regardless of their background or status—to be effective. It encourages young people to listen to God's voice in their lives and to respect the messages others bring, even if those people seem unlikely. It also reminds them that they could be chosen to deliver important messages in their schools or communities.

Adults are challenged to move beyond prejudice or skepticism and to seek God's guidance in all situations. This chapter warns against dismissing God's warnings simply because they come from unexpected sources or uncomfortable truths. The Church must cultivate humility and spiritual sensitivity, recognizing that God's agenda often surprises human expectations and uses the foolish to confound the wise.

God Chooses Who He Will Use

Throughout history, God has chosen unlikely messengers to deliver His warnings and calls to repentance. From prophets who were rejected to outsiders who spoke truth to power, God's methods often confound human expectations.

- **Jonah:** A reluctant prophet sent to warn Nineveh, a pagan city.
- **John the Baptist:** A wild, ascetic figure who called Israel to repentance.
- **Jesus Himself:** Born in a manger, rejected by religious leaders. God's choice of messengers often seems foolish to the world, but powerful in God's hands.

Warnings Often Come Through the Unexpected

In modern times, warnings from God may come through:
- Individuals without formal authority or prestige
- Social or political outsiders
- Controversial or divisive figures
- Events that shock or disrupt the status quo.

75

Because God's ways are higher, His voice might sound different than what we expect. We must be careful not to dismiss His warnings simply because of who delivers them.

The Danger of Ignoring the Messenger

When God sends warnings, the focus should be on **the message**, not the messenger. Dismissing the messenger often leads to missing the warning, which can result in judgment.

"Like people, we look at the outward appearance, but the Lord looks at the heart." (1 Samuel 16:7)

When the prophet Samuel was sent to anoint a new king, he was misled by appearances.

Similarly, if we reject a messenger because they don't fit our expectations, we risk ignoring God's voice.

The U.S. President as a Warning?

Whether one agrees with the politics or not, the rise of a controversial and divisive leader can be seen as a **warning from God** — a wake-up call to a sleeping Church and a complacent nation.

God often uses events and leaders to:
- Expose hidden sins and idols.
- Stir repentance and prayer.
- Challenge spiritual lukewarmness.

Ignoring these warnings can lead to spiritual decay and national instability.

Scripture Focus

- **Jonah 3:** God sends Jonah to warn Nineveh.
- **1 Samuel 16:7:** God looks at the heart, not appearance.
- **Matthew 3:1 12:** John the Baptist calls for repentance.
- **Acts 7:51:** Warning against resisting the Holy Spirit
- **Hebrews 12:25:** "See to it that you do not refuse him who speaks."

What fear has overtaken your faith? Have you allowed fear to dictate your decisions more than the Spirit of God? Are you willing to surrender control and rebuild trust?

God is revealing how fear rules our hearts when trust in Him is absent. In times of turmoil, we are invited to replace fear with faith. Fear has gripped the world—fear of pandemics, economic collapse, civil unrest, war, and personal loss. This is not merely a cultural issue; it is a spiritual one.

Scripture clearly states, "God has not given us a spirit of fear, but of power, love, and a sound mind" (2 Timothy 1:7). If fear is rising, it indicates that trust in God is declining. The early

Church faced persecution, plagues, and political instability, yet they thrived because their hope was not in this world. The modern church must return to that radical trust. Just as Israel feared the giants in the Promised Land (Numbers 13), many today hesitate to move forward because of what they see. However, God continues to call us to take territory by faith.

Satan uses fear to paralyze our purpose. Fearful leaders hesitate to tell the truth. Fearful believers refrain from sharing the Gospel.

Fearful churches avoid taking risks. COVID-19 has revealed not only physical vulnerabilities but also spiritual panic. Many people—even Christians—turned to government directives and news media rather than to the Word of God. God is shaking our false securities: bank accounts, job titles, insurance plans, and even routine church attendance. Why? To awaken a raw, real dependence on Him.

Fear is a sign that something else is occupying the throne of our hearts. God allows crises to confront us with this reality, not to destroy us, but to transform us. Just like Gideon, who was hiding in fear when God called him a mighty warrior (Judges 6), many today are being called out of fear and into faith.

This book, *God Uses the Foolish to Confuse the Wise*, reveals that God often allows foolishness to rise—not to bless it, but to expose it. He raises unlikely messengers, the voiceless and the overlooked, to confront the arrogance of human power. In Scripture, we see this pattern repeatedly. When Pharaoh hardened his heart and oppressed the Israelites, God sent Moses, a stammering fugitive, to challenge him. When King Saul defied God and used his power for himself, the Lord removed him and raised up David, a shepherd boy. When King Nebuchadnezzar grew prideful and claimed glory for himself, God humbled him until he acknowledged that *"the Most High rules in the kingdom of men."* (Daniel 4:17)

These stories serve as both encouragement and warning. God sees every act of injustice. He hears the cries of the oppressed. No leader—no matter how powerful—can escape divine accountability. The cages built on earth cannot contain the judgment of heaven. When political leaders ignore God and religious leaders ignore injustice, God will raise up the least likely voices—prophets from the margins, truth-tellers from among the broken—to speak truth to power.

Just as God removed kings in the Bible, He can and will remove leaders who defy His ways today. Power without righteousness is temporary. Thrones built on oppression are unstable. But in the midst of it all, God is not silent. He is still using the foolish to confound the wise, the weak to shame the strong, and the unexpected to confront the immoral. The question is not whether

God sees—He does. The real question is whether the Church will speak, whether it will align with the Kingdom or continue to compromise with comfort and culture.

The Echo of a Century-Old Warning

Over a century ago, General William Booth, the founder of The Salvation Army, issued a prophetic warning that now rings louder than ever in our generation. He said, *"The chief dangers that confront the coming century will be religion without the Holy Ghost, Christianity without Christ, forgiveness without repentance, salvation without regeneration, politics without God, and heaven without hell."* Booth was not just critiquing his time— he was speaking through time, into ours. His words pierced through the modern landscape of politics, religion, and faith like a trumpet sounding alarm.

In today's world, we are witnessing the tragic fulfillment of Booth's prophecy. We see churches that thrive on entertainment but neglect transformation. We see Christians who know how to attend, but not how to repent. We see leaders in high places invoking the name of God yet acting in ways completely contrary to His character. Worst of all, we see political structures, particularly in the United States, moving forward without any reverence for God, justice, or mercy, and the Church, for the most part, has remained silent. Booth's voice, though long gone from the earth, still speaks today as one of the unlikely messengers God raised in his time to warn ours.

Political Power Without God – A Nation at Risk

Nowhere is Booth's warning more evident than in the unchecked and often inhumane use of political power. In recent years, we have seen the horrifying realities of presidential decisions that led to immigrant children being separated from their parents and placed in cages. Mothers, fathers, and families have been treated with cruelty, often justified by legal language, but devoid of moral conscience. Policies have been implemented that target the vulnerable, while the powerful remain immune to the consequences of their actions.

What is even more alarming is the collective silence of religious leaders who once stood boldly for justice. Where are the prophets? Where are the shepherds who speak for the oppressed, as Christ did? Instead, many have traded their prophetic voice for political favor. They have chosen alignment with power rather than allegiance to truth. This is *"politics without God,"* exactly as Booth warned. The result? A society that is increasingly numb to injustice and a Church that is increasingly irrelevant in the face of suffering.

Biblical Echoes – When Kings Fall and Prophets Rise

This is not the first time in history that political leaders have exalted themselves above God or acted with cruelty and indifference. Scripture is filled with leaders who abused their power and paid the price. Pharaoh oppressed the Israelites until God sent Moses, a stuttering fugitive, to bring him down. King Saul misused his throne until God raised up David, a shepherd boy, to replace him. King Ahab allowed injustice under Jezebel's influence, and God responded by sending Elijah, a rugged prophet from the wilderness, to confront the corruption.

God has always used unlikely messengers—those considered weak, unqualified, or foolish by worldly standards—to bring warning and correction. These voices may not come from palaces or pulpits, but they come from the heart of God. And just like then, today's corrupt systems are being exposed. God is still raising up Moses, Davids, and Elijahs in unexpected places—men and women who are not swayed by popularity but driven by divine purpose.

The silence of the religious elite in the face of injustice is nothing new either. Priests, kings, and even fellow believers often resisted the prophets of Israel. Jeremiah was beaten.

Amos was mocked. Jesus Himself was rejected by the religious system of His day. But that

didn't stop God from sending them—and it won't stop Him today. When the religious leaders stay silent, God will raise up a voice from the wilderness. When pulpits are compromised, He will speak through poets, writers, reformers, and even children.

The Unlikely Prophets of Our Generation

We are living in a time when God is once again using the foolish to shame the wise. He is raising voices from the margins—immigrants, minorities, survivors, activists, mothers, youth—those who have been wounded by the systems of this world and yet have found healing in the arms of Christ. These unlikely messengers are sounding the alarm, not with political power, but with spiritual truth. They are crying out for justice, mercy, and repentance.

You may not hear them on the national news. They may not have a platform or a pulpit. But they carry the same spirit that empowered the prophets of old. They see through the lies. They feel the pain of the broken. They know what it means to live without protection or privilege. And that is why God is using them. Because in their weakness, His strength is made perfect. In their foolishness, His wisdom is revealed.

A Final Call to the Church and the Nation

This generation is standing at a crossroads. We cannot afford to ignore the warnings. We cannot continue to accept politics without God, religion without repentance, and salvation without transformation. God is not mocked. Leaders may enjoy temporary power, but no throne is safe from the hand of the Almighty. Just as He removed Saul, humbled Nebuchadnezzar, and judged Herod, He can—and will—remove those who defy His ways.

The Church must rediscover its prophetic voice. We were never meant to be the cheerleaders of kings but the conscience of the nation. We must cry aloud and spare not. We must confront sin in high places and stand for righteousness in low places. The time has come to listen to the unlikely messengers among us. For in their cries, God is speaking. And in their warnings, God is offering mercy before judgment.

This book, *God Uses the Foolish to Confuse the Wise*, reveals that God often allows foolishness to rise—not to bless it, but to expose it. He raises unlikely messengers, the voiceless and the overlooked, to confront the arrogance of human power. In Scripture, we see this pattern repeatedly. When Pharaoh hardened his heart and oppressed the Israelites, God sent Moses, a stammering fugitive, to challenge him. When King Saul defied God and used his power for himself, the Lord removed him and raised up David, a shepherd boy. When King Nebuchadnezzar grew prideful and claimed glory for himself, God humbled him until he acknowledged that *the Most High rules in the kingdom of men.*" (Daniel 4:17)

These stories serve as both encouragement and warning. God sees every act of injustice. He hears the cries of the oppressed. No leader—no matter how powerful—can escape divine accountability. The cages built on earth cannot contain the judgment of heaven. When political leaders ignore God and religious leaders ignore injustice, God will raise up the least likely voices—prophets from the margins, truth-tellers from among the broken—to speak truth to power.

Just as God removed kings in the Bible, He can and will remove leaders who defy His ways today. Power without righteousness is temporary. Thrones built on oppression are unstable. But in the midst of it all, God is not silent. He is still using the foolish to confound the wise, the weak to shame the strong, and the unexpected to confront the immoral. The question is not whether God sees—He does. The real question is whether the Church will speak, whether it will align with the Kingdom or continue to compromise with comfort and culture.

Reflection
1. Have I ever rejected a message because I disliked the messenger?
2. Am I open to hearing God's warnings, even if they come in unexpected ways?
3. How can I prepare my heart to respond with repentance?

A Prayer for Our Nation, Leaders, and the Brokenhearted

Heavenly Father,

We come before You, the Sovereign Lord over every nation, throne, and authority. You raise kings alone and bring them down. You alone see the secrets of every heart and weigh every deed upon the scales of righteousness. Today, we lift before You the political leaders of our world, especially those in high places of power in the United States and other nations shaped by influence. Lord, we pray for holy conviction to fall upon them. Where pride has blinded them, open their eyes. Where corruption has hardened their hearts, break them with Your mercy.

Where injustice has ruled, let justice roll like a river, and righteousness like an ever-flowing stream.

We pray especially for those who make decisions affecting the lives of the weak, the foreigner, the widow, and the child. Let them remember that power is a trust—not a right—and that they will answer to You for how they have used it. Expose lies. Uncover secret agendas. Bring repentance to those who have oppressed, and raise up those who will lead with humility, truth, and fear of the Lord.

Lord, we also pray for the spiritual leaders of this generation—the pastors, bishops, prophets, and preachers who have grown silent in the face of evil. Awaken the sleeping shepherds. Stir their souls with holy fire once again. Forgive us, Lord, for when we have compromised Your truth for comfort, platform, or politics. Forgive us for aligning more with governments than with Your Kingdom. Let the pulpits burn again with the message of repentance and hope. Raise up a remnant who will not be bought, who will not be silent, and who will not turn away from the cry of the oppressed.

Finally, Lord, we lift up every family living in fear. For the immigrant parent afraid of separation. For the child who remembers the sound of the cage door. For the mother weeping at night, unsure if tomorrow will bring hope or more harm. Surround them with Your protection, O God. Remind them that You are near to the brokenhearted and that You are a refuge for the oppressed. May Your angels guard them. May Your justice defend them. And may Your Spirit comfort them in ways that only You can.

Let Your people rise in love and in truth. Let us not look away. Let us be the hands, the voice, and the heart of Christ in a world that desperately needs You. In Jesus' mighty and merciful name, we pray,

Amen.

In these last days, God is calling the foolish, the weak, and the willing to rise and expose this great deception. He is sounding the alarm through unlikely voices to turn our attention back to Him. Booth's words are a call to repentance, to realignment, and to return. This generation must not settle for a hollow faith or a gospel of convenience. We must cry out for the fire of the Holy Ghost once again, for a Christianity where Christ is King, and where salvation leads to transformation.

Chapter 9: The Call to Repentance Before the Return

"Repent, for the kingdom of heaven has come near."
— Matthew 4:17 (NIV)

Before Christ returns, there will be one message echoed from every mountain, every pulpit, every prophetic heart: **Repent.** Just as John the Baptist prepared the way for Jesus with a baptism of repentance, God is raising voices to prepare the world again. This chapter is a solemn plea: Turn while there is time. Judgment is near, but so is mercy. God is patient, not wanting any to perish. But repentance is not merely emotional; it is transformational. The Church must repent of compromise. Nations must repent of the bloodshed. Individuals must turn from sin. Time is short, but grace is still available.

Repentance is the urgent call echoing through Scripture as the world approaches Christ's return. This chapter focuses on the need for both the Church and the world to turn away from sin and turn toward God with humility and brokenness. Repentance is more than feeling sorry; it is a deliberate choice to change direction and live according to God's will. As judgment draws near, this call becomes louder and more urgent, offering hope and restoration to all who respond.

For teenagers, repentance can sometimes feel like a harsh or confusing idea. This chapter explains it simply as God's loving invitation to start fresh, no matter what mistakes have been made. It encourages young people to be honest with themselves and God, to seek forgiveness, and to let God guide their choices moving forward. Understanding repentance this way empowers teens to live with integrity and hope.

Adults are reminded that repentance is foundational for revival and transformation, both personally and nationally. The chapter challenges believers to examine their hearts, confess hidden sins, and lead their families and communities in turning back to God. Repentance opens the door for God's mercy to flow and prepares the way for Christ's glorious return. It is a call not to despair, but to hope and action.

Repentance: The Heartbeat of Revival
Throughout Scripture, God's primary call to His people has always been **repentance**—a turning away from sin and a turning back to God. Before every great move of God, repentance precedes revival and restoration.

The prophets called Israel and Judah to repent to avoid judgment. John the Baptist and Jesus began their ministries with a call to repent. And in the last days, the call is louder than ever.

Repentance Before Judgment
God is patient, but His patience has limits. Warnings through flawed leaders, divisive events, and prophetic voices are meant to stir hearts before judgment comes.

"Unless you repent, you too will all perish."
— Luke 13:3 (NIV)

Repentance does not just mean sorrow for sin; it means **a complete change of direction**—turning away from worldly ways and turning toward God's kingdom.

The Last Days Are a Time of Warning
The Bible repeatedly tells us that the last days will be marked by deception, rebellion, and hard hearts (2 Timothy 3:1-5; Matthew 24). But God's warnings and calls to repentance remain clear.

God uses all means—including the rise of unexpected leaders and the shaking of nations—to wake His people up.

Hope in Repentance
Repentance opens the door to God's mercy, healing, and restoration. No matter how deep the division or how dark the times, God's arms are open to forgive and restore.

The story of Nineveh in Jonah 3 is a powerful example—when a pagan city repented at God's warning, destruction was delayed and blessings followed.

Scripture Focus
- **2 Chronicles 7:14** – "If my people... will humble themselves and pray and seek my face and turn from their wicked ways..."
- **Acts 3:19** – "Repent, then, and turn to God..."
- **Revelation 3:19** – "Those whom I love I rebuke and discipline."
- **Joel 2:12-13** – "Return to me with all your heart..."
- **Matthew 24:42** – "Therefore keep watch, because you do not know on what day your Lord will come."

When unrest erupts, do you harden your heart or ask God what He is revealing? Are you willing to be part of His redemptive answer— not just in prayer, but in action?

Civil protests, unrest, and social upheaval are often divine signals pointing toward spiritual injustice, calling nations and the Church to repentance and alignment with God's justice. From George Floyd protests to national demonstrations over abortion, elections, racism, and corruption, unrest has intensified across the U.S. and the world.

While some see this only as rebellion or chaos, Scripture shows that unrest often signals divine redirection. God uses the cry of the oppressed to awaken the national conscience. In Egypt, God heard the cry of Israel's oppression (Exodus 3:7-9). That cry activated Moses. Today, protests are cries from people tired of broken systems.

The Church cannot afford to sit silently on the sidelines of injustice. Amos 5:24 cries, "Let justice roll down like waters, and righteousness like an ever-flowing stream." Unrest isn't always unrighteous. Nehemiah led a social outcry when the poor were being exploited (Nehemiah 5).

Jesus flipped tables when the poor were being taken advantage of in the temple (Matthew 21:12-13).

At the root of unrest is often a moral or spiritual failure in leadership. God allows pressure in the streets to reveal compromise in the sanctuary. The danger is that many church leaders dismiss civil unrest as "worldly noise" instead of discerning God's call through it. Silence in times of moral crisis is spiritual cowardice.

God's redirection may come through public pressure, but His ultimate goal is not political reform—it is spiritual revival. The cry in the street must lead to repentance in the heart. Believers are called not to riot, but to respond—to be peacemakers who walk in truth and compassion, and who call both the world and the church to higher ground.

Hope at the Edge: A Call to Repentance for Suffering and Wounded

There may be someone reading this chapter who is facing the hardest trial of their life. Perhaps you've just been diagnosed with cancer, whether breast, lung, liver, or bone—and it's already at stage four. The doctors have tried everything, and now, they look at you with compassion but finality and say, "We have done all we can. The treatment is no longer working." Your world stops. A hundred questions rush through your mind: *Is this the end? Why me? Has God forgotten me? Does anyone still love me?*

In that moment of despair, when everything feels lost, the voice of God still calls out: **"Don't give up—there is still hope."** Even now, even in the midnight hour of your journey, God is reaching for your heart. This is not just a time to reflect, but a time to repent, a time to surrender completely to Him. He is not looking for perfect people—He is calling the broken, the sick, the weary, and those who are barely holding on. You may want to give up, but God is saying, *"I'm not done with you yet."*

If there is life in your body, there is time to turn to God. Repentance is not just for those who have done wrong—it is for all who need to return home to the Father. It is for the prodigal, the forgotten, the afraid, the dying. Like the psalmist cried out in Psalm 42:11, *"Why are you downcast, O my soul? Put your hope in God!"* Even in pain, even in grief, *hope in God.*

Your family might be preparing for your final wishes. Your friends may be looking at you with pity. But God is looking at you with love, still calling you back to His arms. Hear Jesus whisper: *"Your time is not My time. Hang on. Trust Me. Delight yourself in Me. Acknowledge Me—and your miracle is on the way."*

Just like the woman with the issue of blood who suffered twelve long years and tried everything, you, too, may feel like all hope is gone. But she pressed through the crowd and touched the hem of Jesus' garment—and she was made whole. That same power is passing by as you read these words. Reach out and touch the Lord while He is near. Repent, believe, and receive healing—not only in your body, but in your spirit.

And maybe your pain isn't physical. Perhaps it is the deep, hidden wounds from abuse. You may be a young person—or even now an adult—who was sexually, emotionally, or physically abused. Perhaps it was someone close to you, someone who should have protected you, but instead violated your trust and threatened your silence. The scars are invisible, but the pain is real. And now, you have shut down. You have stopped trusting people, and you have begun to wonder if you will ever be whole again.

Hear this truth: **God sees you. He knows everything you've endured. And He is calling you— not just to heal, but to come home to Him.** Repentance is not just for sin—it's a response to pain, a turning back to the One who can restore what was stolen. The world may label you damaged, but God calls you **restored, redeemed, chosen, and loved**.

You may have believed the lies: that you are worthless, ruined, or unlovable. But those are the devil's words, not God's. Begin speaking the truth to yourself again:

- "I am not what was done to me."
- "I am worthy of love, healing, and grace."
- "I am not alone—God is with me."
- "I am healing. I am growing. I am strong."
- "My life still matters. My story is not over."

This is your call to repentance, to restoration, to revival. God is still calling you—not in anger, but in mercy. He wants to save your soul, heal your heart, and renew your hope. Cry out like blind Bartimaeus: *"Jesus, Son of David, have mercy on me!"* He will stop. He will hear. And He will answer.

Maybe your diagnosis came too late. Maybe your abuse was never spoken aloud. But it is never too late for God. As long as there is breath in your body and awareness in your soul, **today is your day of salvation.** Today is the day to trust and obey, for there is no other way to peace, healing, and eternal life than through Jesus Christ.

Now, in the context of this very message, you may be wondering— who exactly are the "foolish" and the "wise" that God speaks of in His Word?

In the context of this chapter, the "foolish" are those whom the world has rejected, overlooked, or dismissed as hopeless. They are the ones suffering in silence—the cancer patient told they have only weeks to live, the abused child now grown up but still carrying invisible scars, the person who has lost everything and is now crying out to God for mercy. These individuals may appear weak or broken on the outside, but in God's eyes, they are exactly who He loves to use. Their willingness to surrender, to believe in the pain, and to repent when others mock their faith makes them powerful vessels of His glory. What the world calls foolish, God calls chosen.

The "foolish" are also those who humbly and desperately seek God when life brings them to their knees. They are the woman with the issue of blood who dared to reach for Jesus' garment, the blind Bartimaeus who cried out in the crowd, the thief on the cross who found eternal life in his dying breath. These people may not have had religious credentials or social approval, but they had faith. That faith moved God. It was not their strength that impressed Him—it was their dependence, their humility, and their desperate repentance. In them, God's power is perfected.

On the other hand, the "wise" are those who trust in their knowledge, status, or strength. They are often the ones society esteems: professionals, intellectuals, leaders, and influencers who believe they have all the answers. They may be doctors who say, "There's nothing more we can do," or religious voices who speak without compassion or understanding. They may be the abuser who thinks they got away with their sin, or the skeptic who mocks faith and believes suffering disqualifies a person from being used by God. These are the so-called wise—the proud, the self-reliant, and the unrepentant who think they see clearly, but are blind to the ways of God.

God confounds these "wise" by using the very people they overlook. When someone at death's door finds peace in Jesus, it confuses the world. When a survivor of trauma forgives and becomes a source of healing for others, it silences the critics. When a broken, dying soul repents and is transformed, it exposes the emptiness of prideful knowledge without God. In every generation, God uses what is weak to reveal His strength and what is foolish to display His divine wisdom.

This is the mystery and beauty of God's kingdom: He flips the script. He chooses what is low to bring down what is high. He uses the broken to show what wholeness looks like. He heals the wounded and then uses their testimony to shake the systems of the world. That is why, in your suffering, in your sickness, in your trauma—God is not done with you. You may be counted out by people, but you are counted in by Heaven. He still uses foolishness to confuse the wise.

Reflection for the Hurting and the Wounded

You may be reading this while carrying pain so deep that words cannot fully explain it. Maybe you have just heard the news that your illness has reached its final stage. Maybe you have prayed, fasted, and cried out, but the answer has not come the way you expected. Your body feels weak.

Your hope feels distant. The people around you do not understand the battle you're in. And deep inside, you wonder, *Is God still with me?"*

Or perhaps your pain is not physical, but emotional and buried under years of silence. Maybe as a child, someone you trusted—a family member, a teacher, a friend—touched you, violated you, and left you with shame that it was not yours to carry. They told you to keep quiet. Maybe you did.

And now, years later, you blame yourself. You ask questions like, *"Was it my fault? Did I do something wrong? Did I deserve it?"*

Let this truth settle in your heart today: **It. Was. Not.Your. Fault.** You did not deserve to be hurt. You did not because of what happened. The person who abused or molested you is responsible for their sin, not you. And God, who is just and holy, saw it all. He wept with you. He never turned His eyes away. And now He is calling you out of silence, shame, and sorrow— not to expose you, but to **heal you**.

You are not unworthy. You are not dirty. You are not forgotten. You are beloved, chosen, and still deeply usable in God's hands. Even if others looked at you with pity or disbelief, God looks at you with compassion and power. He still restores. He still redeems. And He still uses the broken to bring healing to others.

So, whether your pain comes from a diagnosis or a deep emotional wound, know this: God is near to the brokenhearted. He will never waste your pain. His mercy is greater than your shame. His love is stronger than you're suffering. His healing is more powerful than anything the enemy has tried to use against you.

Storms come to every shoreline of faith. Following Christ does not exempt us from swirling winds of illness, loss, disappointment, or the sudden darkness of a world in turmoil. If anything, discipleship paints a target on our backs: *"Your adversary the devil prowls around like a roaring lion, looking for someone to devour"* (1 Pe 5:8). Yet even these assaults serve a larger purpose. When we imagine ourselves wiser than God, He deliberately selects what the world calls *foolish* to confound the self-proclaimed *wise* (1 Co 1:27). Our confusion becomes His canvas, our weakness, His stage.

Picture the ring of life landing from every corner—economic uncertainty, political rancor, wars and rumors of wars, a culture drowning in fear, violence, and injustice. Sometimes you feel the ropes at your back and the enemy's glove at your jaw. But heaven has already declared a different outcome. The moments that appear to spell defeat are the very arenas where faith is forged. It is not the absence of hardship that distinguishes believers, but the presence of a resilient hope that rises each time the count nears ten.

That hope is armed, not empty-handed. *"The weapons of our warfare are not carnal but mighty in God for pulling down strongholds"* (2 Co 10:4 5). Prayer that refuses to quit, Scripture spoken aloud, worship that shifts atmospheres, fasting that loosens chains—these are heaven's artillery. They demolish lies, confront every pretension, and re-align wandering thoughts with the mind of Christ. Where the world shouts, *"Give up!"* the Spirit whispers, *"Stand firm."*

Life, nevertheless, is not fair. It can knock you so low you taste the canvas. Yet the psalmist anchors us: *"Cast your burden on the Lord, and He will sustain you; He will never permit the righteous to be shaken"* (Ps 55:22) . God's sustaining hand does more than lift; it strengthens. Each time He hoists you from the mat, your spiritual muscles thicken, your resolve deepens, and the watching world learns that grace has not quit.

So, trust Him, even when wounded. Grip his unchanging hand and haul yourself upright. Repentance is not a one-time doorway but a lifestyle of turning back, repeatedly, into the arms of mercy. In doing so, we proclaim to every cynic that the light still outshines the darkness, that Christ's return is nearer than yesterday, and that the gospel remains God's power to save. The foolish— those humble enough to depend entirely on grace—become living signposts that confound the calculations of the proud. And through their witness, the wisdoms of this age are invited to kneel, repent, and behold the coming King.

There comes a moment in every believer's journey when we must acknowledge that not everything broken in life is ours to fix. When life knocks us down—through betrayal, grief, sickness, loss, or simply, the weight of the unknown often reaches for control. We try to mend what only God can restore. But faith begins where control ends. It is in those very moments of exhaustion, fear, and surrender that God does His greatest work.

Picture this: You are in the back seat of a car with three others, traveling to meet loved ones for a celebration. You are not driving. Someone else is behind the wheel—someone who knows the way, knows the terrain, and understands how to get everyone safely to the destination. That is how life works when we walk with God. He is not a co-pilot; He is the driver. Yet how often do we reach for the steering wheel, thinking we know better? God does not need a backseat driver; He needs passengers who trust the journey, even when the route looks rough or delayed.

When your marriage feels like it is dissolving into divorce, take your hands off the wheel. When you have lost your job and the foreclosure letter is in the mail, take your hands off the wheel. When your bills are stacking and there is no income in sight, and your children are walking in rebellion, you are not called to fix what is out of your reach. These are the moments where trust in God becomes your only road to peace. Let Him drive. Let Him lead. He knows where you are going. And more importantly, He knows how to get you there.

God does not abandon His people in crisis. He provides blueprints in seasons of stress and anxiety. He wonders when we will surrender. His voice thunders with purpose even when it's not yet clear to us. He orchestrates time and seasons with intention—sending snow to fall, rain to pour, and clouds to shift with divine timing. He waters the earth and refreshes the soul. He loves just and unjust alike. Why? Because he is not like a man. He sees beyond what we see and acts with wisdom we cannot fathom.

This is a call to repentance, not only for the sinful, but for the self-reliant. God is not looking for perfection—He is calling for surrender. He is calling us to return to Him before the return of Christ. Now is not the time to delay. Now is the moment to let go of pride, fear, and control.

Allow the Lord to cleanse, to heal, and to steer.

And as we await the return of Jesus, we must walk in repentance—not just as an act of confession, but as a posture of humility and trust. We must live daily with open hands and surrendered hearts, because true wisdom is knowing when to stop trying to drive and simply ride with the One who knows the road. Trust the process. Trust the pain. Trust the journey. But above all, trust the Driver. He is coming soon—and blessed are those who are ready.

Chapter 10: God's Sovereignty in Political Shifts

"The king's heart is in the hand of the Lord; he directs it like a watercourse wherever he pleases."
— When governments change hands, Heaven does not flinch. Whether through elections, coups, or sudden deaths, God uses every political shift to advance His plan. From Pharaoh to Pilate, from Caesar to the Antichrist, every leader plays a role in God's grand narrative. This chapter brings peace to the troubled heart and clarity to the confused soul: No matter who is in power, God reigns. Political change is not an interruption of God's plan—it is a manifestation of it. As powers rise and fall, we are witnessing the chessboard of prophecy moving toward fulfillment. The King is still in control. Proverbs 21:1 (NIV)

Political changes, whether through elections, resignations, or unexpected events, can unsettle nations and cause uncertainty. Yet, behind every shift, God's sovereign hand is at work. This chapter reveals that no political event is random or out of God's control. Just as God used kings and rulers in the Bible to fulfill His purposes, He continues to guide history toward His divine plan. Understanding this truth can bring peace amid chaos, reminding believers that God's Kingdom will prevail regardless of who holds earthly power.

For teenagers, this chapter helps make sense of why the world feels so unstable. It teaches that while people might struggle to understand politics, God's plan is bigger than any government or leader. Young believers are encouraged to trust God's power and stay faithful in their daily lives, knowing that God is orchestrating history for good, even when it is hard to see.

Adults often feel anxious about political upheaval, fearing the consequences for their families and communities. This chapter challenges them to shift their focus from world leaders to the eternal King. It calls the Church to pray earnestly, engage wisely, and trust fully in God's sovereignty. Knowing that God is in control of political shifts empowers believers to face the future without fear, confident that God's purposes cannot be thwarted.

God Rules Over Every Throne

Political leaders rise and fall, elections surprise, and governments change, but **God remains the ultimate authority behind every throne**. No event catches Him off guard. The Bible is clear: God controls the hearts of rulers and directs history to fulfill His purposes. This sovereignty should bring comfort, especially in turbulent times when political shifts feel chaotic or threatening.

The Divine Hand Behind Human Plans

God uses kings, presidents, and governments to carry out His will—even when those leaders do not know Him or follow His ways. The story of Joseph in Egypt (Genesis 37–50) illustrates this perfectly: sold into slavery and imprisoned, Joseph rose to power to save many lives during famine, fulfilling God's plan through human politics. Similarly, Daniel's prayers and prophetic ministry in Babylon show God's control over foreign rulers.

Political Changes Are Part of God's Timing

Daniel 2:21 reminds us:
"He changes times and seasons; he deposes kings and raises others."

The timing of political events is not random. God's plan unfolds according to His divine calendar, which calls believers to watch and pray rather than panic or despair.

What This Means for Believers Today
- Trust God above political ideologies or leaders
- Pray for those in authority, regardless of their character (1 Timothy 2:1-2)
- Focus on the Kingdom of God, not earthly kingdoms.
- Remember that God can use even flawed leaders for His glory.
- Even in unexpected or controversial rises to power, God's sovereignty remains unchallenged.

Scripture Focus
- **Proverbs 21:1** – God directs the hearts of kings.
- **Daniel 2:21** – God changes times and seasons.
- **Romans 13:1** – All authority comes from God.
- **1 Timothy 2:1-2** – Pray for those in authority.
- **Psalm 75:6-7** – God lifts one and puts down another.

How do you respond to the suffering around you? Do you view it as an opportunity for growth and revival, or do you see it as a sign of despair? Are you willing to stand with those who suffer and guide them to Jesus?

The suffering of nations and peoples signals God's call for repentance and prepares the way for His deliverance. Throughout Scripture, God's heart breaks over the suffering of the oppressed, including widows, orphans, and captives (Psalm 34:18; Isaiah 1:17). National suffering—whether due to war, disease, economic hardship, or social decay—often acts as a prophetic alarm, urging people to return to God.

The cries of the Israelites in Egyptian bondage moved God to action. Similarly, today's suffering reveals the depth of spiritual breakdown and injustice in our society. While suffering is never God's desire, it can be a tool He uses to awaken a hardened people to their need for salvation and change. The Church should not ignore suffering or try to sanitize it. To follow Christ means to carry a cross, and standing with those who suffer embodies His love.

Like Jeremiah, who wept over the destruction of Jerusalem, God's people must grieve and intercede for national and global pain. Suffering often reveals the futility of placing hope in political promises or economic security, instead directing people to the only true source of peace—God Himself.

The COVID-19 pandemic, racial tensions, and economic struggles have caused significant loss but have also created opportunities for spiritual awakening if the Church remains attentive.

Believers are called to be agents of hope and healing amidst suffering, following Christ's example of compassion and sacrificial love.

Reflection

1. How does understanding God's sovereignty over politics affect my faith?
2. Am I trusting God or political systems for my security?
3. How can I pray for our leaders and nation?

Prayer

Sovereign Lord,

You rule over all kingdoms and leaders. Help me to trust Your hand even when the political landscape is confusing. Teach me to pray faithfully for those in authority and to seek Your Kingdom first. Let your will be done on earth as it is in heaven. In Jesus' name, Amen.

Chapter 11: Political Idolatry and Kingdom Identity

"No one can serve two masters. Either you will hate the one and love the other, or you will be devoted to the one and despise the other." — Matthew 6:24 (NIV)

Many believers have traded kingdom identity for political allegiance. Some defend policies more than they preach the Gospel. Others divide over party lines more than they unite around the cross. This chapter confronts the dangerous idol of political identity. While we must vote, engage, and influence, donkeys or elephants do not define us—but by the Lamb. Jesus never came to take sides—He came to take over. God is calling His Church back to its true citizenship: Heaven. Until we abandon political idolatry, we cannot walk in kingdom authority.

In today's world, it is easy for believers to become so attached to political parties or leaders that they start putting them above their faith. This chapter warns against political idolatry—the dangerous practice of allowing politics to replace God as the ultimate authority. When political views become idols, they divide the Church and blur the line between earthly allegiances and heavenly citizenship. The Church must remember that our true identity is found in Christ alone, not in any political system.

For teenagers, this chapter explains how it is normal to care about issues and leaders but cautions against letting politics shape their entire worldview or friendships. Young believers are encouraged to seek God first, understand His kingdom, and engage in politics with wisdom, kindness, and humility. This chapter helps teens navigate a world full of strong opinions without losing sight of their spiritual values.

Adults are challenged to evaluate where their loyalties lie. Are political views shaping their faith, or is faith shaping their opinions? This chapter calls the Church to rise above partisan conflicts and to unite around Christ's mission rather than party platforms. By reclaiming their kingdom identity, believers can stand firm as ambassadors of God's eternal Kingdom in a divided and politicized world.

When Politics Becomes Idolatry

Political involvement and patriotism are not inherently wrong. Scripture encourages believers to pray for leaders and seek the welfare of their communities (Jeremiah 29:7; 1 Timothy 2:1-2). However, the problem arises when political allegiance replaces or competes with our allegiance to God.

Political idolatry happens when:

- We elevate political leaders to a place reserved for God.
- Our hope and security depend more on political outcomes than on God's promises.
- We adopt tribalism that divides the Body of Christ.
- This idolatry can blind us to truth, distort our priorities, and damage our witnesses.

Kingdom Identity Above All

The Church is called to be **a kingdom within the kingdoms of this world**, governed by Christ as King. Our ultimate loyalty must be to God's Kingdom, not any political party or national ideology.

"But seek first his kingdom and his righteousness, and all these things will be given to you as well."
— Matthew 6:33 (NIV)

Kingdom identity means:
1. Loving neighbors regardless of political views
2. Speaking truth in love, not fear or hatred
3. Remaining rooted in God's Word above culture or media narratives
4. Remembering our citizenship is ultimately in heaven (Philippians 3:20)

The Danger of Dividing the Church

Political idolatry fuels division within the Church, causing believers to turn against each other over partisan differences. This weakens the Church's mission and undermines its prophetic voice.

God calls His people to **be peacemakers** and **unifiers**, showing the world a different kind of allegiance—one that transcends politics.

Scripture Focus
- **Matthew 6:24** – No one can serve two masters.
- **Philippians 3:20** – Our citizenship is in heaven.
- **Ephesians 4:3-6** – Unity of the Spirit in the bond of peace
- **Jeremiah 29:7** – Seek the welfare of the city.
- **1 Timothy 2:1-2** – Pray for kings and all in authority.

Are you confused by culture or rooted in the Word? Are you prepared to be a voice of clarity and courage amid chaos?

As culture increasingly rejects absolute truth and moral clarity, God calls His Church to stand firm and proclaim His unchanging Word. Today's world is marked by moral confusion, with shifting views on gender, sexuality, marriage, and truth itself. This situation is not new; Paul warned us about it in 2 Timothy 3:15. Secular culture often dismisses biblical values as outdated or oppressive, and the Church faces pressure to conform or remain silent.

God's call is not to blend in but to stand out—to be "salt and light" (Matthew 5:13-16), preserving truth in a decaying world. Just as Noah's generation mocked the coming flood, modern society often ridicules the Church's warnings about sin and judgment. While this confusion can overwhelm believers, it is also a sign of the end times, fulfilling prophecy, and urging the Church to remain vigilant.

Church leaders and believers must be grounded in Scripture, equipped to confront error lovingly but firmly without compromising grace. The temptation to be "user-friendly" must not come at the cost of biblical fidelity. The Church must proclaim repentance, even when it is unpopular. History shows that when the Church abandons truth for popularity, decline follows, as seen in Israel's idolatry and the moral struggles of the Corinthian church.

I invite you to renew your commitment to God's Word and to pray for the courage to be a faithful witness in a hostile culture.

Reflection

1. Where have I allowed political views to overshadow my faith?
2. How can I maintain Kingdom identity while engaging in politics?
3. What steps can I take to promote unity in my church and community?

Prayer

Lord Jesus, help me to serve You above all else. Guard my heart against political idolatry and division. Teach me to love those with different views and to seek Your Kingdom first. May my life reflect Your unity and truth in a world that is often divided. In Your name, Amen.

Chapter 12: The Church's Role in the Last Days

"You are the light of the world. A town built on a hill cannot be hidden." Matthew 5:14 (NIV)

The final chapters of time are not about Hollywood, Washington, or Wall Street; they are about the Church. This chapter explores the Church's prophetic assignment in the last days: to preach, to prepare, to prophesy, and to endure. The Bride of Christ must make herself ready. No longer can we afford lukewarm gatherings or entertainment-driven services. The world is groaning, and creation is waiting for the children of God to rise. In these final hours, the Church must become a beacon of truth, holiness, and unwavering love. The harvest is ripe—but the workers must awaken.

As the world moves closer to the end of this age, the Church stands at a pivotal crossroads. This chapter emphasizes that the Church is not a bystander but an active participant in God's unfolding plan. The last days call for a Church that is awake, united, and bold—ready to proclaim the Gospel, disciple believers, and stand as a light in darkness. The Church's role is to prepare the Bride for Christ's return by living holy lives, practicing spiritual discipline, and loving others fiercely, even amid growing opposition.

For teenagers, this chapter offers hope and a sense of purpose. It tells young believers they have a critical role to play—whether through sharing their faith, standing up for what is right, or simply living authentically. The Church needs their energy, passion, and fresh perspectives as part of the global movement preparing for Jesus' return.

Adults are reminded that complacency or division weakens the Church's witness. This chapter calls Church leaders and members to recommend prayer, unity, and obedience. The Church must rise above cultural distractions and political battles to focus on its divine mission. The last days are not a time for fear but for faith-filled action, knowing that the Church is God's chosen instrument for revival and transformation in the world.

Called to Be Watchmen and Witnesses

In the last days, the Church has a critical mission: to be both **watchmen** who alert the world to coming judgment and **witnesses** who proclaim the Gospel of Jesus Christ.

Like Ezekiel was called to warn Israel (Ezekiel 33), believers today are called to watch, pray, and speak God's truth even when it is unpopular or costly.

Standing Firm Amidst Chaos

As political and cultural upheaval intensifies, the Church must resist fear and confusion. Instead, it is called to stand firm in:

- **Prayer and fasting** for revival and protection.
- **Unity despite diversity** within the Body of Christ
- **Bold proclamation** of God's Word with love and conviction

The Church is not powerless or passive but empowered by the Holy Spirit to impact the world for God's Kingdom.

The Church as a Spiritual Army

The Apostle Paul describes the Church as engaged in spiritual warfare (Ephesians 6:10-18). The Church fights not with flesh and blood but with prayer, truth, righteousness, faith, salvation, and the Word of God.

In a time when leaders rise and fall, and nations shake, the Church must:
- Stand as a beacon of hope and truth.
- Call sinners to repentance.
- Comfort the brokenhearted
- Pray for leaders and governments.

Hope in Christ's Return
While the world grows darker, the Church lives with **hope and expectancy** for the return of Christ. This hope fuels perseverance and mission.

"Therefore, keep watching, because you do not know on what day your Lord will come." Matthew 24:42

Have you neglected your altar? Is your spiritual fire burning low? Will you return and rebuild what has been broken between you and God?

Before revival can fall, the Church must repair the altar of prayer, repentance, and worship that has been neglected or defiled. In 1 Kings 18, before calling down fire from heaven, Elijah first rebuilt the altar of the Lord that had been torn down. Revival did not start with spectacle—it started with repair.

Today's church has altars that have been replaced by stages, lights, and performances. In many places, the sacred has been exchanged for the superficial. God is not calling us to build bigger churches— He is calling us to rebuild deeper altars. Altars of humility, brokenness, intercession, and obedience.

A broken altar is symbolic of a broken relationship with God. Where prayer is absent, pride is present. Where repentance is missing, religion replaces relationships. Rebuilding begins in the heart. It means personal surrender before public ministry. God wants inner purity, not just outward platforms. The modern church often rushes to conferences and events, but God is waiting in the secret place. He is calling His people to rebuild their quiet time, their tears, and their groaning.

Like the priests of old, we are called to minister before the Lord, not just before people. True fire only falls on a consecrated altar (Leviticus 9:24). In times of shaking, God is restoring the

Church to her first love. The altar is where the Bride meets the Bridegroom, where Heaven kisses Earth again. Revival will not come because we pray for it; it will come because we live it through holiness, sacrifice, and a deep return to the presence of God.

Scripture Focus
- **Ezekiel 33:7-9** – The watchman's responsibility
- **Matthew 5:14-16** – The Church as light of the world
- **Ephesians 6:10-18** – The armor of God

- **Acts 1:8** – Empowered by the Holy Spirit to witness.
- **1 Thessalonians 5:6** – Be alert and self-controlled.

Reflection
1. How am I acting as a watchman and witness in my community?
2. What spiritual armor do I need to put on daily?
3. How can I encourage unity and boldness in my church?

Prayer
Lord, help me to be your faithful watchman and witness. Give me boldness to speak truth in love and strength to stand firm in these challenging times. Unite Your Church and fill us with Your Spirit, so we may shine Your light and prepare the way for Your return. In Jesus' name, Amen.

Chapter 13: God's Judgment and Mercy in the Last Days

"The Lord is not slow in keeping his promise, as some understand slowness. Instead, he is patient with you, not wanting anyone to perish, but everyone to come to repentance." — 2 Peter 3:9 (NIV)

Judgment and mercy are not opposites; they are twins. In the last days, God will release both. His judgments are not vindictive; they are redemptive. Like a surgeon cutting out cancer, God judges to save, not destroy. This chapter walks readers through biblical patterns of judgment and how they always came after multiple chances to repent. Yet in every act of judgment, there is also a door of mercy. Today, that door is still open. But soon, it will shut. The Church must proclaim both love and warning, because without justice, grace becomes cheap.

God's judgment in the last days is a powerful but often misunderstood reality. This chapter teaches that judgment is not about punishment alone—it is about correction, purification, and the restoration of God's order. Just like a loving parent disciplines their child, God's judgment is meant to bring His people back to Himself. Alongside judgment, God's mercy shines as a beacon of hope, offering forgiveness and new beginnings for those who repent.

For teenagers, this chapter explains that while judgment might sound scary, it is God's way of saying, "I love you and want the best for you." It encourages young people to respond to God's mercy by choosing to follow Him wholeheartedly. Understanding both judgment and mercy helps teens see that God's love is patient but serious, and that their choices matter.

Adults are urged to balance their understanding of God's justice and mercy. This chapter calls the Church to preach both truth and grace, warning about consequences while offering hope.

Recognizing God's judgment as an act of love can motivate believers to live holy lives and to share the Gospel urgently. God's mercy remains available, but the time to receive it is limited, making repentance and faith more important than ever.

The Reality of Judgment

The Bible teaches that God's judgment is real and coming. It is just a response to sin and rebellion against Him. The last days will be marked by increased wickedness and a hardening of hearts (Matthew 24:12).

Judgment is often described as a refining fire—painful but necessary to purify God's people and cleanse the earth. We cannot ignore the fact that our churches and our governments are both plagued with division and compromise. In the U.S., confusion is rampant—spiritual leaders are divided in truth, and political leaders are torn in their allegiance to the Constitution and the rule of law. This global pattern of disunity reveals a deeper spiritual crisis. The Bible warns that a house divided will fall, and this truth applies now more than ever. God will not bless confusion or tolerate deception for long. Judgment begins with the house of God.

The Overflowing Mercy of God

But God's mercy is equally real and abundant. Throughout Scripture, God patiently calls sinners to repentance, longing for restoration rather than destruction.

The story of Nineveh in Jonah 3 exemplifies this mercy—when the people repented, God relented from sending judgment.

Judgment Serves a Purpose

God's judgment is not arbitrary or cruel. It serves to:
- Warn the wicked to repent.
- Encourage the righteous to remain faithful.
- Purify the Church and the earth.
- Bring about the ultimate restoration of all things.

The warnings we see in current events, including the rise of controversial leaders and national upheaval, can be seen as part of this process.

Balancing Fear and Hope

Believers must balance a healthy fear of God's judgment with confident hope in His mercy. This balance motivates holiness and compassion, not despair or judgmentalism.

If Christ returned today, would you be ready? Have you responded to the warning signs, or silenced them with distraction? What will you do with this last call of grace?

The current shaking of the world is not the end, but a final warning. God is giving time for repentance before Christ returns in power and glory. Throughout history, God always sent warnings before judgment—Noah before the flood, Jonah before Nineveh's destruction, and Jesus before Jerusalem fell. Today's global unrest—plagues, wars, apostasy, earthquakes, false teachings, lawlessness—is not random. It aligns with Jesus' words in Matthew 24 and Luke 21.

These signs are not just tragedies—they are trumpets, calling the Church to wake up, prepare, and warn others: "Behold, the Bridegroom is coming; go out to meet Him!" (Matthew 25:6). God is still speaking, but many are distracted. As in the days of Noah, people are eating, drinking, and marrying—ignoring the ark being built in front of them.

This chapter is not about fear; it is about urgency. The world will not last forever. Jesus is coming back, and He is looking for a ready Bride, not a sleeping one. The Church must stop entertaining and start evangelizing. Stop compromising and start consecrating. This is the final hour—not the time to blend in. Just like the ten virgins, half were prepared and half were not. The difference? Oil—symbolizing the Holy Spirit, intimacy with God, and spiritual readiness.

Prophetic voices are being raised globally. God is using the foolish-those who have no fame, no platform, no degrees—to sound the alarm with purity and urgency. For those with ears to hear, this moment is holy. A last call. A final warning. Not because God is angry, but because His mercy desires no one to perish (2 Peter 3:9).

The Fear of Division and the Cry for Peace

In these last days, fear is gripping the hearts of men and women around the world. With every passing day, the divisions in governments, communities, and churches grow deeper, creating confusion and emotional unrest. Many people are desperately searching for peace, but instead, they are met with anxiety, violence, injustice, and uncertainty. This deep unrest is not just spiritual; it is physical. Fear is now contributing to widespread health issues, such as depression, high blood pressure, panic attacks, and mental illness. The soul is heavy, and the mind is weary. Peace seems out of touch.

Across the world and even in the United States—once seen as a beacon of liberty—there is a tightening of freedom of speech. The truth is being silenced, and bold voices for righteousness are being shamed, shadow-banned, or punished. Migrants are being mistreated, and even citizens are experiencing abuse by those in power. When the systems created to protect justice instead contribute to oppression, people cry out for help, but it feels like their voices are falling on deaf ears. There is injustice in the courtroom, silence in the pulpit, and confusion in the pews.

But even in the chaos, God has not forsaken His people. The peace we seek cannot come from man—it comes from above. Jesus said, "Peace I leave with you; my peace I give you. I do not give to you as the world gives" (John 14:27). True peace, justice, and divine order will only come through the hand of God. He alone can restore the rule of law, silence confusion, and raise righteous leadership in the nation, the church, and the world. The time is coming when God will shake the heavens and the earth—not to destroy, but to awaken.

Just as Jesus once declared, *"I tell you, if these should hold their peace, the stones would immediately cry out"* (Luke 19:40), so it shall be again. If spiritual leaders remain silent, if politicians fail to repent, if the Church refuses to rise, then God will use the unlikely. As He once used a donkey to rebuke a prophet (Numbers 22:28–30), He will now raise what the world considers foolish to speak truth. Stones will cry out, the voiceless will be heard, and the rejected will carry the Word of the Lord. God is not dependent on titles—He uses yielded hearts.

This is not a time to fear, but to return to God with sincerity and humility. The Church must rise in unity and repentance. Nations must turn their hearts back to justice and righteousness. For those suffering under the weight of fear, there is hope: *"The Lord gives strength to His people; the Lord blesses His people with peace"* (Psalm 29:11). Let us not ignore the signs or silence the truth, for we are nearing the day when every knee will bow, and every tongue confess that Jesus Christ is Lord. God is shaking the earth so that what cannot be shaken will remain (Hebrews 12:26-27).

Freedom from the Dungeon of Fear

"I sought the Lord, and He heard me, and delivered me from all my fears." — Psalm 34:4
"God has not given us the spirit of fear, but of power, and love, and a sound mind." — 2 Timothy 1:7
"There is no fear in love. But perfect love drives out fear..." — 1 John 4:18

In this present world, many are living under the dark cloud of fear—fear of losing their jobs, fear of unjust deportation, fear of government control, fear of molestation, domestic abuse, censorship, persecution, or even the silencing of truth or rising global instability. Fear has become a dungeon where hearts are tormented daily, and peace seems far from reach. But God's Word reminds us in **Psalm 34:4**, "I sought the Lord, and He heard me, and delivered me from all my fears." Fear may be a powerful weapon in the enemy's hands, but it is no match for the love and authority of God. Fear paralyzes, but faith mobilizes. While man may attempt to control others through fear, God liberates through love and truth.

The devil thrives in spreading fear through systems, corrupt leaders, and abusive relationships. He uses fear to silence truth, to oppress freedom, and to cripple the destiny of those called by God. But Scripture is clear: "God has not given us the spirit of fear, but of power, and love, and a sound mind" (**2 Timothy 1:7**). Fear is not from God—it is a spiritual bondage that is broken when we choose to trust in the Lord above what we see and feel. The world may shake, but the Kingdom of God stands unmovable.

When we understand the depth of God's love through Jesus Christ, fear begins to lose its grip. "Perfect love casts out fear" (**1 John 4:18**). This love is not just an emotion—it is a divine force that reassures, protects, and empowers us in the darkest hours. It is the love that drove Jesus to the cross, and it is the same love that holds us securely in these troubled times. God's love shines brightest when the world is darkest. We do not have to fear tomorrow when we know the One who holds it.

Every fear—whether of injustice, loss, silence, or violence—must submit to the authority of Christ. Fear is a tool used by man when love is absent, but God uses the "foolishness" of faith, hope, and sacrificial love to overthrow the wisdom of the world. He has chosen the broken, the exiled, and the persecuted to shine His glory. This is why we must lift our heads, not bow them in despair. Christ is our Deliverer, and His promise remains: "Lo, I am with you always, even to the end of the age" (**Matthew 28:20**).

So be encouraged: do not let the world trap you in fear. We are not forsaken, and we are not powerless. God is raising a remnant— even through unlikely voices—to speak peace in the storm. As you walk through this season, declare over your life: *"I will not fear, for the Lord is with me. He has delivered me, and He will deliver me again."* Let faith arise. Let hope be rekindled. And let love lead the way— because *God uses the foolish things of the world to confound the wise*, and His love will always overcome fear.

These fears have become chains that weigh down the hearts of both citizens and immigrants, men and women alike. But Scripture reminds us that God hears our cries and delivers us. Fear is not of God; it is a tool of the enemy, used to dominate and divide. But God's perfect love casts out all fear.

The devil's tactics have not changed—he uses fear to intimidate and suppress the people of God. Whether it comes through ungodly governments, abusive relationships, or threats to our freedom, fear is meant to silence faith. But *God has not given us the spirit of fear*. Instead, He gives us power to overcome, love to endure, and a sound mind to discern what is true. When fear knocks, faith must answer. We stand boldly because of who God is, not because of what is happening around us.

Fear gains ground when love is absent. It is the absence of God's love and truth in the hearts of people that causes leaders to oppress, abusers to harm, and society to unravel. But through Jesus Christ, God restored love to the center of our lives and gave us the authority to overcome fear. His love is a shield, a light, and a fortress. No matter what threatens our peace—whether it be global instability, personal betrayal, or cultural decay—we are safe in His hands.

Now more than ever, we must rise above fear. The world calls it foolish to trust in God in such chaotic times. But Scripture tells us that *God uses the foolish things of the world to shame the wise*. The faithful—those who trust Him even when they do not see the way—will be the ones who lead others out of fear into hope. Lift your head. Stand in truth. Refuse to be silenced. Speak peace. Walk in the power of God's love.

Scripture Focus
- 2 Peter 3:9 – God's patience and desire for repentance
- Revelation 3:19 – God disciplines those He loves
- Romans 11:22 – God's kindness and severity
- Joel 2:13 – Return to God with all your heart
- Matthew 25:31-46 – The final judgment

Reflection
1. How do I view God's judgment and mercy in my life?
2. Am I living in a way that reflects both reverence and hope?
3. How can I share the message of God's mercy with others?

Prayer
Father God, I surrender every fear that weighs on my heart—fear of the future, fear of loss, fear of rejection, and fear of the unknown. I choose to trust in You. Fill me with Your perfect love that casts out fear. Remind me that You are my Deliverer, my Refuge, and my Defender. Help me to walk in boldness, knowing that You have not given me a spirit of fear, but of power, love, and a sound mind. Use me as a light in this dark world to show others that hope is found in You alone. Thank you for your patience and mercy. Help me to live in awe of Your holiness and hope of Your grace. Give me boldness to share Your call to repentance and to extend Your mercy to those around me. May Your Kingdom come soon. In Jesus' name, Amen.

Chapter 14: Preparing for Christ's Return – Living with Eternity in View

"Therefore, keep watch, because you do not know on what day Your Lord will come." Matthew 24:42 (NIV)

The King is coming. Not as a baby in a manger, but as a righteous judge on a white horse. This last chapter is the crescendo of hope, urgency, and holy anticipation. Christ is not delaying because He is disinterested, but because He is merciful. But the delay will not last forever. The Church must awaken from its slumber. Believers must trim their lamps. Sinners must bow before the Savior while there's still time. Heaven is mobilizing. Angels are preparing. Prophecy is converging. The Bridegroom is on His way—will we be ready?

The return of Jesus Christ is the ultimate hope and the greatest promise for believers. This chapter urges the Church and individuals alike to prepare spiritually, emotionally, and practically for that glorious day. Preparation means living holy lives, growing in faith, and actively sharing the Gospel with urgency. The world is moving rapidly toward the end times, and believers must stay vigilant, like the wise virgins who kept their lamps trimmed and ready.

For teenagers, this chapter offers an inspiring vision: they are part of a divine story with an incredible ending. It encourages young believers to build a solid foundation now through prayer, Bible study, and fellowship, so they can stand firm no matter what challenges come.

Preparing for Christ's return means choosing daily to live with hope and purpose, even when the world feels uncertain or unfair.

Adults are called to lead by example in this preparation, nurturing their faith and encouraging their families and communities. This chapter emphasizes the importance of holiness, repentance, and readiness, warning against complacency or distractions. It reminds the Church that Jesus' return is imminent and will be unexpected, making faithfulness today the key to rejoicing tomorrow.

Watchfulness and Readiness
The return of Jesus Christ is certain but unknown in timing. Scripture calls believers to always be watchful and ready, living holy lives that reflect the Kingdom of God.

Preparation means:
- Staying spiritually alert
- Growing in faith and obedience
- Sharing the Gospel with urgency and love

Living in the Light
Jesus taught that those who live as children of light are prepared for His coming. Darkness may increase, but God's people shine as beacons of hope and truth.

The Foolish and the Wise
The title of this book reminds us that God uses "foolish" people—those whom the world underestimates—to confound the wise. As we await Christ's return, humility and reliance on God's wisdom are essential.

Encouragement to Persevere

The last days will be challenging. Believers may face persecution, confusion, and opposition. Yet, perseverance grounded in God's promises will lead to victory.

Will you be counted among the remnants? Will you stand when others fall? Will you be the Church that carries the fire of God to the final hour?

Amid global shaking and moral collapse, God is raising a remnant Church—pure, bold, Spirit-filled, and unshakable. While systems fail and worldly leaders falter, God is not panicking—He is preparing. He is refining a Church that will not bow to fear, culture, or compromise. This remnant Church will be like Daniel in Babylon—faithful in prayer, unwavering in truth, and influential even in the heart of wicked government.

God is not looking for a big Church; He's looking for a burning Church—a people who are holy, humble, and wholly surrendered. In every generation, there has been a remnant: Noah and his family, Elijah at Mount Carmel, the faithful in Sardis (Revelation 3:4). Quantity never impressed God—purity does.

This Church won't just survive the storm—it will shine in it. Like the wise virgins with oil in their lamps, they will carry light in the darkest hour. Their strength won't be in politics or popularity but in presence—a deep walk with God through prayer, the Word, fasting, worship, and obedience. These believers may not be known on Earth, but they are known in Heaven. They are intercessors, evangelists, servant leaders, and watchmen on the wall.

The shaking has revealed who is built on sand and who is built on the Rock. This Church will stand, not because of resources, but because of roots. In these last days, God will use the foolish, the rejected, and the overlooked to lead revival, carry glory, and declare truth.

There is a sobering truth every human must face: *everything in this life has an expiration date.* Whether it's political power, spiritual influence, romantic relationships, family connections, or cultural trends, all of it is temporary. The Apostle Paul reminded us in Hebrews 9:27, "It is appointed unto men once to die, but after this the judgment." This means no matter our titles, achievements, or the love stories we treasure—whether in government, marriage, ministry, or education—we will all one day stand before the Judge of all creation.

Even the most unconventional of political leaders—like the U.S. President—are not exempt from this truth. Thrones crumble, Nations rise and fall. Elections come and go. But what remains constant is God's timeline, which moves steadily toward the return of His Son, Jesus Christ.

Ecclesiastes 3 echoes this: "To everything there is a season, a time for every purpose under heaven." The wisdom of Solomon continues with this eternal warning: "Fear God and keep His commandments, for this is the whole duty of man."

In our modern world, we are tempted to believe that certain positions or seasons will last forever.

But the truth is that *seasons shift*, and when they do, we must be ready. Marriages flourish and fade. Work achievements accumulate and then vanish with retirement or death. Cultural movements trend and are then forgotten. Our lives are like vapor, appearing for a little while and then vanishing away (James 4:14). So, what does it profit a man to gain the entire world and yet lose his soul?

Jesus gave this command: "Watch therefore, for you know neither the day nor the hour in which the Son of Man is coming" (Matthew 25:13). He was not just speaking to preachers or prophets— He was addressing *all people*. The parable of the ten virgins in Matthew 25 reminds us that the wise prepare while the foolish delay. The Bridegroom will come at midnight, when least expected. In that moment, it will not matter if you were a president or a janitor, a CEO, or a single parent. What will matter is whether your lamp was full, if your life was yielded to Christ, and your soul clothed in righteousness.

This message must pierce through our busy calendars and our worldly distractions. Families must realize that the best inheritance to leave behind is not wealth, but a legacy of faith. Church leaders must preach holiness, not popularity. University students must pursue truth over ideology. Workers must see their career as a platform for witness, not worship. Because the trumpet will sound, and Christ will return for a people who are watching, waiting, and ready.

We, the Bride of Christ—male and female alike—are in a divine engagement season. And every engagement must lead to a wedding or be broken. We must ask ourselves: Are we preparing for the Bridegroom, or flirting with the world? Are our garments white and pure, or stained with compromise? The call of this chapter is not just awareness; it is **readiness**. For one day soon, the sky will split, and the King of Glory will appear. May He find us faithful, awake, and longing for His coming.

Scripture References:
Hebrews 9:27 – "It is appointed unto men once to die, but after this the judgment."
Ecclesiastes 3:1 – "To everything there is a season, and a time for every matter under heaven."
Ecclesiastes 12:13 – "Fear God and keep his commandments: for this is the whole duty of man."
James 4:14 – "You are a mist that appears for a little while and then vanishes."
Matthew 25:13 – "Watch therefore, for ye know neither the day nor the hour wherein the Son of man cometh."

Scripture Focus
Matthew 24:42-44 – Be ready for the Son of Man's coming. 1 Thessalonians 5:1-11 – Living as children of the light.
James 1:12 – Blessed is the one who perseveres under trial. Revelation 22:20 – "Yes, I am coming soon."

Reflection
1. How am I preparing spiritually for Christ's return?
2. What areas of my life need greater faith and obedience?
3. How can I encourage others to watch and wait with hope?
4. Am I living with eternity in mind, or clinging to things that are fading?
5. Have I prepared my heart for the return of Christ?
6. What areas of my life would I be ashamed of if Jesus returned today?

Prayer

Heavenly Father, awaken our hearts to the urgency of this hour. Teach us to number our days, that we may gain a heart of wisdom. Strip away the illusions of permanence in this world and anchor us in Your eternal truth. May we be ready when You return, with our lamps full and our hearts faithful. In Jesus' name,

I long for your return. Help me to be watchful and faithful, ready to meet You at any moment. Strengthen my faith and obedience so that I may live as a light in this dark world. Use me to share your hope and truth with others until you come again. Amen.

The world praises brilliance, beauty, and power. We elevate celebrities, scholars, and influencers, convinced that greatness looks a certain way. But God has always worked in reverse—raising the lowly and humbling the proud. "But God hath chosen the foolish things of the world to confound the wise…" (1 Corinthians 1:27). This is not a poetic thought. It is a divine strategy.

From Genesis to Revelation, God never followed man's logic. He used barren women to birth nations, stutterers to deliver messages, and fishermen to launch the Church. He chose a manager over a mansion. A cross over a crown. The kingdom of God is upside down: the last become first, the meek inherit the earth, and the poor are blessed. This is foolishness to the world, but wisdom to God.

In the days of Noah, the wise laughed at the ark. In Egypt, Pharaoh scoffed at Moses. In Nazareth, no one believed a carpenter's son could be the Messiah. God's choices never made sense to those seeking status. Even the cross, the ultimate act of salvation, was seen as scandalous. "The message of the cross is foolishness to those who are perishing…" (1 Corinthians 1:18). But it is the power of God to those who believe.

We must unlearn the idea that being used by God requires worldly credentials. It requires surrender. Availability, not ability, is what heaven looks for. Scripture is filled with the unqualified who became powerful through obedience: David, the shepherd boy; Esther, the orphaned girl; Peter, the impulsive fisherman; Paul, the former persecutor.

If you feel too broken, too unworthy, or too unknown to matter, you are exactly who God is looking for. His power is made perfect in weakness (2 Corinthians 12:9). God does not need your résumé—He wants your "yes." The more we cling to our wisdom, the more we resist His will. But when we yield, we tap into something eternal.

God's wisdom is not loud. It whispers through wildernesses. It speaks in dreams. It confirms through Scripture. It guides in stillness. Often, it looks like foolishness until it becomes fulfillment. Today, we must ask: Have we traded the foolishness of the cross for the approval of man? Are we seeking a platform over presence?

Revival will not come through polished speeches, but through humble vessels. The next great move of God may not come through the pulpit, but through prisons, protests, or a child's prayer. God still confounds the wise. He still overturns worldly systems. He still picks the least likely to carry His glory. So let this be your foundation: God's foolishness is not a flaw. It is a divine invitation to be part of something so much bigger than yourself. And He is still calling the willing.

We are living in a time of great upheaval—social unrest, political confusion, economic uncertainty, and a global drift from moral and spiritual truth. In a world where knowledge has increased but wisdom has diminished, where people idolize intellect but ignore divine instruction, the words of Paul to the Corinthians have never been more relevant: *"But God chose the foolish things of the world to shame the wise; God chose the weak things of the world to shame the strong"* (1 Corinthians 1:27).

The modern age celebrates self-reliance and human achievement. We exalt influencers, CEOs, and experts. Yet, in this same era, we are facing rising mental health crises among children, identity confusion in youth, and hopelessness in adults. Homelessness, broken families, and mass disillusionment are no longer the exception; they are the norm.

God is not surprised. He is not silent. He is still speaking. He is doing it through the voices we often overlook—the recovering addict who now preaches grace, the child who prays with unshaken faith, the homeless woman who knows scripture by heart, the grieving father who comforts others despite his loss. These are the vessels God uses to remind the world that His strength is made perfect in weakness.

The Church must open its ears. Political leaders must humble their hearts. Advocates, activists, and educators must begin to see beyond systems and lean into the Spirit. Because while the world is shouting its opinions, God is whispering truth through the least likely among us.

Children today are exposed to confusion earlier than ever. Many are searching for meaning in a world that's lost its compass. Youth are bombarded by false identities and empty promises.

Adults are drowning in fear and uncertainty, especially those who have lost jobs, homes, or loved ones. But these very crises are the places where God does His most surprising work.

In times of despair, God births purpose. In places of lack, He releases provision. He does not wait for conditions to improve; He invades chaos to show He is still God.

The reason many do not see Him is that He rarely shows up in the form they expect. The Israelites missed the Messiah because they were looking for a king, not a carpenter. And today, many miss His voice because they are looking for scholars, not shepherds.

God has always confounded expectations. When nations tremble and churches compromise, when families fracture and society falters, God raises voices in the wilderness. They may not speak with polish, but they speak with power. They may not be known by name, but they carry heaven's authority.

Let us not forget: God used a donkey to speak to Balaam, a slave to rebuke Pharaoh, and a virgin to birth the Savior. He is still using the foolish to wake up the proud.

If you are a young person who feels unseen, a parent grieving over your child, a teacher struggling with what is being taught in schools, or a leader overwhelmed by the noise of culture, know this: God can and will use you.

He is not looking for the most educated, the most experienced, or the most eloquent. He is looking for the most surrendered. Your pain, your loss, your confusion—it can all become a platform for God's power.

Watchfulness and Readiness: In a time when world systems are unraveling, we must live alert to God's movement. The shift in the U.S. administration is not just political; it is prophetic. The world stage is being set for God to reveal His glory through uncommon vessels. Will you recognize the time?

Living in the Light: The light of God's truth exposes the illusion of human wisdom. Living in that light means turning from man-made solutions and leaning into God's unchanging Word.

Encouragement to Persevere: If you feel insignificant or overwhelmed by what you see in the news or your neighborhood, take heart. God has always used small people to accomplish mighty things. Stay faithful, even when it feels foolish.

Scripture Focus: 1 Corinthians 1:27-29 Isaiah 55:8-9, 2 Corinthians 12:9-10

Reflection and Prayer: Lord, in a world obsessed with strength, remind me that You are glorified in weakness. Use me for your purposes even when I feel foolish, and teach me to hear Your voice when others ignore it. Prepare my heart for revival. Let me not miss the moment of Your visitation.

A Call for Personal and Corporate Repentance (Churchwide and National)

Even leaders need space to admit failure before the Lord. Add a segment that directly calls on spiritual leaders, churches, and the nation to repent for:
- Compromising the truth for popularity
- Neglecting the broken and marginalized
- Idolizing political ideologies over kingdom values
- Replacing Spirit-led worship with performance
- Turning churches into businesses rather than places of transformation. Supporting political leaders in their hidden agenda, such as racism, withholding food from children, and the excessive cost of living.

"If My people, who are called by My name, will humble themselves and pray and seek My face and turn from their wicked ways..." — 2 Chronicles 7:14

A Prophetic Warning Against Delayed Obedience
Some leaders believe they have more time. Make it clear: the window for repentance is closing, and delayed obedience is still disobedience. Speak prophetically into the urgency of the hour.

"Night is coming, when no one can work." — John 9:4
"Today, if you hear his voice, do not harden your hearts." — Hebrews 3:15

Testimonies or Real-life Examples of Modern 'Foolish' Vessels God is Using

Share 2–3 short vignettes of people today (young, overlooked, broken backgrounds) who are boldly living for Christ and igniting change where theologians or church boards have not. It will contrast man's rejection with God's selection.

A Commissioning Prayer or Consecration Declaration
End with a declaration or prayer of consecration that pastors, ministers, and readers can repeat out loud, inviting the Holy Spirit to cleanse, fill, and reassign them for this end-time work.

Prayer
Lord, I lay down my pride, my platform, and my plans. I picked up the cross again. Use me, not for my name's glory, but for Yours. Let me live holy. Let me lead boldly. Let me love sacrificially. Let revival begin in me. In Jesus' name, amen."

A Final Trumpet Cry: Prepare the Way

Echo John the Baptist's cry. Invite leaders and readers to see themselves as modern-day forerunners preparing people not just for church, but for the return of Christ.

"Repent, for the kingdom of heaven is at hand." — Matthew 3:2
"I am the voice of one crying in the wilderness: Prepare the way of the Lord!" — John 1:23

Chapter 16: Called, Commissioned, and Sent

You've read the stories. You've seen how God worked through the least, the lost, and the unlikely. But now the question becomes: What will you do with what you have heard? The Bible is not a history book. It is a living word. And the same God who used Moses, Rahab, Gideon, and Paul is still calling for vessels—now.

We are living in a time of shaking. Cultural confusion, political chaos, and spiritual compromise surround us. The harvest is plentiful. The laborers are few. We do not need more polished influencers. We need bold, Spirit-filled believers who are unafraid to look foolish to the world and faithful to heaven.

"Whom shall I send? And who will go for us?" (Isaiah 6:8). The call still echoes today. God is not looking for the most impressive—He is looking for the most surrendered. Every revival in history began with ordinary people doing extraordinary things through obedience. Not one of them had it all together. But all of them were willing.

You are not too late. You are not too broken. You are not overlooked. Your voice matters in this hour because it is heaven's voice that speaks through you. Jesus didn't choose scholars to follow Him. He chose fishermen, tax collectors, and zealots. Why? Because God sees what man ignores.

The time for passive Christianity is over. This is not the season to hide your light under a basket (Matthew 5:15). The world is in darkness, and you carry the flame. You were not saved to be silent. You were saved to be sent. Someone is waiting on the other side of your obedience.

Do not wait for a stage. Your mission may be your job, your family, or your city. You carry the answer to a world in crisis—Jesus Christ. What if revival is waiting on you? What if heaven is ready to move—but it's waiting for someone to say yes, even if it looks foolish?

The foolishness of God is your strength. And the world is about to witness what happens when God's people stop blending in and start standing up. You have read the stories. Now it is time to live one. Be the modern Noah, the present-day Esther, the 21st-century Gideon. God is still using the foolish to confuse the wise. Do not just admire the message—become the messenger.

The time for passive faith is over.

We are no longer in a season of quiet observation. The world is shifting rapidly. Children are questioning their purpose, youth are disengaging from the Church, and adults are abandoning truth for convenience. Apostasy is rising. The family is under attack. Trust in spiritual leadership is waning. The world has become louder, prouder, and bolder in its rebellion against God.

Yet God has not changed. He is still holy. He is still sovereign. And He is still calling people who look foolish to the world but carry a divine purpose. This chapter is not just a conclusion—it is a commissioning. God is calling the Church to stand again. He is calling leaders to return to the altar, not for applause but for repentance. He is calling community advocates and politicians to remember that justice begins with humility before God. Activists must be more than outraged— they must be anointed.

We must stop relying on clever language and start speaking the truth. Stop blending into culture and start confronting it with love and conviction.

This is a divine wake-up call. To the parents raising a child alone, you are not disqualified. To the unemployed worker, your worth is not in your paycheck. To the grieving soul, your pain is not wasted. To the young adult feeling lost, God sees you. To the pastor tired of compromise—preach again, but this time with fire.

God is using today's disappointments to awaken tomorrow's deliverers. You may feel like a nobody, but you're exactly the kind of person God chooses to confuse the powerful. The same God who used David to take down Goliath, who raised Esther for such a time as this, and who turned Saul into Paul is calling **you**.

But calling is not enough. You must be commissioned and sent. This moment in history demands action. Will you answer the call? Will you say, "Here I am, Lord. Send me"?

Because if we do not rise in faith, the world will continue to fall into fear. If we do not speak, the stones will cry out. If we do not shine, the darkness will grow bolder.

God is not done. His glory will cover the earth. But He is looking for vessels who are willing to look foolish in the eyes of man to be faithful in the eyes of God. You are called. You are commissioned. You are sent.

Watchfulness and Readiness: In this prophetic hour, the change in national leadership signals a greater shaking. God is alerting His people to wake up, rise, and speak out. Don't be lulled into apathy—be watchful for divine assignments.

Living in the Light: We cannot afford to hide the truth behind tradition. Living in the light means embracing holy boldness, speaking what is unpopular but righteous, and walking as children of the day. Preach with fire but live with integrity. Let your life reflect the Word you teach. Let your household be your first pulpit. When the light of Christ shines in you, others will be drawn not just to your message, but to your Master.

Encouragement to Persevere: Revival begins with resistance. When you feel opposition, remember that even Jesus was rejected before the resurrection. Keep building, praying, preaching, and loving. Don't give up. The field is hard, but the harvest is coming. Your labor is not in vain. Keep praying, keep serving, and keep standing. God sees you, and He is faithful.

A Call for Personal and Corporate Repentance (Churchwide and National): It is not enough for individuals to repent. God is calling the entire Church—across denominations, political divides, and doctrinal lines—to humble itself. From pulpits to pews, from city councils to national platforms, we must return to righteousness. We must cry out not for popularity, but for purity.

"Return to me, and I will return to you," says the LORD Almighty. — Malachi 3:7

"Rend your heart and not your garments. Return to the LORD your God, for he is gracious and compassionate." — Joel 2:13

A Prophetic Warning Against Delayed Obedience: Every delayed step of obedience widens the gap between God's will and our walk. Some have mistaken God's patience for permission, but there is a limit to divine tolerance. The door to act is open now, but it will not remain so.

"So then, let us not be like others, who are asleep, but let us be awake and sober." 1 Thessalonians 5:6

"The time has come for judgment to begin with God's household." — 1 Peter 4:17

Testimonies or Real-Life Examples of Modern 'Foolish' Vessels God is Using: There is a teenager leading prayer circles on public school grounds, a formerly incarcerated man now mentoring young fathers, and a widow on a fixed income who gives generously to feed the homeless. These are not famous or flawless people, but they are faithful. God is using them to confuse the wise and reignite faith.

Let their stories remind us: God's Spirit is not confined to pulpits, platforms, or plans. It flows wherever hearts are surrendered.

A Commissioning Prayer or Consecration Declaration:

Heavenly Father, I answer Your call. I lay aside reputation, comfort, and fear. Make me your witness in this generation. Let holiness mark my speech, my walk, and my worship. Fill me with boldness and wisdom. Use me as a vessel of revival and truth. Here I am, Lord—send me. In Jesus' name, amen.

A Final Trumpet Cry: Prepare the Way. This is not just another season. This is a divine

moment. The Bridegroom is returning. And the Church must awaken. Our cry must echo John the Baptist: *"Prepare the way of the Lord."*

There is no time left to build our kingdoms. No time for entertainment Christianity. No time for compromise.

"Blow the trumpet in Zion; sound the alarm on my holy hill. Let all who live in the land tremble, for the day of the LORD is coming." — Joel 2:1

"The Spirit and the bride say, 'Come!' And let the one who hears say, 'Come!'" — Revelation 22:17

Watchfulness and Readiness: Be alert. The shaking in nations is a divine signal. God is calling His people to readiness. The Bridegroom is nearer than we think. Awaken your spirit and stir your house.

Living in the Light: Live publicly what you preach privately. Let your home, work, and community be flooded with truth and grace. Shine boldly and stand upright, even in hostile terrain.

Encouragement to Persevere: Stay in the race. The narrow road is often lonely, but you are not alone. Heaven watches and rewards the faithful. Keep pressing forward.

Scripture Focus: Malachi 3:7 1 Thessalonians 5:6 Joel 2:1-13 Revelation 22:17

Reflection and Prayer: Lord, the time is urgent. Let me not sleep through this moment. Use me, shape me, and send me. Let me carry Your Word boldly and walk it faithfully. Let revival break forth through surrendered hearts. May I be found ready when You come.

Scripture Focus: Isaiah 6:8 Matthew 5:14-16 Acts 4:13 Romans 13:11-12

Reflection and Prayer: Father, I hear Your call. I surrender my comfort, my reputation, and my fear to be used by You. Send me into dark places with Your light. Anoint my voice, my life, and my story to reflect Your glory. Let this be the beginning of revival in my life, in my home, and across the earth.

Chapter 17 God's Warning Through Leadership: A Wake-Up Call from Heaven

God's warning concerning the rise of the U.S. President left many stunned—not because of the man himself, but because of what God is doing and saying through this moment in history. There are seasons when God does not whisper—He roars. He shakes nations, disrupts systems, and commands the attention of the entire world. We are living in such a season where the name of a single leader—whether a president, politician, or public figure—can stir an entire nation. But this is not about a man. It is about the message.

The real question is not, "Who is this leader?" but "What is God revealing through this leadership?" We must not allow personalities to distract us from the prophetic truth. Throughout history, God has used both righteous and unrighteous rulers to accomplish His divine will. Daniel declared this truth to King Nebuchadnezzar: *"He changes times and seasons; He removes kings and sets up kings"* (Daniel 2:21). This is not just a history lesson; it's a spiritual principle. Every election, every regime change, every unexpected rise to power is filtered through God's sovereign hand. Heaven is never caught off guard.

The political rise of the U.S. President shocked some and thrilled others. But from the kingdom's perspective, this moment should not be viewed merely as a political shift, but as a spiritual one. God uses unlikely vessels to accomplish His perfect plans. He used Pharaoh to show His power,

Cyrus to deliver His people, and Nebuchadnezzar to humble proud nations. So why do we assume He would not do the same today?

The current presidency is not just a political development—it is a prophetic message. It is a divine disruption. God is calling His people to pay attention, not just to policies, but to prophecy. He is not looking for perfect vessels—He is looking to fulfill His perfect will. Sometimes, God raises bold, controversial voices to challenge the compromise and complacency in culture. Other times,

He allows divisive figures to expose the divisions already rooted in our hearts. What we call "chaos," God may be calling "clarity." Through this leadership, the idols of the heart have been exposed as idols of nationalism, fear, race, pride, and political allegiance. God has peeled back the layers of America's soul and said, "Look. This is what's inside." Just like in biblical times, God doesn't do anything by accident.

His actions are intentional, purposeful, and prophetic. It's not about endorsing or rejecting a man—it is about recognizing that God will shake the earth to awaken His sleeping Church. If we fix our eyes solely on the leader, we risk missing the message.

God's providence is greater than any person's platform. The question is not "Do I like this leader?" but "Lord, what are You trying to say through this leader?" When we begin to ask that question, we step into spiritual discernment. God has never been limited by the character of a ruler. He will use flawed men to accomplish flawless purposes.

During this presidency, many believers became more politically engaged than ever before. For some, that was good—it awakened civic responsibility and moral clarity. But for others, it led to a dangerous detour, where political identity began to overtake kingdom identity. That is why God sometimes allows controversial leaders to rise, to reveal what we truly worship. If we trust in God, we will not be shaken by who rises or falls. But if we trust in men, we will be tossed around by every political storm. God's purpose in raising this leader may not have been to elevate the man, but to expose the

Church. He is speaking loudly, and we must not only hear the headlines, but we must also hear the Holy Spirit. God never wastes a moment in history. Every administration is an opportunity for divine revelation. The question is: Are we listening?

Throughout history, God has used leaders—prophets, kings, and judges—to deliver urgent warnings to His people, calling them back to righteousness before judgment falls. Today, as we look at the moral and spiritual crisis engulfing America and much of the world, it becomes clear that God's warning is just as urgent. We live in an age marked by widespread deception, where lies flourish not only in political arenas but often even within the Church itself. This deception fuels division and blinds many to the truth.

Meanwhile, the gap between the wealthy and the poor widens drastically, echoing the prophetic indictments against societies that oppress the vulnerable. Yet, too many leaders—both political and religious—are silent or afraid, choosing to protect their positions rather than stand boldly for righteousness, allowing a dark spiritual cloud to settle over nations.

This growing crisis is unmistakable. Deception and half-truths saturate media, political discourse, and even some church leadership, making it difficult to discern truth from falsehood.
The rich continue to accumulate wealth and power, while the poor struggle under increasing burdens, fulfilling the warnings of the Bible about unjust societies (James 5:1-6). Many political

146

and church leaders choose silence or compromise, fearing loss of influence or backlash if they speak the truth. This fear deepens the darkness, creating a spiritual and moral fog that envelops nations. Such conditions pave the way for further decay unless there is swift and genuine repentance.

God's pattern of warning through leadership is well-established in Scripture. In the Old Testament, prophets like Jeremiah, Ezekiel, and Amos repeatedly warned Israel and other nations of looming judgment because of rampant injustice, idolatry, and immorality. Despite these clear warnings, many refused to listen, resulting in exile and destruction. The New Testament reminds us that God neither sleeps nor slumbers (Psalm 121:4), assuring us that He is fully aware of the moral state of the world. Jesus used the story of Sodom and Gomorrah as a sobering example of God's displeasure with a society that refuses to repent. Their destruction serves as a warning to all generations that persistent sin brings inevitable consequences.

Many today ask whether God still cares or if He has fallen silent amid the turmoil. The Bible assures us that God is not asleep or distant but is sovereign and active in the affairs of the world (Psalm 121:4; Hebrews 13:5). What may appear as silence is often His patience, a gracious allowance of time for repentance (2 Peter 3:9). The shaking in our world—the political unrest, natural disasters, and moral decay—are clear signs that God is still speaking and warning humanity. The challenge lies in hearing and responding to His voice amid the noise. God's timing may not always align with ours, but His purpose is perfect and just.

The fear gripping many leaders today—especially within the Church—is a major barrier to spiritual renewal. Rather than boldly proclaiming God's truth and calling society to repentance, some leaders prioritize retaining their influence or position. This compromise leads to silence when courage is needed most. The Church is called to be a prophetic voice, like Isaiah and Ezekiel, who spoke God's word boldly regardless of consequences. Fear and complacency among leaders only deepen the spiritual darkness and delay revival. The urgency to overcome fear and stand firm in righteousness has never been greater.

We stand at a crossroads reminiscent of the biblical cities of Sodom and Gomorrah—places known for their extreme wickedness, pride, and injustice. The Bible tells us these cities faced God's judgment because they refused to repent. Many see striking parallels in today's world, where moral decay, lawlessness, and societal breakdown are rampant. God's warning is unmistakable: judgment will come if hearts do not turn back to Him. Yet, even in His righteous wrath, God's mercy remains, calling people to repentance and restoration (Joel 2:13). The path of destruction is not final—God desires revival and renewal, but it requires a genuine turning from sin.

God's warnings are never meant as instruments of condemnation but as wake-up calls to bring His people back to Him. The Bible urges repentance and courage in the face of mounting darkness. Leaders and believers alike must commit to returning to God's standards of righteousness and justice. This means standing boldly for truth and mercy, praying fervently, and living lives marked by holiness. The future depends on the choices we make now. God's sovereign plan will prevail, but He invites us to partner with Him through faithfulness and courage.

God remains sovereign over the earth. His warnings are signs of His ongoing involvement and love, not abandonment. The decisions we make today—whether to heed or ignore His call—will shape the destiny of our generation and those to come. Will we listen and repent, standing firm as God's witnesses in these critical times? Or will we continue in complacency, risking the consequences foretold by Scripture? The time to act is now, with faith, boldness, and unwavering trust in the God who uses even the foolish to accomplish His divine purposes.

Walking in Wisdom and Hope

As we come to the close of this journey, it's clear that God's ways are often unexpected and mysterious. He chooses the foolish, the unlikely, and even the flawed to accomplish His perfect will. The rise of leaders, political upheavals, and cultural shifts are not random events but part of God's sovereign plan to awaken His Church and prepare the world for Christ's return.

This book has shown us that behind every surprising leader or shocking event, there is a spiritual message of call to repentance, unity, and Kingdom focus. God's warnings are not meant to condemn but to clarify, to expose what is hidden in our hearts and the nations, and to offer mercy through repentance.

Remember, it is never about the man or the politics; it is always about the providence of God. When we shift our focus from personalities to God's purposes, we walk in true spiritual wisdom.

In these challenging times, you are called to be a watchman and witness, shining God's light with boldness and love. Trust in God's sovereignty, guard your heart against idolatry, and live with hope and expectancy for Jesus' return.

May this understanding empower you to navigate the complexities of our day with faith and courage. May you be part of the movement that God is using to bring revival, restoration, and the fullness of His Kingdom.

The Freedom We are Failing to Use

We live in a nation that proudly champions *freedom of speech* and *freedom of the press*, rights many have fought and died to protect. These freedoms allow us to speak boldly, publish without censorship, question leadership, and exchange ideas across every platform imaginable. Yet in all our liberty, we are witnessing a generation that speaks much but listens little to God.

We have access to Bibles in every translation. Sermons stream 24/7. Devotionals, podcasts, apps, and commentaries flood our screens. Yet, the very Word of God that brings life, correction, and direction sits unopened, unread, and often unwanted.

We scroll, but we do not seek. We post, but we do not pray.
We quote Scripture, but we do not live it.
We defend our right to speak but neglect our responsibility to listen to God.

In many countries, believers risk imprisonment, persecution, or even death to possess a single page of the Bible. Underground churches whisper the Word in darkness, memorizing verses in hiding. Meanwhile, we in America have the divine privilege of freedom and still fail to align our lives with the truth we claim to believe.

This, too, is foolishness—but not the kind God uses.

God is not looking for clever mouths; He's looking for obedient hearts. He's not impressed with theological debates on social media but with hearts that tremble at His Word (Isaiah 66:2). In these last days, it's not freedom of speech that will save us, but freedom through surrender.

"Then you will know the truth, and the truth will set you free." — John 8:32

We are free to open His Word.
We are free to repent.
We are free to walk in righteousness.
We are free to tell the truth in love.

But freedom unused becomes freedom lost. Silence in the face of sin is complicity. Ignorance by choice is rebellion. God will not hold a generation guiltless when they had full access to His truth and chose instead the foolishness of the world.

It is time to rise—not just as speakers of freedom, but as doers of the Word.

God is still using the foolish things of the world to confound the wise. But now, the question is: Will you be the vessel? Will you speak His truth, not your own? Will you use your freedom to draw near, to be filled, to be sent?

The foolishness of the cross still speaks.
Let it be said, we didn't waste our freedom.

Reflection & Call to Action: Youth in Unstable Times -Mobilized by the Chaos: How God is Raising a Remnant

In a world shaken by political instability, moral confusion, spiritual compromise, and mental health crises, a generation is rising that will not be silenced. This chapter serves as a divine invitation to the youth of this age—an age often called "foolish" by the world's standards but deeply chosen by God.

Why Engage Youth in Such Unstable Times?

Because they are already being shaped by the shaking.

In these unstable times, youth are not passive observers. They are absorbing the fear, confusion, and uncertainty around them. But rather than being victims of it, God is calling them to be victors through it. In every crisis lies the seed of spiritual calling. And for this generation, the shaking is not punishment—it's preparation.

1. Youth Shape the Future
They are tomorrow's leaders, workers, advocates, and culture-shapers. The world they will inherit is being formed now. Engaging them in faith, truth, and purpose during chaos ensures they are not just survivors of the storm, but builders after it.

"Remember now your Creator in the days of your youth..." – Ecclesiastes 12:1

2. They Deserve a Seat at the Table
Youth carry a perspective. Their insights, pain, and passion matter. Many are already leading movements in justice, healing, and innovation. The church cannot afford to sideline them. They must be discipled, empowered, and *released.*

"Let no one despise your youth, but be an example..." – 1 Timothy 4:12

3. Chaos Awakens Hunger for God

When idols fall and world leaders fail, youth begin to ask deeper questions: *What is real? What is worth following? Who can I trust?* These questions are sacred invitations to the Cross.

How Instability Fuels Spiritual Mobilization

1. The Foolish Are Chosen to Shame the Wise

When youth see God use flawed, unqualified, even "foolish" leaders to conduct His plan, they are awakened to their potential. They realize God is not recruiting based on GPA, popularity, or religious perfection, but on *willingness*.

"God has chosen the foolish things of the world to shame the wise..." – 1 Corinthians 1:27

2. Broken Systems Create Hunger for Kingdom Truth

As youth lose trust in the government, schools, or even churches, their hearts become fertile soil for God's Word. They are desperate for what is pure, eternal, and true.

3. Mental Health Struggles: Birth Authentic Faith

Struggles with anxiety, depression, identity, and isolation are real, but they are not disqualifiers. Often, they are doorways to *authentic encounters* with the living God who heals, understands, and redeems.

A Trumpet Cry to Youth: You Were Born for This
This is not just a crisis. It is your commissioning.

You are not called to comfort. You are not called to blend in. You are not called to merely survive culture.

You are called to lead revival.
"Arise, shine, for your light has come..." – Isaiah 60:1
You were born for such a time as this.

Reflection & Questions for Youth:
- What systems or leaders have failed you, and what might God be saying through that?
- In what areas have you tried to fit in when God called you to stand out?
- Are you willing to be used by God, even if it costs your popularity? Challenge:

Start a prayer group. Lead a Bible study. Speak out in love. Serve someone struggling. Be the answer someone's praying for.

Commissioning Prayer & Final Prayer

Heavenly Father,
Thank you for your unfailing wisdom and grace. Help me to walk in Your truth, to hear Your voice above the noise, and to be a faithful witness in these times. Strengthen my faith as I wait for the return of Your Son, Jesus Christ. Use me to bring hope, healing, and unity in a world that desperately needs You.

God of this generation, stir the hearts of young people across our nation. Awaken their purpose. Raise prophets, leaders, artists, and preachers who will carry the truth without fear. Use their pain, passion, and creativity to shake the earth. Let them know you have not forgotten them, and that you are calling them to rise. In Jesus' name, **Amen."**

Chapter 18: Reclaiming True Discipleship in a World Turned Upside Down

In the face of global unrest, political instability, and a church age wrestling with compromise, the true worshippers of God are being summoned to rise—not with louder noise, but with deeper roots. As racial tensions escalate, diversity and inclusion become politicized, insurance and

healthcare access dwindles, and economic instability threatens household after household, the need for a *new kind of discipleship* becomes urgent.

This chapter is not a call for trendier programs or more polished sermons, but a prophetic challenge to return to the core of the Gospel: being filled with the knowledge of God's will, walking worthy of the Lord, and bearing fruit in every good work, even as the systems of man falter.

Being Filled with the Knowledge of God's Will

In these last and closing days, when every institution seems fragile and every ideology challenged, discipleship must begin with spiritual clarity. Paul's prayer in Colossians 1:9 becomes more vital than ever: "that you may be filled with the knowledge of His will in all wisdom and spiritual understanding." In a world where insurance benefits are revoked, health crises abound, and economic barriers suffocate communities, believers cannot afford to operate on worldly wisdom. We must discern God's will—what He is doing *now*—and align our lives accordingly.

This means we must disciple believers not only in Scripture memorization or church etiquette but in prophetic awareness, cultural intelligence, and Holy Spirit sensitivity. It means training youth and adults to interpret the times through the lens of eternity. In the face of racial discrimination and social exclusion, we must be discipled into reconcilers, not reactors—peacemakers grounded in divine wisdom.

Walking Worthy of the Lord

To walk worthy of the Lord is to embody what it means to be in Christ, not merely knowing Him intellectually but resting in the finished work of the cross. This type of discipleship calls us out of religious routines and into relational intimacy. It exposes how man-made doctrines, denominational strongholds, and politicized theology have enslaved many to a form of godliness that denies His power.

Jesus came to liberate us from all forms of slavery—mental, emotional, spiritual, and cultural. Discipleship must now emphasize *being*, not just doing. The worthiness we walk in is not based on performance, but on identity: knowing we are loved, chosen, and free through Jesus. From this place of rest, we can challenge religious legalism and ideological control that have distorted the Gospel and divided the church.

Bearing Fruit in Every Place

If discipleship does not bear fruit, it is only theory. True discipleship bears fruit in classrooms, boardrooms, community kitchens, city councils, and family tables. The chaotic behavior of this world, the hypocrisy of failed church leadership, and the disillusionment of many must be met with a church that lives what it preaches.

It is time to raise disciples who know who they are in Christ (knowledge), live who they are (worthy walking), and multiply who they are (fruitfulness). We need teachers who disciple in truth without compromise, professionals who model integrity and love in the workplace, and ministers who care more about transformation than titles.

The church must disciple people to be resilient yet compassionate, holy yet humble, bold yet gentle. We must learn again what it means to *lead people to Jesus*, not just to a church building or livestream. We must stop outsourcing evangelism and start discipling people to live evangelism—because the world is watching, and Christ is coming. The Urgency of the Hour

What we do with this moment matters. God is not impressed with empty programs, political alignments, or flashy conferences. He is looking for people whose hearts burn for Him, whose lives reflect His Son, and whose discipleship leads to generational fruit. The global shaking is God's divine call to reclaim authentic discipleship.

Let the church arise—not as an institution of control, but as a movement of love and power. Let us disciple each other in the fullness of Christ—body, soul, and spirit—so that the Bride may be ready when the Bridegroom returns. Chaos is not our end; it is our commission. We were made for this moment. Christ is coming. Let our discipleship reflect that urgency.

Reclaiming the Lost and Broken

In these trying times, the church must rediscover its role not as a cultural club but as a sanctuary for the broken. Youth, addicted individuals, those caught in cycles of abuse, and families fractured by sin and poverty are not beyond redemption—they are the very ones Christ came to save. The church cannot afford to idolize comfort while ignoring crisis. We must go beyond preaching to embody the love of Jesus with compassion, persistence, and truth.

To reach those who are hurting, we must become present. That means engaging youth caught in social media distraction with real relationships and purpose. It means welcoming those struggling with addiction and abuse into a community of grace and accountability. It means walking with single mothers, mentoring fatherless children, and opening our homes as safe places of healing and hope. The Gospel is not an event—it is a life lived.

The world is craving authenticity, not performance. Programs may attract, but only presence transforms. Discipleship must include showing up at the shelter, staying late after service to talk, weeping with those who weep, and mentoring youth in truth and love. It is messy, but it is holy.

The Great Commandment: Beyond the Sabbath
Many churches have become so focused on traditions—such as sabbath observance—that they've missed the weightier matters of love and justice. Jesus summarized all the Law with one command: "Love the Lord your God with all your heart, soul, mind, and strength—and love your neighbor as yourself" (Mark 12:30-31). This is the root of discipleship.

True worship is not a single day but a surrendered life. If we love God, we will obey Him. If we obey Him, we will love others. If we love others, we will reach them. This kind of love breaks through politics, doctrinal debates, and generational wounds. It awakens a church to her mission.

Learning to Love Yourself to Love Others
But to love God and others, one must also learn to love oneself. This does not mean pride or ego—it means seeing ourselves the way God sees us: forgiven, chosen, and valuable. A person who hates themselves cannot love others well. A generation struggling with mental health, identity confusion, and trauma must be discipled into their identity in Christ.

Healing comes when we understand that our past does not define us, and our worth is not determined by the world's approval. Only then can we pour out love without fear or condition.

The church must disciple people into inner healing, not just deliverance from sin, but deliverance from shame.

Scripture Focus: Colossians 1:9-10 – "We continually ask God to fill you with the knowledge of his will through all the wisdom and understanding that the Spirit gives, so that you may live a life worthy of the Lord and please him in every way: bearing fruit in every good work, growing in the knowledge of God."

Reflection Questions:
1. Where in your community can discipleship be reimagined to reach the broken?
2. In what ways have you seen tradition overshadow the Great Commandment in your faith walk?
3. What step can you take to love yourself as God loves you? 4.

Youth Action Step: Find one young person in your church or neighborhood this week. Reach out to them. Invite them into conversation, listen to their world, and share your story. Your presence could be the bridge that leads them to Christ.

Closing Prayer: Lord Jesus, awaken our hearts again. In these chaotic days, make us disciples who are filled with Your wisdom, walk worthy of Your call, and bear fruit for Your Kingdom. Let us be Your hands and feet to the broken, the outcast, the hurting, and the lost. Teach us to love You with our whole being—and to love others as You first loved us. Let our love for You transform the world. Amen.

Conclusion: A Final Trumpet Call to the Church

From beginning to end, this book has been a journey through Scripture, history, and the present age to show how God has consistently chosen the unexpected, the flawed, the overlooked- yes- yes- yes yes, even the foolish—to accomplish His will and confound the wisdom of the world. As we've seen through prophets, judges, widows, warriors, and misfits, the message is clear: *God does not see as man sees. He chooses vessels that the world would never expect to proclaim His glory.*

In this hour, the world is groaning under the weight of spiritual confusion, moral decay, political upheaval, and relational breakdown. It is precisely in such moments that God raises a remnant— people willing to surrender fully, live sacrificially, and love radically. The call has never been louder. The question is: *Will we respond?*

The Church must awaken from slumber and become more than a gathering place. It must be a movement of love, truth, justice, and mercy. These chapters have challenged us to let go of comfortable religion, compromise, and fear. We must rise as holy people, not perfect but purified by grace, and walk worthy of the Lord with boldness.

To every pastor, youth leader, advocate, educator, parent, policymaker, and neighbor reading this: *you are part of God's divine strategy.* The world doesn't need another influencer—it needs Spirit- filled witnesses. It needs believers who know their God and will do exploits (Daniel 11:32). It needs churches who open their doors not just for programs but for healing, restoration, and repentance.

Young people need mentors. Hurting families need hope. The addicted and broken need deliverance. The spiritual curiosity needs truth. And the skeptical need proof, not just through argument, but through love in action.

Let this book not merely inform your faith but transform your life. Let it ignite urgency, hope, and readiness. Christ is returning. Until that day, may we live with holy purpose and fierce compassion, proclaiming that God's foolishness is still wiser than human wisdom, and His ways will never fail.

Amen and Amen.

Chapter 19: The Rising Generation—God's Unexpected Messengers

In an era where chaos, corruption, and confusion dominate public discourse, God is doing something that defies logic and overturns expectations. He is raising a new generation of teenagers, young men, and young women to be the standard-bearers of His truth. These youth, often dismissed as inexperienced or unqualified, are being chosen as prophetic voices to confront injustice, expose hypocrisy, and reveal the heart of God to a lost and dying world. They may not have traditional platforms or religious titles, but they are bold, unashamed, and deeply rooted in the Word. With their authenticity, creativity, and fearless conviction, they will confound political elites, religious institutions, scientists, and false prophets alike.

This generation will not rely on charismatic preaching alone but will live out the gospel in radical and visible ways. Their lives will be sermons—full of love, justice, mercy, holiness, and courage. They will model honesty in a culture of deception, purity in a world obsessed with perversion, and humility in an age of self-worship. Where the pulpit has grown silent on matters of righteousness, these young voices will cry out like John the Baptist in the wilderness: *"Prepare the way of the Lord!"* Their influence will reach the four corners of the globe—not just through church stages, but through social media platforms, music, visual art, protest movements, and political engagement. They will take the cause of Christ into schools, government chambers, neighborhoods, and digital spaces.

We are witnessing a spiritual uprising—a holy resistance against darkness. These youth will not be swayed by trends or intimidated by power. Instead, they will be filled with the Spirit of truth and anchored in the knowledge of God's Word. They will declare what is right, honest, trustworthy, lovely, and praiseworthy—not by parroting religious clichés, but by demonstrating real transformation. Their testimonies will speak louder than ten thousand sermons, and their presence will ignite hunger in the hearts of their peers. God will use their seeming "foolishness"—their passion, zeal, and simplicity—to confound those who think themselves wise.

Unlike past generations, these young messengers are not content with performative religion.

They are hungry for the real Jesus—the One who turned over temple tables, healed the broken, challenged corrupt leaders, and willingly bore the cross. Their faith will be raw, unfiltered, and drenched in grace. They will not wait for permission to speak truth or serve—they are already moving in obedience. Through them, God is shifting global atmospheres and preparing hearts for His return. These youth are the answer to the cries of a broken world. They are torchbearers of the coming revival.

This movement will not be led by one denomination, political party, or institution. It is a sovereign act of God. As the world grows darker, the light within these young warriors will shine brighter. And they will not be alone. God is raising mentors, spiritual fathers and mothers, and communities to support and intercede for them. But the spotlight will rest on those whom the world never expected— the foolish, the young, the underestimated. Through them, God is writing the final chapters of history before Christ's glorious return, will not just talk about the gospel—they will embody it. Their lives will be marked by honesty, purity, courage, justice, and love.

163

God is using these young people to confound political leaders, church institutions, scientists, and false prophets, revealing His plans and ushering in global spiritual awakening. This generation movement is not about platforms but about purpose, not about performance but about obedience. God is using what the world considers foolish to prepare the earth for the return of Christ, and this rising generation is central to that divine plan.

God often begins His most radical moves in moments of national confusion. The United States, like much of the world, stands at a tipping point—morally, politically, and spiritually. In these chaotic times, God is allowing leadership at the highest levels, even the presidency, to reflect the heart and spiritual condition of the nation (Romans 13:1). Many are bewildered by decisions, behaviors, and national directions that seem foolish, yet God is sovereign even in this. Just as He used Pharaoh to reveal His power (Exodus 9:16) and Nebuchadnezzar to humble a nation (Daniel 4:17), He is allowing current leadership to stir discomfort and reveal the deep need for repentance and a return to truth. This confusion is not without purpose—it is the beginning of a divine shift.

Amid this global shaking, God is raising an unexpected remnant: young men and women who have been in spiritual obscurity but are now being prepared to lead with integrity, fire, and faith. This generation may not be esteemed by the older religious or political establishments, but God has anointed them for such a time as this. As 1 Corinthians 1:27 declares, *"But God chose the foolish things of the world to shame the wise; God chose the weak things of the world to shame the strong."* These youth, overlooked by institutions and dismissed by tradition, will carry the message of righteousness and revival with boldness.

This rising generation will fulfill the prophecy of Joel 2:28-29: *"And it shall come to pass afterward, that I will pour out my Spirit on all flesh; your sons and your daughters shall prophesy, your old men shall dream dreams, and your young men shall see visions."* This outpouring is not reserved for the elite or the experienced—it is for the willing and the yielded. God is breathing upon high schoolers, college students, young professionals, and even children, awakening them to a divine assignment that will confound the wise and overturn the traditions of man.

These young leaders will take their place not just behind pulpits, but in boardrooms, classrooms, courtrooms, and digital platforms. Like David before Goliath (1 Samuel 17), they will face giants that the older generation has grown too afraid or too entangled to confront. Like Jeremiah, they may say, *"I am only a youth,"* but God will respond, *"Do not say, 'I am only a youth'; for to all to whom I send you, you shall go"* (Jeremiah 1:6-7) . These young voices will rise with truth that exposes corruption, with love that heals division, and with faith that shifts nations.

The older generation, including church leaders who have become comfortable with compromise, will be confused and even offended at how God moves through the young. Just as Eli failed to hear from God while Samuel, a child, heard the voice of the Lord clearly (1 Samuel 3:1-10), so too will many seasoned leaders be bypassed if they resist the new thing God is doing. Yet God is not discarding the elders—He is inviting them to partner with this generation in humility. Those who resist may be silenced, but those who align with the Spirit will see His glory revealed.

entertain, but to reform; not to preserve old systems, but to usher in the Kingdom of God on earth as it is in heaven.

This is the fulfillment of Isaiah 43:19: *"Behold, I am doing a new thing; now it springs forth, do you not perceive it?"* God's new move won't fit old wineskins (Luke 5:37- 38). It will look messy to the religious. It will sound radical to the complacent. But it will be holy. The rising generation is not coming to As the world plunges deeper into deception, a great spiritual confrontation is unfolding—one that mirrors the showdown between Elijah and the prophets of Baal on Mount Carmel (1 Kings 18).

In a time of drought and desperation, false prophets cried out to their gods with loud chants, self- harm, and vain repetition—but their idols were silent. Then Elijah stepped forward and simply prayed to the living God, and fire fell from heaven. That fire not only consumed the altar but also consumed the hearts of the people who had been deceived. They fell on their faces and declared, *"The Lord—He is God! The Lord—He is God!"* (1 Kings 18:39).

In the same way, we are entering a season where false worship—idolizing fame, wealth, self, celebrities, sexuality, governments, and even religion—will be exposed as powerless. The idols of science, intellect, and politics will not be able to stop the judgment or bring healing to a broken world. But God will once again answer by fire. Not only literal fire, but the fire of His presence, power, and undeniable truth. The people of the world will see that the gods they served cannot save them. And like in Elijah's day, hearts will begin to turn back to the true and living God.

Atheists—those who once mocked or denied God—will begin to believe. Why? Because when the world system demands that people take the *mark of the beast* (Revelation 13:16-17), a remnant will refuse. persecution will be a testimony so powerful that it will awaken many who have long been spiritually asleep.

They will not bow to the image of the beast, they will not surrender their worship, and they will not trade eternity for convenience. These men, women, and youth will honor God with their **body, soul, and mind** (Mark 12:30), even if it costs them their lives. Their faithfulness in the face of

This generation will remember what God has been saying all along. He has told us repeatedly to remember. *"Remember Lot's wife"* (Luke 17:32)—a warning against looking back at the world and its comforts while judgment falls. She was turned into a pillar of salt because her heart was still tied to Sodom. Likewise, many will be tempted to cling to worldly systems in the end times, but only those who fully surrender will be saved.

God also said, *"Remember the Sabbath day, to keep it holy"* (Exodus 20:8) . This is not just about a day—it's about a lifestyle of setting apart time for God and acknowledging Him as Creator. The world has forgotten God's Day, but the rising generation will reestablish worship, rest, and reverence. And finally, *"Remember now thy Creator in the days of thy youth, while the evil days come not"* (Ecclesiastes 12:1). This is a direct call to young people to turn their hearts to God **before** the full weight of tribulation comes. Those who seek Him early will be used powerfully in these final days.

True worship is not about songs or services. It is about allegiance. The mark of the beast will divide the world into two camps: those who worship the beast and those who worship the Lamb (Revelation 14:15). And God will honor those who refuse to compromise. These worshipers will be like the three Hebrew boys—Shadrach, Meshach, and Abednego—who refused to bow to Nebuchadnezzar's golden image. Even when threatened with death, they declared, *"Our God can deliver us... but even if He does not, we will not bow"* (Daniel 3:17-18).

once mocked, God will cry out like the Roman soldier at the foot of the cross, *"Truly this was the Son of God!"* (Matthew 27:54).

That same spirit of bold, fiery worship will fill the hearts of God's end-time remnant.

Through this fire, a harvest will come. Atheists will believe. Skeptics will surrender. Idol worshipers will repent. And those who The stage is being set for the greatest outpouring of repentance, revival, and revelation the world has ever seen. God is calling His people to return—body, soul, and mind—and to prepare for His glory to be revealed.

True Worship Will Rise as Idolatry Falls

As idol worship saturates every level of global culture—from entertainment to politics to the pulpit—God is once again calling His people to confront false altars with prophetic fire. Just as Elijah challenged the prophets of Baal and exposed the impotence of their gods, so too will today's remnant boldly stand against the idols of this age. These idols may not be carved statues, but they are worshiped through compromise, silence, celebrity obsession, self-glorification, and the rejection of God's authority.

But just as in Elijah's day, when God's fire fell and consumed the sacrifice, the rising generation will see the fire of God's presence fall on their obedience. Their worship will not be shallow or performative. It will be born from sacrifice and complete devotion. As atheists and skeptics watch this remnant resist the mark of the beast—choosing to honor God with their **body, soul, and mind**—they will witness miracles, divine protection, and unwavering peace that logic cannot explain. And many will believe.

- *"Remember now thy Creator in the days of thy youth"* (Ecclesiastes 12:1).

This revival will be rooted in remembrance. God has been sounding the alarm through Scripture for generations:

- *"Remember Lot's wife"* – do not look back (Luke 17:32).
- *"Remember the Sabbath day, to keep it holy"* (Exodus 20:8).

Those who remember will remain. Those who remain will be refined. And those who are refined will rise.

Reflection Questions
1. What idols—whether cultural, political, or personal—does the Spirit of God want to confront in this generation?
2. How does Elijah's story encourage you to stand in boldness, even when you feel alone?
3. What does it mean for you to honor God with your body, soul, and mind in these times?
4. Which "reminders" from Scripture (e.g., Lot's wife, the Sabbath, your Creator) speak most clearly to your current spiritual walk?

Self-Assessment Prompt:
- Have I identified the idols that challenge my loyalty to Christ?
- In what areas do I need to remember and return to God's call for true worship?

young men and women to stand boldly for truth, to walk in righteousness, and to worship You in spirit and truth.

Prayer & Meditation
Heavenly Father, We come before You in awe of Your wisdom and sovereignty.

In a world overcome with darkness, deception, and idol worship, you are raising a generation that will not bow. You are calling Lord, we thank You for the spirit of Elijah that is being awakened in this hour. May this generation be fearless in the face of compromise, courageous before corrupt systems, and steadfast under pressure. Let their hearts burn with holy fire. Let their lives reflect the beauty of holiness and the authority of Your Word.

We pray for those who have been written off, overlooked, or labeled foolish by the world. Use them, O God, to confound the wise. Let their obedience shake nations. Let their purity bring conviction. Let their voices cry out in the wilderness, "Prepare the way of the Lord!"

Awaken even the hearts of atheists and skeptics, Lord. Let them see your power displayed through the faithful remnant who refuse the mark of the beast and cling to your name alone. Just as You answered Elijah by fire, answer us now with the fire of Your Spirit. Purify our worship. Burn away every idol. Let our bodies, minds, and souls be consecrated unto You.

Father, help us to remember—remember Lot's wife and the danger of looking back; remember the Sabbath and the need for holy rest; remember You, our Creator, in the days of our youth. May we not forget what You have spoken. Let us walk in remembrance and reverence as we wait for the return of Christ. Seal this generation for Your glory, and may their lives bring a great harvest in these last days. In Jesus' mighty name we pray, Amen.

Chapter 20: When Leaders Fail and Lampstands Fall — God's Judgment on the Church and the Nations

"He who has an ear, let him hear what the Spirit says to the churches." – Revelation 3:22

In this sobering and prophetic chapter, the reader is confronted with the spiritual decline of today's Church leadership and the warning signs echoing from Scripture. Drawing parallels to Eli and his corrupt sons, this chapter exposes how many pastors are failing in their most important calling: to lead both their families and congregations with integrity. Instead of being examples of holiness, many ministers are consumed by power struggles, titles, and performance-driven ministry.

The message reflects on the condition of the modern church through the lens of the seven churches in Revelation, most notably the lukewarm Laodicean church that Jesus threatens to

reject. In contrast, the chapter emphasizes the rare and faithful characteristics of the Philadelphia church that still please the Lord. The rise of unscriptural church culture—such as the glorification of titles like "First Lady"—is called into question as the Church drifts further from its biblical foundation.

This chapter also brings a warning to national and global leaders, particularly the President of the United States, highlighting how ungodly legislation and political compromise provoke the judgment of God. It discusses the reality of spiritual warfare in the heavenly realm, referencing Daniel 10, where Michael the archangel must fight through demonic resistance to deliver an answered prayer.

Finally, the chapter reminds readers of God's plan to use the humble, broken, and overlooked to call the world to repentance. As false prophets and self-appointed ministers rise, deceiving many,

God is preparing a faithful remnant to speak truth without fear and to call the Church back to holiness, bold evangelism, and Spirit-led living. Judgment begins in the house of God—and this chapter is both a warning and a call to awaken.

Across the United States and the globe, the Lord is exposing the spiritual decay that has silently crept into the heart of the modern church. He is sounding a trumpet to warn the shepherds who have abandoned their first love, neglected their calling, and pursued influence over integrity. The hunger for power, prestige, and position has overtaken the humble spirit of servanthood once modeled by Jesus Christ. What once was a sanctuary of truth has, in many places, become a stage of performance.

The Holy Spirit revealed to me the state of the church through the lens of Eli and his sons. Eli, though positioned as a priest, ignored the sins of his household. His sons defiled the temple, exploited the people, and committed immorality without restraint. God held Eli responsible—not only for their actions, but for his silence. In today's church, leaders are ministering to crowds while their children are drowning in sin. They preach in pulpits while failing to minister at home. Just like Eli, many church leaders are facing God's judgment for prioritizing ministry image over household obedience (1 Samuel 2:12-36).

We are living in the era of the seven churches described in Revelation chapters 2 and 3. Most resemble Laodicea—lukewarm, self-satisfied, and spiritually blind. Jesus cannot find the fire of purity and holiness among them. Rare churches like Philadelphia, which are kept.

God's Word and did not deny His name. The Lord is grieved that many ministries today cannot be praised, because they have traded intimacy for influence and truth for trendiness. He is warning the Body: Repent before the lampstand is removed (Revelation 2:5).

There is also the unscriptural elevation of positions in the church, like the role of "First Lady." Nowhere in the Bible is such a title endorsed. The wife of a pastor is called to walk in humility and partnership, not dominance or spiritual manipulation. Many First Ladies have become more prominent than the pastors themselves, even rebuking others while lacking the calling or spiritual covering to do so. These cultural constructs have distorted biblical order and have led many into confusion.

God is not silent. He is warning the United States President and the global leaders: your actions will not go unnoticed. Legislation that mocks God's Word, systems that rob the poor while enriching the wealthy, and silence in the face of moral decay are provoking divine judgment. The Scriptures declare, "Be wise, O kings... serve the Lord with fear" (Psalm 2:10-11) . Political idolatry and church compromise have opened the door for darkness to rise, but God is preparing to raise a remnant that will stand boldly, speak truth, and not bow to Babylon.

In these last days, many prayers and praises are being hindered—not because God is deaf—but because demonic forces in the heavenly realm are blocking them. The Bible reveals this clearly in Daniel 10:12-13, where the angel sent with Daniel's answer was delayed by the demonic "prince of Persia" until Michael the archangel came to help. Spiritual warfare is raging in the unseen realm. The enemy is intercepting the sound of prayer from earth to heaven, but praise be to God—He is sending His angelic army to break through the darkness.

The Scripture reminds us that "God has chosen the foolish things of the world to confound the wise" (1 Corinthians 1:27). While many church and political leaders are failing, God is raising misfits, the overlooked, the broken, and those without titles—but filled with truth—to declare His Word. They will call out sin, restore the altar, and bring the fire of repentance back to the church. These are the ones crying in the wilderness, preparing the way of the Lord.

It is time for the church to return to her first love. Time for pastors to repent, for fathers to return to their children, for false titles to be laid down, and for the true gospel to be preached again.

God's judgment begins in His house (1 Peter 4:17). The sanctuary may be empty, but the Spirit of God is still moving among the faithful few. Let those who have ears hear—before the lampstand is taken away and retribution falls sooner than we think.

The Missing Power of Pentecost and the Call Back to Evangelism

Something extraordinary happened on the Day of Pentecost—a spiritual outpouring that transformed fearful disciples into bold, Spirit-filled witnesses. In Acts 2, the Holy Spirit descended like a rushing mighty wind and filled the room where the disciples were gathered. Tongues of fire appeared on each of them, and they spoke in other languages as the Spirit gave them utterance. That same day, Peter, who once denied Christ, stood boldly and preached the gospel, resulting in over three thousand souls being saved.

What happened that day was not a show. It was not a church program. It was not confined within the walls of a temple. It was the fire of heaven igniting ordinary people for extraordinary impact. But today, this power seems largely absent in many of our churches. We have become content with church routines, polished programs, and professional preaching, but we lack the fire, boldness, and supernatural empowerment that marked the early church. We have the form of godliness but deny the power thereof (2 Timothy 3:5).

Modern pastors often stay under the safe covering of the sanctuary— preaching to the same people week after week— while ignoring the very command Jesus gave: "Go ye therefore and teach all nations..." (Matthew 28:19).

The Great Commission was never meant to be fulfilled within the four walls of a building. It is a mobilization mandate, not a ministry job description. Yet many leaders refuse to go out into the streets, neighborhoods, and broken communities. The lost are outside, but the church remains inside. This is why communities are perishing—because those called to bring light are hiding it under a religious basket.

Evangelism is not optional. It is essential. But to evangelize effectively, like the disciples, we must be filled with the Holy Spirit, walk honestly, and be living examples of the gospel. This generation, especially the youth, does not want a religious performance; they want authenticity. We must meet them where they are, not where we expect them to be. We must motivate them through love, truth, and transparency, not guilt or fear. Discipleship means relationship, and relationship means going outside the building.

The Apostle Paul said, "If any man be in Christ, he is a new creature: old things have passed away; behold, all things are become new" (2 Corinthians 5:17).

This is what must happen in the hearts of believers today—a renewal, a spiritual awakening, a casting off of the old mindset, and a putting on of the mind of Christ. Many churches are packed, but few are transformed. Many claim to be believers but still walk according to the flesh. The early church walked in the Spirit, shared all they had, operated in unity, and turned the world upside down. That is the model to which we must return.

But instead of this model, we now see an explosion of self-proclaimed prophets, teachers, and apostles—many of whom have no spiritual maturity, accountability, or divine calling. Platforms like social media have become pulpits for deception. People are more concerned about followers, likes, and viral videos than they are about the truth of God's Word and the salvation of souls.

Ellen G. White's early prophetic visions illustrate a human attempt to discern divine timing, though her confidence in specific dates (June and September 1845, October 1844) and her vivid 1856 "food for worms" vision all went unfulfilled. Yet Scripture warns Christians to "watch and be ready" (Matt 25:1–13), even as the Lord's return appears delayed (2 Pet 3:9). When the prophecy fails in timing, we must test its prophet by the Word (Deut 18:22). Real wisdom lies not in setting dates but in humble readiness.

A tragic example is Ellen G. White, who prophesied that Christ would return at a specific time— a prophecy that failed. Though some still defend her teachings, her incorrect predictions make her a clear example of false prophecy, according to Deuteronomy 18:22. Sadly, such cases haven't stopped others from following the same path. Today, many "prophets" prophesy political outcomes, claiming God told them who would win elections. When their words do not come to pass, they do not repent; they shift blame or spiritualize the error. This discredits the true prophetic ministry and causes many to mock the name of God.

Scripture warns of this:
"Many false prophets shall rise and shall deceive many" (Matthew 24:11).

People are being deceived because they no longer test the spirits or search for the Scriptures. Prophecy has become entertainment, and ministry has become marketing. The truth has been replaced with emotionalism, and doctrine has been buried under opinion. But God is not mocked. A day of reckoning is coming for every false word spoken in His name.

The Church must repent. It must return to the simplicity of the gospel, the power of Pentecost, and the humility of Christ. We must be filled again with the Holy Spirit—not for shouting, dancing, or status—but for witnessing, loving, healing, and boldly proclaiming Jesus crucified and risen. We must leave the comfort of the sanctuary and enter the battlefield of souls.

A Call to Rise: A Challenge to Spiritual Leaders, Believers, and the Church

There is a cry rising from heaven to earth— "Rise, O men of God!" The time for complacency is over. The time for fear- driven silence must end. The world is in crisis, and so is the Church. God is calling His spiritual leaders to stand, speak, and shine, not retreat into silence or spiritual compromise. The Bible exhorts us in Philippians 4:5: *"Let your moderation be known unto all men. The Lord is at hand."* This is not a time to blend in, but to boldly stand out for righteousness, truth, and holiness.

Spiritual leaders must rise—not just in position, but in purity. It is not enough to wear a collar or carry a title; the Lord is looking for those whose lives reflect His character. Now is the time for pastors, bishops, prophets, evangelists, and every believer to let their voice be heard—not in politics, personal gain, or popularity, but in preaching repentance, teaching truth, and leading souls back to the cross. We must sound the alarm: the Lord is at hand, and His return is nearer now than ever before.

The Word of God provides the blueprint for how ministers of the Gospel should think and live. Philippians 4:8 commands: *"Finally, brethren, whatsoever things are true, whatsoever things are honest, whatsoever things are just, whatsoever things are pure ... think on these things."* We are to meditate not on the culture's chaos, but on the Kingdom's clarity. Our messages, our behavior, and our priorities must reflect this standard. If there is virtue, if there is praise—these are the things we must pursue and proclaim.

We must no longer preach a diluted gospel that comforts the flesh but neglects the soul. Hell is real. Just as real as the breath in our lungs and the beating of our hearts, so is the eternal fire of judgment for those who reject Jesus Christ. The modern church may have tried to erase hell from its sermons, but Jesus spoke of it often. The road to destruction is wide, and many are on it— many even sitting in pews every week, spiritually asleep, unrepentant, and unaware.

There is an urgent call from heaven for a global spiritual awakening— but it must begin in the United States of America. A nation that once declared "In God We Trust" has turned its back on the very God who blessed it. Revival is not just emotionalism in a service; it is repentance in the streets, holiness in our homes, truth in the pulpits, and justice in the land. Revival begins when leaders fall on their faces in brokenness, and churches rise in unity and righteousness.

This is a call to action. A call to return. A call to truth. If the Church does not rise now, who will? If the ministers stay silent, how will the lost be warned? If we are not watchmen, then whose blood will be on our hands? The Lord is at hand, and there is no time to waste. He is looking for a faithful remnant to carry the fire of truth, to preach the undiluted gospel, and to lead people away from hell and into His marvelous light.

Commissioning Prayer of Rededication for Ministers, Church Members, and All Believers

Heavenly Father,
We come before You today with open hearts and bowed spirits. We acknowledge that we have fallen short. As ministers, leaders, and believers, we have allowed distractions, pride, fear, and spiritual apathy to creep into our callings. But today, Lord, we rise. We stand in the gap. We repent for the silence when we should have spoken. We repent for the compromise when we should have stood in holiness. We repent for building platforms instead of building altars.

Father, we rededicate our hearts, our voices, and our ministries back to You. Purify us. Fill us once again with the power of the Holy Ghost, just as You did on the day of Pentecost. Make us bold witnesses of Your truth. Let us preach your gospel without shame, without fear, and without seeking the approval of man.

Lord, awaken the Church. Stir up the fire of revival in America and let it sweep across every nation. Begin with us. Let every minister walk in righteousness, every church member live in love, and every believer press forward with the hope of heaven in their hearts.

We declare today that we are not ashamed of the Gospel. We will no longer be silent. We will no longer compromise. Hell is real— but so is Your grace. And we will spend our lives drawing people out of the fire and into Your Kingdom. Seal us, O God, for Your glory. And when you return, may we be found faithful. In Jesus' mighty name we pray,

Amen.

Reflection & Response: A Call to Rise Key Scripture Focus

Philippians 4:5 – "Let your moderation be known unto all men. The Lord is at hand."

Philippians 4:8 – "Whatsoever things are true... honest... just... pure... think on these things."

2 Corinthians 5:17 – "If any man be in Christ, he is a new creature..." Matthew 28:19-20 – "Go ye therefore, and teach all nations..." Deuteronomy 18:22 – "When a prophet speaks... if the thing follow not... it is not from the Lord."

Reflection Questions

What are the signs that the Church today has become lukewarm or silent?

How have you personally responded to God's call for boldness and truth?

What false teachings or distractions are keeping the Church from rising to her full calling?

What does it mean to let your 'moderation be known unto all men'? In what area of your life or ministry do you need to rededicate yourself to God?

Personal Commitment Section

Prayerfully write your rededication to God below:

....

....

....

Action Step

This week, share the Gospel with one person outside of your church walls. Be bold. Be loving. Be honest. Let your light shine publicly.

Group Challenge (For Ministry Teams & Small Groups)

Spend time in prayer as a group or ministry team. Read the rededication prayer aloud together. Share where each person feels called to rise in their walk or ministry.

Chapter 21: Screens and Shadows: When the Enemy Enters Through the Devices

"Be alert and of sober mind. Your enemy the devil prowls around like a roaring lion looking for someone to devour."
—1 Peter 5:8 (NIV)

The enemy has always sought to infiltrate homes, communities, and generations with subtle, deceptive influence. In this modern age, he has found one of his most effective tools: the screen. Whether it's your phone, tablet, laptop, smart TV, or even the wristwatch on your arm, these devices—though created for good—have become the enemy's open door to every soul he can reach. And he's not knocking anymore; he's walking straight through the front door, unnoticed, welcomed, and even admired.

Children, teens, young adults, and even parents and grandparents are being swallowed whole into a world of scrolling, clicking, liking, and chatting. But what seems innocent on the surface is often laced with spiritual poison. Every scroll on TikTok, every post on Instagram, every story on Facebook and WhatsApp, and every YouTube video you binge can become a shadow to your eyes—blinding you from the light of God's Word. These screens have not only distracted us; they've become digital prisons, slowly replacing real relationships with illusions, real communication with emojis, and real love with artificial validation.

Have you ever stopped to calculate how many hours you spend on your phone every day? Research says the average person now spends more than 8,450 hours of their life glued to screens—scrolling endlessly, searching for nothing. These are moments you'll never get back— hours lost that could have been spent seeking the face of

God, listening to His voice, spending time with family, or enjoying the sunrise that God paints every morning. Instead, we reach for our phones to take selfies or see what others are doing, while the voice of Jesus is often drowned in digital noise.

Many parents believe they are giving their children the best when they hand them a smartphone or tablet. But have you considered that what you're giving them might be a spiritually toxic device— one that introduces unfiltered images, distorted morals, and voices louder than your own? Parents, your children need protection—not just from the world outside, but from the screens inside your home. Without proper boundaries and godly instruction, we allow the enemy to disciple our children in silence, while we remain unaware.

The screen has now taken over the dinner table. What used to be family time—talking, praying, watching a movie, or reading a Bible story together—has been replaced with heads bowed, not in prayer, but in attention to glowing devices. Even in our cars, God may be trying to speak as we drive to work, school, or home. But we're too distracted texting, watching videos, or catching up on the latest gossip. And accidents, even deaths, happen in an instant. The enemy tells us it is harmless, but we pay the price in ways we never imagined.

Let us be reminded: the devil cannot create anything. He only twists and distorts what God made for good. God created us for connection, community, and communication with Him and each other. But Satan has taken our desire to be known and loved and replaced it with likes, shares, followers, and filters. We think we're more connected than ever, but many are lonelier than ever before— trapped in a world that celebrates the image and forgets the soul.

God is watching. He is not measuring time like we do. His hourglass is not filled with sand or water but with the divine moments of our lives—each second that passes, either bringing us closer to Him or further away. Every moment spent mindlessly scrolling is a moment we could have spent in His presence. This is not legalism—it is an awakening. The Holy Spirit is calling His people to return to intentional living, to break the addiction to screens, and to reclaim the sacred moments we've lost.

Jesus said in John 10:27, *"My sheep listen to my voice; I know them, and they follow me."* But how can we follow Him if we've tuned Him out? If His whisper is silenced by reels, ringtones, and rapid texts, we will miss His leading in the most crucial seasons of our lives. There are times when Jesus wants to comfort you, speak to you while you're weeping at night, or guide you in your car—but instead of sensing His presence, we're too busy checking our notifications.

This is a call to parents, leaders, and every believer. Your children don't need another app; they need your presence. They don't need the approval of strangers online; they need your affirmation. They need to see your face, not just the back of your phone. Set boundaries. Create space for real connection. Turn off the screen and turn up the voice of God in your home. Let worship echo louder than reels. Let Scripture speak louder than social media trends. Reintroduce family prayer, story time, and Christ-centered conversations.

The devil has disguised distraction as entertainment, and addiction as harmless convenience. But it's time for God's people to wake up. You don't need to delete every device, but you must discipline your time, guard your soul, and filter your life through the lens of the Holy Spirit. Let the light of God shine brighter than the screen. Let your home be filled not with shadows, but with glory.

We must remember: Only Jesus can fill the void. Not a phone. Not a post. Not a follower count. And not a video that disappears in 24 hours. God is calling this generation—yes, even the foolish ones—to rise above the noise, walk in discernment, and redeem the time. Don't let the screen steal your calling. Do not let it silence your purpose. And don't let it replace the One who gave His life for you.

Youth, hear this truth: **you are worth more than your followers could ever account for**. Those filtered, perfect lives you see online aren't real. The enemy and the shadows want you to believe you're missing out, that you're not enough, or that someone else is living the dream life. But **the real, joyful, genuine life doesn't cause inner discomfort**. Jesus is the real life. He is the way, the truth, and the life (John 14:6). In Him, there is peace that passes understanding, satisfaction that no post can offer, and identity that no comment can define.

Many of you ignore His gentle warnings because you think you are smarter, more advanced, or too modern for what seems old-fashioned. You dismiss those God sends your way as foolish or outdated. But remember—**God often sends the foolish to confound the wise** (1 Corinthians 1:27). When you think someone's words are irrelevant, pause and ask if it's God speaking through them to get your attention.

Jesus is always trying to get your attention. But Satan is an expert in distraction. He will keep you scrolling, tapping, snapping, and chatting until you are so numb you no longer recognize the still, small voice of God. And then, when life falls apart, **the same enemy who tempted you will laugh at you** in your despair. Do not fall for the same trap he tried with Jesus.

Remember when Satan took Jesus up to a high mountain and tried to offer Him all the kingdoms of the world in exchange for worship? How could he offer Jesus what already belonged to Him?

Jesus and the Father are One. The devil's tricks did not work on Jesus, and they won't work on those who **truly know God**. The same schemes he used on the mountain are the ones he uses today—on our children, our politicians, our churches, and our leaders. But his lies have no power over a heart anchored in truth.

Parents, wake up. Your children are not just being entertained— they are being discipled by screens. You think you are doing them a favor by handing them a device, but what they need is **discipline, guidance, and your voice is louder than the one coming through the app**. Do not let the enemy raise your child through an algorithm. Set spiritual boundaries. Reclaim your home.

To the youth again, **you cannot keep living with your head down, eyes glued to a screen**, and expect to discover the purpose of God for your life. Look up. Look beyond the shadow of the screen and fix your eyes on **Jesus, the author and finisher of your faith** (Hebrews 12:2). When you look at Him, you will be amazed at the peace, transformation, and clarity He brings—not only for your now, but for your eternity. He did it for the woman at the well, who ran back to the town shouting, *"Come, see a man who told me everything I ever did! Could this be the Messiah?"* (John 4:29).

Jesus is that, Messiah. And He still sits at the wells of our weariness, waiting to reveal Himself— if only we would put down the phone long enough to notice. None of us knows how much time we have left. Don't waste your days living through someone else's posts or giving your soul to the lies of the enemy. Every shadow on your screen is a moment lost if it is not pointing you to Christ.

You may think you have more time, that you'll act later, but **later may never come**. Choose whom you will serve today. Step out of the shadow of your screen and into the light of God's truth. The enemy came to steal, kill, and destroy—but **Jesus came that you might have life, and life more abundantly** (John 10:10).

Restoring the Family Table: God's Design Hasn't Changed

Before the rise of smartphones, social media, and 24/7 connectivity, the family was the **central institution** of society. Homes were places of warmth, laughter, discipline, and togetherness. Family dinners were sacred—everyone gathered around the table, sharing their day, listening, laughing, crying, and most of all, **connecting**. There was no screen to scroll, no device to distract faces across the table, and voices filled with stories, questions, and love. And at the heart of these homes was often **prayer**, where parents led their children in seeking God's guidance and giving thanks together. The phrase "it takes a village to raise a child" was not just a saying—it was a lived reality, supported by neighbors, churches, and extended family who shared responsibility for each other's children and well-being.

Research confirms that families who ate together regularly— especially before the digital age— had **stronger bonds, better communication, fewer behavioral issues, and higher academic performance** among children. According to a report by The Family Dinner Project at Harvard, children who participate in frequent family meals are more likely to have **lower rates of depression, anxiety, substance abuse, and eating disorders**. Family dinners were a powerful anchor that helped children feel safe, heard, and supported.

But as technology advanced, something shifted. The dinner table now has silent participants: smartphones lying beside plates, constantly lighting up with messages, memes, and media. Family members sit in the same room but exist in **different digital worlds**, barely speaking, barely listening. Parents are scrolling through social media, teens are watching videos, children are distracted by games, and the family altar, once centered around prayer and conversation, has been dismantled. **The screen has replaced the Shepherd** in many homes.

This is not a coincidence. It is **a strategy of the enemy** to break down the family institution that God Himself created. The enemy knows that when families are divided, **generations are weakened**. With no boundaries around technology, children are being discipled by influences instead of parents. Respect for authority has eroded. Children are going astray. Violence, rebellion, and emotional isolation have crept into our communities. The rise in mental health issues among youth, along with increased suicide rates and school violence, is a spiritual and social cry for **a return to the original blueprint of the family**.

God's plan for the family has not changed. From the Garden of Eden to today, His desire remains the same: that families would reflect His love, truth, and unity. In Deuteronomy 6:6-7, God commanded, *"These commandments that I give you today are to be on your hearts. Impress them on your children. Talk about them when you sit at home and when you walk along the road..."* God's Word was always meant to be passed down at home—**in conversations, at the table, during walks, in everyday moments**. But if we are not talking to our children, someone else is.

It is time to bring the family back to the table. Not just for meals, but for **fellowship, healing, prayer, and restoration**. Parents must take the lead. That may mean turning off devices during dinner. It may mean reclaiming one night a week for Bible study or family devotion. It may mean having open, honest conversations about identity, temptation, and purpose. And most importantly, it means inviting the presence of God back into your home, not just as a guest, but as **the head of the household**.

When families are spiritually united, **generations are secured**. When children grow up in homes where God's presence is real, they are less likely to fall for the enemy's distractions. We must reestablish the values that held our families together before screens took over: **prayer, presence, patience, and purpose**.

Satan wants to divide the family. He's doing it through distraction. But God wants to **restore it through devotion**. It's not too late. The same God who parted seas and raised the dead can restore your family— **but He needs your attention**. The healing starts when someone in the home says, "Enough. As for me and my house, we will serve the Lord" (Joshua 24:15).

Put down the phone. Pick up the Word. Gather your family again. Return to the table— and meet God there.

Reflection Questions

1. How much time do you and your family spend on devices each day? Are there specific times or habits you could begin reclaiming for God and one another?
2. In what ways has technology impacted your family's communication and time together?
3. What are some old family traditions or habits (like eating dinner together or praying at bedtime) that you can bring back?

4. Do your children see you model a life rooted in God's presence more than on a screen? What can you change today?
5. Are you giving God more attention than your device? If not, what boundary can you start implementing this week?

Prayer: "Lord, Restore Our Family and Reclaim Our Home"

Heavenly Father,
We come before You today with humbled hearts, acknowledging how far our families have drifted from Your original design. We confess that we have allowed the distractions of screens and the noise of the world to take priority over our time with You—and with one another.

Forgive us, Lord, for placing devices before devotion, notifications before prayer, and entertainment before Your presence.

Lord, restore what has been broken in our homes. Rebuild the altar of family prayer. Revive the joy that once filled our dinner tables. Rekindle the warmth of conversations once shared freely between parents and children, siblings, and elders. Remind us again that the family is Your idea—

Your holy institution—and that no device, no distraction, and no shadow of the enemy can destroy what You have ordained when we place it back into Your hands.

We lift our children to You, Lord. Protect their hearts and minds from the lies and illusions of the online world. Let them see their worth through your eyes, not through likes, follows, or filters.

Give them ears to hear Your voice and courage to turn away from the traps set by the enemy. Give parents wisdom to lead with love, strength to set boundaries, and grace to model lives anchored in You.

Reclaim our homes, God. Let Your Word dwell richly in every room. Let laughter return where silence has settled. Let truth arise where confusion has entered. Let unity, forgiveness, and peace reign again under our roofs. Teach us to unplug from the world so we can reconnect to Heaven.

Today we declare that as for us and our households, we will serve the Lord. Help us turn off the screens, close the apps, and open our hearts to the only One who brings true life—Jesus Christ, the Author and Finisher of our faith.

In His mighty and restoring name we pray, Amen.

Chapter 22: Recognizing the People God Sends Into Our Lives

This chapter explores how believers can discern when God has intentionally placed someone in their lives for a divine purpose. Through the gentle guidance of the Holy Spirit, God often uses people as vessels of His will—bringing encouragement, correction, wisdom, or companionship at just the right moment. By learning to recognize the signposts of God's direction—such as alignment with His Word, peace in our spirit, confirmation through prayer, and the fruit of the Spirit in others—we can walk in greater confidence that our relationships are Spirit-led. The chapter reminds readers that God never works by accident; every person He sends carries a purpose, whether for a season or a lifetime. As we cultivate prayer, discernment, and openness to the Spirit's voice, we become equipped to welcome these divine connections and to step into the plans God has already prepared for us.

God sees what we cannot see. He knows every hidden thought, every whispered word, and every secret plan spoken behind closed doors. In His wisdom, He often allows the "foolish" to enter our lives to expose what we do not want to see. In our own eyes, we may believe we are wise and capable of discerning who belongs in our lives. Yet God uses the foolish to confuse the wise, revealing how limited our own understanding truly is. Just as Judas betrayed Jesus while smiling in His presence, God reminds us that betrayal can come wrapped in a smile and cloaked in laughter. Because of His love, He sends us warning signs, but too often we ignore them. When God shows you who someone really is, believe Him the first time.

Many of us hold on to toxic relationships out of misplaced loyalty or a false hope that love will change a person's heart. But God's

Word teaches us otherwise. When He exposes someone's true nature, it is a divine warning, not to be overlooked. Failing to take heed can lead to heartbreak, wasted years, and spiritual exhaustion. God uses the foolish to confuse the wise when we think we can fix people that only He can save. It is not your job to be their savior, healer, or redeemer—only God carries that role.

Throughout Scripture, we see God's hand of deliverance guiding His children away from those who meant them harm. David, though anointed king, had to flee from Saul, and it was through Jonathan, Saul's own son, that God provided a way of escape. In the same way, God reveals exit doors in our lives. He never leaves us without a "runway" to escape draining, destructive, and unhealthy relationships. People who are not meant to remain in your life will weigh you down like dead weight. They leave you feeling mentally exhausted, emotionally unstable, and spiritually dry. You pour into them, yet they never pour back into you. You encourage them, but you walk away empty. That is not a coincidence—it is a sign from God.

God never calls us into relationships that strip us of life, peace, and joy. He does not place people in our path to deplete us like a vehicle running until its tank is empty. Instead, the people He ordains for our lives will replenish us, strengthen us, and bless us. When God sends the right person, they will not consume your kindness without restoring your soul. They will stand by you in season and out of season, lifting you when you are weak and bringing joy to your darkest days. God uses the foolish to confuse the wise by showing us the stark difference between takers who drain and givers who uplift.

Today, we must be mindful of those who come into our lives with selfish motives. Some people thrive on guilt, manipulation, and emotional control. No matter how much you give, it will never be enough for them. They will take and take until you are left with nothing. Such people are not a blessing but a burden, and God's Spirit will whisper to your heart when it is time to let go. The longer you hold on to what God has told you to release, the more you will suffer spiritually, emotionally, and physically. God uses the foolish to confuse the wise, so we learn that love without His guidance can leave us wounded, and patience without His direction can lead to destruction.

Pretentious people may disguise themselves as friends, lovers, or supporters, but over time, their true nature will surface. You will know them by the fruit they bear. When their presence consistently leaves you angry, irritable, and drained, that is not God's design. That is an unbalanced, one-sided relationship that will eventually shatter your spirit. God is not the author of confusion or chaos. If someone's presence brings only confusion, heaviness, and despair, it is not a relationship from Him—it is a distraction from the enemy.

The truth is that some people are like leeches, parasites, or bedbugs. They thrive on the kindness of others, sucking out love, joy, and peace while offering nothing in return. God uses the foolish to confuse the wise by allowing us to see the difference between divine relationships and demonic distractions. We must not allow anyone to manipulate our compassion or drain our spirit under the disguise of "love." Remember—you are not their sacrificial lamb. Christ already paid that price.

Every time you leave a conversation or interaction feeling heaviness and depletion, it is the Holy Spirit warning you: *This person is not ordained for your life.* God desires relationships that build, restore, and strengthen, not ones that break, deplete, and destroy. It takes courage to let go, but God promises to strengthen you when you obey His leading. As Amos 3:3 declares, "Can two walk together, except they be agreed?" No, they cannot. If you are walking with someone who constantly pulls you away from God's peace, then it is time to release them into His hands.

God uses the foolish to confuse the wise so we may learn to fully trust His guidance over our own judgment. He allows wrong people to cross our path not to destroy us, but to train our discernment, deepen our dependence on Him, and teach us to recognize the blessing of the right people when they come. Do not cling to those He has already shown you are not meant to stay. Instead, seek Him for wisdom, and He will align your life with those who bring joy, strength, and peace—the kind of people who reflect His love.

Whenever you feel heaviness, exhaustion, or walk away from someone with the sense that something is missing from your life, it's not just a coincidence. It's a divine alert. The Holy Spirit is gently tugging at your spirit to pay attention. God does not call us into relationships that rob us of joy, peace, and spiritual strength. When you notice this heaviness consistently after being with a person, it is God's way of saying: *This is not from Me.* Relationships that are from God will bring encouragement, not despair; peace, not chaos; and love, not manipulation. Just as a demolished home crumbles to the ground and becomes uninhabitable, so do relationships outside of God's will—they cannot stand the test of time or storm.

This is why it is so important to seek God's guidance in every connection. Instead of asking, *Do I want this person in my life?* we must ask, *Lord, is this person meant to walk with me in this season?* God uses the foolish to confuse the wise by showing us that what looks good in our eyes may not be good for our souls. When someone constantly drains your spirit and pulls you away from prayer, worship, and faith, they are not adding value but subtracting from your God-given assignment.

Letting go is never easy. Our hearts often want to hold on to what feels familiar, even if it is hurting us. Yet God has promised to give us the strength to release what is not meant for us. Scripture reminds us, *"Can two walks together, except they be agreed?"* (Amos 3:3). If there is no agreement in spirit, no unity in prayer, and no alignment in purpose, God does not ordain the relationship. If you do not willingly release the wrong people, God Himself will step in and remove them. When He does, it may feel painful, as though your world is crashing down, and everything is being stripped away. But do not mistake His discipline for abandonment—this is His protection. What you may see as a storm is God rescuing you from destruction you could not see.

In those seasons, ask yourself hard but necessary questions: *Who in my life is draining me? Who leaves me feeling worse instead of better? Who do I continue to defend and make excuses for, even though I know deep down they are breaking me?* When God reveals the answers, do not debate with Him. Do not justify or rationalize their behavior. God uses the foolish to confuse the wise because He wants you to see what you've been ignoring. Fear and guilt will try to keep you chained to them but remember: God never takes away without preparing something better. His replacements are always greater than what we let go of, because He restores with abundance, not lack.

Deception is one of the enemy's greatest tools. Some people will appear as angels of light, yet their true intent is to steal your peace and derail your purpose. They may come with sweet words that sound like music to your ears, promising love, loyalty, or friendship. But over time, their actions will expose them. Words can be rehearsed, but actions cannot be hidden. As Jesus said, *"By their fruits you shall know them"* (Matthew 7:20). Wolves in sheep's clothing may disguise themselves for a season, but eventually, the fruit of deception, manipulation, and selfishness will reveal their true identity.

When you finally release the person sent by the enemy, you will experience something powerful—peace. A peace that surpasses understanding (Philippians 4:7). That peace is confirmation that you have made the right decision. What you thought would break you actually becomes your breakthrough. That peace is the sign that the Holy Spirit has lifted a burden that was never yours to carry. It is God's seal of approval on your obedience.

Holding on to the wrong people will keep you stuck in cycles of frustration, confusion, and disappointment. But when you let go, you make room for the right people God has prepared for you— people who pray with you, encourage you, and walk beside you in alignment with His will. God uses the foolish to confuse the wise to teach us that discernment is greater than appearance, and obedience is greater than desire.

We see this truth clearly in the story of Samson and Delilah. Samson was chosen and anointed by God from birth, yet his downfall came because he allowed the wrong person into his life. Delilah was not sent to build him up but to destroy him. Her words were sweet and her affection persuasive, but her heart was set on betrayal. She pressed him daily until he revealed the secret of his strength, and in doing so, she stripped him of his God-given purpose (Judges 16:15–21).

Samson's story is a powerful reminder that not everyone who enters your life has been sent by God. Some are sent by the enemy to weaken your faith, drain your spirit, and derail your destiny. God uses the foolish to confuse the wise by showing us that what looks like love can actually be a trap.

The Apostle Paul also warned the early church about such relationships. He spoke of "false brethren" who slipped in unnoticed, pretending to care but actually working to bring bondage and division (Galatians 2:4). These individuals were masters of deception, appearing religious on the outside but corrupt within. In the same way, God warns us today that not every smiling face, not every word of encouragement, and not every hand extended in friendship comes from Him. Some are traps designed to take advantage of your kindness, test your faith, and keep you distracted from your calling.

Yet even in betrayal, God never leaves His children without a way of escape. Samson's story ended in tragedy, but it also showed God's faithfulness—because even in his brokenness, Samson cried out to God, and God restored his strength one last time to fulfill his purpose.

Likewise, Paul testified that though false brethren tried to infiltrate, God gave him discernment and strength to stand firm. When we listen to God's Spirit and obey His voice, He equips us to overcome the traps of the enemy.

When you release people who were never meant to remain in your life, it may feel like loss at first—but it is actually deliverance. And when that weight is lifted, the peace you feel is God's confirmation that He is aligning you with His perfect will. He removes Delilah so you can meet your Jonathan. He exposes false brethren so you can recognize true brothers and sisters in Christ. He takes away what is counterfeit so He can give you what is genuine.

When God sends someone into your life, the first sign is that their presence brings peace, not confusion. The peace of God is one of the greatest confirmations of His will. Scripture reminds us that *"God is not the author of confusion, but of peace"* (1 Corinthians 14:33). When you are around the right person, you will not feel drained, anxious, or constantly second-guessing yourself. Instead, you will sense a calm assurance in your spirit. This peace is not based on circumstances or appearances but comes directly from the Holy Spirit bearing witness within you that God ordains the relationship.

Another signpost of God's will is mutual encouragement and spiritual growth. When God sends someone, they will not pull you away from prayer, worship, or the Word of God. Instead, they will push you closer to Him. Like iron sharpening iron (Proverbs 27:17), their words and actions will challenge you to grow in faith, obedience, and love. You will notice that your walk with God strengthens, not weakens, because of their influence. A God- sent person will pray with you, not just for you. They will remind you of God's promises when you feel weary and celebrate with you when God answers your prayers.

A third confirmation is the fruit they bear. Jesus said, *"You will know them by their fruits"* (Matthew 7:16). The fruit of a God-sent person will align with the fruit of the Spirit: love, joy, peace, patience, kindness, goodness, faithfulness, gentleness, and self-control (Galatians 5:22-23). These qualities will consistently show up in their character, not just in moments when it benefits them. Even in times of trial, their actions will reflect Christ rather than selfishness or manipulation. This doesn't mean they will be perfect, but it does mean their hearts will be sincere and their intentions pure.

The Holy Spirit also uses confirmation through agreement. Amos 3:3 asks, *"Can two walk together, except they be agreed?"* When God sends someone into your life, there will be unity in spirit and purpose. You will find yourselves moving in the same direction, not constantly clashing over values, vision, or faith. The Spirit of God within you will resonate with the Spirit of God within them, producing agreement that cannot be manufactured. This unity is not forced it flows naturally because it is rooted in God's design.

The presence of a God-sent person will bring restoration, strength, and blessing into your life. Instead of draining you, they will pour into you. Instead of leaving you empty, they will fill your cup with joy, encouragement, and faith. Their presence will be a blessing in seasons of plenty and in times of hardship. When the Holy Spirit confirms someone is from God, you will not feel robbed or burdened; you will feel uplifted and strengthened. This is how you will know: their presence leaves you closer to Christ, not further.

When God sends someone into your life, one of the clearest signposts of His will is that the relationship bears fruit in righteousness. This does not mean perfection, but rather that their presence draws you closer to Christ and strengthens your walk with Him. Instead of encouraging compromise or distraction, this person's words, actions, and lifestyle encourage you to pursue holiness, love, and faith. Their influence feels like healthy soil where your spiritual growth can flourish.

Another signpost is peace that goes beyond natural understanding. The Holy Spirit often uses peace as confirmation that a connection is aligned with God's purpose. Even when challenges arise, there is a steady assurance that God's hand is in the relationship. This peace is not the absence of difficulty but the presence of God's stillness voice calming your spirit. It guards your heart against confusion and gives you rest, even in uncertainty.

The presence of godly counsel and confirmation is another way God reveals His will. Often, when the Lord orchestrates a relationship, He allows trusted mentors, spiritual leaders, or even Scripture itself to echo and affirm the direction. These confirmations are not forced but come naturally, often aligning with what the Holy Spirit has already been stirring within you. When several voices of wisdom point to the same truth, it is a sign that God is guiding your steps.

A person truly sent by God will also reflect the character of Christ in their daily living. Their humility, patience, kindness, and self-control will testify to the Spirit's work in them. While they will have flaws, as everyone does, the overall pattern of their life shows a desire to honor God. They live in a way that does not merely impress others but glorifies the Lord, reminding you of Christ's presence through their example.

God also reveals His will through timing and alignment. When a relationship is from Him, circumstances begin to align in ways you could not orchestrate yourself. The door opens at the right moment, and both lives are in a season where the connection makes sense. If something feels rushed, forced, or out of season, it may not be God's timing. But when His hand is on it, the path becomes clear, and obstacles that once seemed immovable often shift into place.

The Spirit of God also convicts and protects within a God-sent relationship. If the person tempts you into sin or consistently pulls you away from God's standards, that is a red flag. But if the connection challenges you to grow, corrects you when necessary, and points you back to God's truth, it is a sign the Holy Spirit is at work. Conviction is never meant to condemn but to guide you toward God's best for your life, ensuring the relationship remains pure and purposeful.

Finally, one of the greatest signposts is that the relationship aligns with God's Word. Scripture is the final authority by which all things must be evaluated. Any ties that contradict God's commands or cause you to compromise biblical values cannot be from Him. But when the relationship reflects the love, sacrifice, forgiveness, and covenant principles found in His Word, you can walk forward with confidence that His will is.

Prayer

Heavenly Father,
Thank You for being a God who knows what I need before I even ask. I confess that at times I have overlooked or even resisted the people You have sent into my life for my good. Today, I ask for clarity and discernment. Open my eyes to see Your hand at work in the relationships around me. Teach me to recognize the fruit of the Spirit in those You send and give me humility to receive guidance, correction, and encouragement. Silence every voice of confusion and doubt so I can hear the gentle leading of Your Holy Spirit. Help me to trust Your timing and not rush ahead of Your plan, but to walk in step with the wisdom You provide through Your Word and through those You place in my path. In Jesus' name, Amen.

Reflection

Take a moment to pause and consider: Who has God recently placed in your life that carries qualities of love, truth, and encouragement? Reflect on the conversations, support, or even challenges you've experienced through them. Ask yourself: *Does their presence draw me closer to God? Does their advice or example align with Scripture?*

Sometimes God speaks through mentors, friends, or even strangers to redirect us toward His will. Journal about a time when God used someone to strengthen your faith and ask the Holy Spirit to continue sharpening your awareness. Remember—when God sends someone, it will always lead you toward His peace, His truth, and His purpose.

Chapter 23: When God Speaks Through the Foolish — Listening Beyond the Noise

God is deeply displeased with the state of the world today. Just as He has done in the past, speaking through dreams to awaken His people, He continues to use unusual, even "foolish," vessels to get His message across. These are people—praying, fasting, and walking in obedience—whom the wise might overlook or ridicule. Remember how God used a donkey to speak? What seemed foolish in human eyes was God's method to confound the wise and bring clarity where there was confusion.

In biblical times, God spoke through dreams to various men and women whom others often considered foolish or insignificant. These individuals simply had to listen to God's voice. Even when they tried to share the messages they received, they were mocked and dismissed. Yet, the dreams came true. Whether or not you believe in dreams, know this: God does not seek permission to speak. He asks only if you are willing to listen. When God speaks through dreams, it is not a mere suggestion—it is a summons, a divine call to action.

Consider Joseph, the dreamer, who received visions that ultimately saved Egypt from famine. Or Nebuchadnezzar, whose disturbing dream led to temporary insanity until Daniel interpreted it. Recall Pilate's wife, who warned her husband not to harm Jesus because of a troubling dream. And the wise men, who were redirected in a dream to avoid Herod's deadly trap. In Scripture, dreams were not afterthoughts; they were spiritual megaphones announcing God's plans and warnings.

Look around you today—from America to the far corners of the globe. Do you think God is unaware or indifferent to what is unfolding? Far from it. He is sounding alarms through many who are hearing Him in dreams. But in our noisy world—filled with media chatter, podcasts, social media, music, cultural confusion, and constant distractions—our ears are deafened. It becomes nearly impossible to recognize when heaven is trying to get our attention. So God waits until we are asleep, when the noise quiets, and He whispers—or sometimes thunders—His message through dreams.

Many have had dreams that linger long after waking, images that refuse to leave the mind. We sometimes wake up startled, compelled to share what we saw or heard. The wise may dismiss these dreams as strange or irrelevant, but what if God was using those dreams to reach the very people we thought were strange? What if He was calling us, too, but we rolled over and went back to sleep, missing the divine message?

This is a problem in modern churches. When gathered within the four walls of our buildings, many have grown dull to God's voice. We have traded revelation for routine and lost the expectancy of God's power. The fire that burned in the early church, as seen in Acts 2, is now dim. Miracles are often viewed as things of the past, and worship has become a performance rather than an enthusiastic encounter. We wait for the worship team to hit the right note, dance a little, then fall asleep just as the Holy Spirit is ready to move.

Listen carefully: when God wants to shake a nation, He first stirs the church. It is the church— not the buildings—that He awakens. Whether through dreams, disasters, or upheaval, God's messages come with fire and trembling: earthquakes, floods, death, and hardship. These warnings are not meant to frighten us but to strengthen our faith and draw us closer to Him.

Sometimes, God places flawed political leaders in power—not to glorify them but to send a divine disruption. These leaders expose the spiritual condition of a nation and stir the church to wake up before disaster strikes. When you criticize a political figure without praying for them, you miss the bigger picture: God is using these moments as a spiritual mirror, revealing the soul of the nation. Lawlessness, idolatry, immorality, and seduction often accompany these signs.

Look back to Israel's demand for a king "like other nations." God gave them Saul, not because He approved, but to teach them a lesson about trusting in human charisma over divine character.

Saul was outwardly strong but inwardly insecure and selfish. Israel watched as consequences unfolded, witnessing the danger of valuing human power over God's authority.

Today, we see similar patterns. A leader rises who disrupts established norms, dividing politicians, the media, and even the church. Some call for silence; others label him chaotic. But God uses the foolish to confuse the wise, accomplishing His purposes through vessels who are often unclean or flawed. This divine disruption exposes how easily the church can be seduced— not by policies but by power, greed, and confusion.

The kingdom of God is not about allegiance to any man, but to the King of kings and Lord of lords. Yet, many Christians have acted as if the future of the church depends on a political figure. This, too, is a reflection God shows us—how deeply divided we are and how much the church has compromised when allegiance to party outweighs allegiance to God's principles.

God does not only use the righteous to carry His message; He uses whomever He chooses— Pharaoh, Cyrus, Nebuchadnezzar—flawed leaders through whom His plan unfolds. What did God want His people to see when He used these leaders? Division was already present in the nation. Racism, tension, and denominational splits bubbled to the surface. These divisions exposed a deeper spiritual sickness—a loyalty to earthly systems rather than heavenly standards.

Now, every Christian must ask: Who truly reigns in my life? Is it politicians or God? Church leaders and believers alike are called to examine where their allegiance lies, to embrace the kingdom of God more than anything else, and to respond to God's call with faith, even when it comes through the seemingly foolish.

The world today is filled with challenges and questions that can often feel overwhelming. People everywhere ask: What does the future hold? Why is there so much confusion and conflict? Amid these uncertainties, many of us search for answers and hope. As Christians, we turn to the Bible, an ancient book full of wisdom that remains deeply relevant in our lives, no matter how much the world changes around us.

In times of uncertainty, faith becomes our anchor. The Bible encourages us to place our trust in God's plan, even when we feel lost or overwhelmed. This trust is not passive but active, leaning on God's understanding rather than our own. Through faith, we find the strength to navigate confusion and turmoil, knowing that God is working behind the scenes for our good, even when we cannot see it.

Proverbs 3:5-6 reminds us of this truth: "Trust in the Lord with all your heart and lean not on your understanding; in all your ways submit to him, and he will make your paths straight." These verses emphasize the importance of wholehearted trust in God. We are called to let go of our limited human understanding and submit our plans to Him. When we do this, God provides clarity and direction, guiding our steps through life's uncertainties.

Similarly, Philippians 4:6-7 offers powerful encouragement: "Do not be anxious about anything, but in every situation, by prayer and petition, with thanksgiving, present your requests to God.

And the peace of God, which transcends all understanding, will guard your hearts and your minds in Christ Jesus." This passage assures us that through prayer and thanksgiving, we can lay our worries before God and receive His peace—a peace that surpasses human understanding and protects our hearts and minds.

As we face the noise and distractions of the world, these promises to remind us to listen beyond the chaos and trust in God's sovereign care. When God speaks—whether through Scripture, prayer, or even dreams—He calls us to quiet our hearts and be attentive. In doing so, we open ourselves to His guidance, wisdom, and peace amid the storms of life.

Church splitting and division are not part of God's plan. Yet, throughout history, what seems foolish or confusing to the wise has often been the very tool God uses to reveal deeper truths. When the church fractures over differences—denominations, doctrines, racial tensions, and leadership disputes—it may appear as weakness or failure, but God can use even these painful moments to challenge the status quo and shake the complacency of His people.

From the beginning, divisions have existed, bubbling under the surface across generations. The wise may try to control or explain these splits through human reasoning, but God often uses what looks like foolishness to confuse the wise and bring His purposes to light. When churches divide, it exposes a deeper spiritual disease: loyalty to earthly systems rather than heavenly authority.

This foolishness in human eyes is actually a divine disruption, shaking the church from within to confront uncomfortable truths about where our allegiance truly lies.

The church, called to be the unified body of Christ, finds itself challenged to answer a crucial question: Who is Lord of our lives? Is it God, or is it the political, social, or denominational powers that divide us? The foolishness that causes church splits serves as a mirror reflecting how far we have drifted from God's vision. It forces leaders and believers alike to evaluate whether they serve God wholeheartedly or are distracted by money, power, or personal agendas.

God's wisdom is often revealed through what the world sees as folly. Just as He used unlikely leaders and flawed vessels to fulfill His divine plan, He can use division in the church to confuse the wise and awaken the faithful. If God's people humble themselves and seek Him sincerely through prayer, these divisions can become a catalyst for repentance, renewal, and a return to the unity God desires. What seems like foolishness to human wisdom may, in God's hands, be the very means to bring His church back to His truth.

God often uses what appears to be foolishness—such as divisions and splits within the church— to confuse the wise and reveal deeper spiritual realities. Church division is not part of God's original design; rather, it exposes the struggle between earthly loyalties and heavenly allegiance. The fragmentation seen among believers— whether over denominations, doctrinal differences, racial tensions, or leadership disputes—serves as a divine disruption to wake the church from spiritual complacency.

Biblical examples abound where God used unlikely, flawed, or even foolish vessels to fulfill His purposes. King Saul, who was outwardly strong but inwardly unstable, was given to Israel to show the consequences of trusting human power over God's authority (1 Samuel 9-15). God humbled Nebuchadnezzar's prideful reign to teach a lesson of submission (Daniel 4). Paul's "thorn in the flesh," a weakness in his life, became a testimony of God's strength made perfect in weakness (2 Corinthians 12:7-10). Likewise, when the church experiences division, it can serve as a mirror revealing its true spiritual condition and the need to return to God's vision.

Scripture warns of the dangers of disunity. Paul urged believers to maintain the unity of the Spirit (Ephesians 4:3) and reminded them that the body of Christ is one, with many parts working together (1 Corinthians 12:12-27). The book of Proverbs declares, "Where there is no vision, the people perish" (Proverbs 29:18), underscoring the necessity of God-centered guidance to prevent spiritual decay.

The chapter challenges every believer and church leader to examine their hearts: Are we serving God, or do politics, money, or pride divide us? True healing begins when God's people humble themselves, pray, and seek His face (2 Chronicles 7:14) . Through such repentance, the church can overcome division and become a powerful witness of God's love and unity.

Prayer:
Heavenly Father, we confess the divisions and distractions that keep Your church from unity. Forgive us for turning our hearts toward earthly loyalty instead of Your heavenly kingdom. Help us to humble ourselves, to listen to Your voice above the noise, and

to seek Your will more than anything else. Unite us in Your love and purpose, that we may stand as one body, reflecting Your glory to the world. In Jesus' name, Amen.

Lord God,
You are the God who brings order out of chaos and light out of darkness. In times when division threatens to tear Your church apart, remind us that Your wisdom often works through what the world sees as foolishness. Help us to see beyond human differences and to seek unity rooted in Your truth.

Teach us to humble ourselves, lay aside pride, and listen closely for Your voice. Strengthen our faith so that we may trust You wholeheartedly, even when circumstances seem confusing or challenging. Heal our hearts from division and fill us with Your peace that surpasses understanding.

May Your church rise as a unified body, shining Your love and grace to a broken world. Use our weaknesses, our mistakes, and even our divisions for Your glory and the advancement of Your kingdom. In Jesus' name, we pray. Amen.

Reflection Questions

1. In what ways have you witnessed division within the church or Christian community? How did it affect your faith or view of God's work?
2. Reflect on a time when God used what seemed like a "foolish" or unlikely situation for a greater purpose in your life or others.' How does this give you hope during confusing or difficult times?
3. What earthly loyalties or influences might be distracting the church from unity and obedience to

God? How can you personally help shift the focus back to God's authority?

4. How can humility and prayer transform division into a catalyst for renewal in the church? What steps can you take to encourage this in your faith community?

5. What does it mean to you to declare that God, not politicians or leaders, is Lord of your life? How can this declaration impact your daily decisions and relationships?

Chapter 24: Israel, the Sleeping Church, and the Sound of Prophetic Alarm

Israel has always been a nation surrounded by conflict. From the days of Pharaoh to the modern threats of missile strikes, wars, and political pressure, Israel remains at the center of global attention. For some, it seems like a coincidence. For others, it is just politics. But for those who understand the Scriptures, Israel's conflict is spiritual at its core.

The Bible makes it clear—God chose Israel for a divine purpose. And because of that, Israel has always been under attack. Whether it was the Egyptians, the Amalekites, the Philistines, the Assyrians, or modern nations today, Satan has relentlessly tried to destroy what God has preserved.

But why? Because Satan knows that Israel is a central piece in God's redemptive plan. If the enemy can destroy Israel, he thinks he can thwart the fulfillment of prophecy. But that plan has already failed. From ancient tyrants like Sennacherib to modern dictators like Hitler, there have been countless attempts to wipe Israel off the map. And yet, Israel still stands. That is not luck, it is prophecy.

"He who watches over Israel neither slumbers nor sleeps." – Psalm 121:4

Despite all the attacks, Israel remains a sign of God's faithfulness, a living witness to His promises, and a prophetic reminder that the clock is ticking toward Christ's return. While the world watches Israel with suspicion or disdain, the Church must watch with understanding. But herein lies a deeper problem.

The Church has grown sleepy. Many Christians today are unaware— or uninterested—in the prophetic significance of what is happening in Israel. They are distracted by comfort, divided by politics, and disengaged from God's prophetic Word. Yet the signs are everywhere.

Jesus told us to watch the fig tree—symbolic of Israel—for signs of the end (Matthew 24:32-34). But instead of watching, many have turned away. Instead of praying, many are posting. Instead of sounding the alarm, many are hitting the snooze button on prophecy. We are living in the days when headlines and holy Scripture are overlapping, and still, many churches remain silent. Why? Because a sleeping church does not disturb the world, and a comfortable church does not prepare for war. But the spiritual battle is intensifying. What is happening in Israel is not a political coincidence—it is a prophetic confirmation.

God is shaking the nations, waking up His remnant, and calling His Bride to be ready. Yet many believers remain in spiritual slumber, unaware of how close we are to the return of Christ. The Bible tells us that in the last days, Israel will face even greater trials. There will be a false peace treaty signed with the Antichrist (Daniel 9:27). The temple will be rebuilt. Israel will be invaded by enemy nations. And yet, through it all, God's plan will not fail.

God's Word also tells us that in the end, Israel will recognize Jesus as the Messiah (Zechariah 12:10). What a glorious day that will be! This is not the time to be fearful, but to be faithful. These signs are not given to cause panic, but to stir preparation.

"When these things begin to happen, stand and look up, for your redemption is near." – Luke 21:28

God is once again using what seems foolish in the eyes of the world to fulfill His eternal purposes. A small nation like Israel—rejected, despised, and misunderstood—is God's prophetic timepiece. And though the world mocks and threatens, God is preserving her. Likewise, God is raising unlikely voices—remnant believers, persecuted Christians, and even unexpected nations—to declare His truth in a world that does not want to hear it.

This is how God works. He uses what the world overlooks. He lifts what others call weak. He speaks through the mouths of babes and prophets, through donkeys and dreams, through storms and silence. He uses foolishness to confuse wisdom.

The Church must open her eyes. We are not waiting for the prophecy to begin. We are living in the middle of it. Each war, each shift in alliances, each movement of nations is a rehearsal for the final act. The wise will discern the season. The foolish will ignore the signs. But God is speaking loud and clear.

He is saying: Wake up, Church. Prepare your heart. Watch and pray. Time is short. This world is not our home. Our hope is not in politics, policies, or presidents. Our eyes must be fixed on the eastern sky, where Jesus will return in power and glory. And when He does, every eye will see Him. Every nation will tremble. Every prophecy will be fulfilled. And Israel will finally rejoice.

Let us be counted among those who watched, who believed, who stayed awake, and who helped others wake up too.

"Therefore, keep watch, because you do not know the day or the hour." – Matthew 25:13

The Church may have slept through many warnings. But it's not too late to rise now. Let Israel's struggle stir your soul. Let prophecy provoke your faith. Let the headlines push you back to the Word of God. Because the next sound we hear may be the trumpet. And the King is coming.

Israel's Role as Related to the End Times

From Genesis to Revelation, Israel is not just a location—it is a covenant nation. God's relationship with Israel is foundational to the entire biblical narrative. The promises made to Abraham, Isaac, and Jacob were eternal, and despite centuries of rebellion, dispersion, and conflict, God has never revoked His covenant with the Jewish people (Romans 11:12). In the end times, Israel remains central, not just politically, but spiritually. Prophecy points to Israel as the epicenter of global attention and divine activity in the final days.

The modern reestablishment of the nation of Israel in 1948 was not merely a geopolitical event; it was a fulfillment of prophecy (Isaiah 66:8; Ezekiel 37). The return of the Jewish people to their ancestral land is a clear indicator that we are living in prophetic times. God's Word declared that they would return from the nations, and that the land long desolate would bloom again—both of which have happened.

According to Scripture, Israel will face a time of great trial known as the Tribulation or "Jacob's Trouble" (Jeremiah 30:7). During this time, the Antichrist will rise to power, establish a false peace treaty with Israel (Daniel 9:27), and then break it, leading to intense persecution. Yet through that time of distress, Israel's eyes will be opened, and they will recognize Jesus Christ— Yeshua—as their long-awaited Messiah (Zechariah 12:10; Romans 11:25-26).

God's Perspective on the Nations

God's sovereignty extends to all nations. He raises kingdoms and brings them down (Daniel 2:21). He uses nations as instruments for judgment, correction, and blessing, all in line with His redemptive plan. While Israel is His chosen nation, God is watching how **every nation** treats Israel. In Joel 3:2, God says He will gather all nations and judge them based on how they treated His inheritance—Israel.

The nations are accountable to God. Their political decisions, alliances, and treatment of His people carry weight in the courts of heaven. God has a special place in His heart for those who bless Israel (Genesis 12:3), and a firm word of judgment for those who curse her or divide her land (Zechariah 12:3; Joel 3:2).

The Role of the United States

The United States has long stood as a key ally of Israel and a platform for global evangelism, freedom, and moral influence. Historically, the U.S. has supported the Jewish state, provided refuge for Jewish people, and defended religious liberty. Many believe these actions have brought about favor and blessing upon the nation (Psalm 33:12).

However, there is growing concern among believers that America is drifting away from these spiritual roots. As political decisions begin to conflict with biblical values and alliances with Israel become more conditional or politically motivated, the U.S. stands at a crossroads. God is not partial to nations based on size, history, or wealth—He responds to obedience, righteousness, and humility. If the U.S. turns from its support of Israel or God's moral law, it opens itself up to judgment, just like any other nation.

God will not overlook injustice, pride, or spiritual complacency. The same God who used Babylon, Assyria, and Rome to discipline His people will also hold modern nations accountable. Yet, God is merciful and patient, calling leaders and citizens alike to repentance.

The Destiny of the Nations

In the end of times, nations will be gathered for judgment (Matthew 25:31-46). Those who rejected Christ, persecuted His people, and acted in arrogance will face His wrath. But nations that align with God's truth, show mercy, and stand with His people will be honored. This is not about political favoritism—it is about spiritual alignment with the heart and Word of God.

God is not impressed by military might, economic strength, or cultural influence. He is looking for nations and people who tremble at His Word, walk in justice, and recognize His Son as Lord. The nations are a drop in the bucket to Him (Isaiah 40:15), yet He loves each one and desires their salvation.

Hope for All

In His mercy, God is calling both Israel and the nations to repentance. The cross of Christ is the great equalizer—Jews and Gentiles alike must come through Jesus to be saved. Israel's national salvation will come in the end, but today, the door is open for all who will believe.

As we see wars, conflicts, and alliances forming around Israel, we must not view these as political issues alone. They are spiritual. The shaking of the nations is God's trumpet, warning and inviting the world to return to Him before Christ returns.

The Church must rise from slumber and proclaim the truth boldly. We must pray for Israel, pray for our nations, and seek to live as lights in a dark world. Jesus is coming soon. And when He does, every knee will bow, and every nation will be judged.

A World on Edge: Signs of His Return"

With increasing turmoil in the world, from rising tensions in the Middle East to division within and among nations, it is clear that we are living in prophetic times. The headlines are not just political; they are spiritual signposts. Many are speaking about Israel, the United States, and global unrest, but behind the political movements is a spiritual shaking. God is not silent—He is speaking, warning, and preparing His people for the soon return of Jesus Christ.

God's Purpose in the Shaking & The Return of the King

The chaos we see is not random—it is God allowing the systems of this world to be shaken so that what is unshakable may remain (Hebrews 12:26-27). God is preparing His Church, waking up His people, and calling the world to repentance. The wars, rumors of wars, earthquakes, and pestilences are all pieces of the end-time puzzle (Matthew 24:6-8). These are not just signs— they are invitations to return to Him with all our hearts. Every sign points to one truth: Jesus is coming back. Not as the suffering servant, but as the conquering King. He will return to rule with justice, destroy wickedness, and restore all things. The Church must be like the wise virgins in Matthew 25—alert, filled with oil, and watching for the Bridegroom.

"But when these things begin to come to pass, look up, and lift your heads; for your redemption draweth nigh." – Luke 21:28 (KJV)

Fear is not new. The uncertainty and anxiety many are feeling today—in the church, in the United States, and across the world—are not unique to our generation. The fear of political instability, economic collapse, moral decay, and global conflict is real. Many wonder who they can trust, and some even question if God is still in control. But Scripture reminds us that such fear gripped nations and leaders long before our time.

King Jeroboam, for example, rose to leadership during a turbulent period in Israel's history. Because of Solomon's unfaithfulness, God had already spoken through the prophet Ahijah, declaring, "I will take the kingdom from [David's] son's hands and give you ten tribes" (1 Kings 11:35). The Lord went further, promising Jeroboam that if he obeyed His commands, He would "give Israel to [him]" and establish his reign (v. 38). This was no political guesswork—this was the unchanging word of Almighty God.

Yet even with such assurance, Jeroboam's heart was overtaken by fear. He began imagining "what if" scenarios that directly contradicted God's promise. "If these people... offer sacrifices at the temple of the Lord in Jerusalem," he reasoned, "they will return to King Rehoboam" (1 Kings 12:27). In other words, Jeroboam feared losing the people's loyalty, just as many leaders today fear losing influence, followers, or control.

His response was tragic but familiar. Instead of trusting God, he turned to human solutions. He set up golden calves at Bethel and Dan—alternative worship sites—to keep the people from going to Jerusalem. This political move may have seemed smart from a human perspective, but it led the nation straight into idolatry and rebellion (vv. 26–33). In the end, Jeroboam faced God's judgment (1 Kings 14:7-16) because his fear caused him to reject faith in God's word.

Today, we see the same pattern repeating itself. Political leaders make decisions out of fear of losing control. Church leaders alter their messages out of fear of losing attendance. Believers compromise out of fear of being rejected by society. The result is the same as in Jeroboam's day—false altars are built, truth is diluted, and God's people are led away from wholehearted worship.

The church in America, and much of the Western world, is in danger of becoming the **sleeping church** —lulled into complacency by fear of cultural rejection, political tension, and the uncertainty of the future. We forget that the same God who reigned in Jeroboam's day reigns today. His promises have not changed. His sovereignty has not weakened. His authority has not been challenged by human politics or world events.

The prophetic alarm is sounding: *Wake up, Church!* Do not let fear of current events cause you to compromise your faith or reshape your worship to fit the culture. Do not trade the truth of God for the approval of man. We are called to trust the Lord with the same confidence that biblical leaders were meant to have—because the God who parted the Red Sea, raised kings, and brought nations to their knees is still ruling today.

We do not have to face the fears of this world alone. God has given us the safety of His promises in Scripture—promises that cannot be broken, no matter how unstable the world becomes. If we anchor our hearts in His Word, He will give us courage to stand, faith to endure, and hope that shines even in the darkest seasons. The God who was faithful then is the same God who is faithful now.

Scriptures to Stand On

- *Isaiah 41:10* – "Fear not, for I am with you; be not dismayed, for I am your God."
- *Psalm 46:12* – "God is our refuge and strength, a very present help in trouble. Therefore, we will not fear…"
- *Hebrews 13:8* – "Jesus Christ is the same yesterday and today and forever."
- *John 16:33* – "In this world you will have trouble. But take heart! I have overcome the world."

Prophetic Prayer

Lord, awaken Your Church in these last days. Break the power of fear that has silenced your people. Teach us to trust Your promises more than the headlines, more than the voices of political leaders, and more than the uncertainties of the world around us. Give us boldness to speak truth, courage to live faithfully, and eyes fixed on You. Let us remember that You are the same God who delivered Israel, upheld Your servants, and fulfilled every word You spoke. May Your prophetic alarm ring loudly in our hearts, stirring us to be a watchful, prepared Bride— ready for the return of the King. In Jesus' name, Amen.

The same God who reigned over the nations in Jeroboam's day still reigns today—so do not let fear silence your faith or compromise your obedience.

Prophetic Challenge – Will You Choose Fear or Faith?

The headlines may be loud, but God's Word is louder.
Political tension, moral decay, and global instability are shaking the nations, but the same God who ruled in Jeroboam's day still rules today.

- Refuse the false altars of compromise, political dependence, or cultural approval.
- Stand on God's promises even when fear whispers "What if?"
- Be the watchful Bride—awake, alert, and ready for the return of the King.

This Week's Faith Step: Identify one area where fear has shaped your decisions more than faith. Surrender it to God in prayer, find a promise in His Word that speaks to it, and declare that promise aloud every day this week.

Remember: Fear will paralyze the sleeping church, but faith will awaken her to shine in the darkness.

Jeroboam's Mistake vs. Today's Church

Jeroboam's Day	Today's Church
God's Promise Ignored – God assured Jeroboam that He would give him ten tribes if he obeyed (1 Kings 11:35-38).	**God's Promises Ignored** – The church has God's unchanging promises in His Word, but often doubts them in times of crisis.
Fear of Losing People – Jeroboam worried the people would return to King Rehoboam if they worshiped in Jerusalem (1 Kings 12:27).	**Fear of Losing Attendance & Influence** – Many leaders fear losing members or cultural influence if they preach the truth without compromise.

Man-Made Solutions – He set up golden calves at Bethel and Dan to keep the people close (1 Kings 12:28-33).

Man-Made Compromises – Churches build "alternative altars" through watered-down preaching, entertainment-driven services, or political dependency.

Result: Idolatry & Judgment – Jeroboam's Result: Spiritual Decline & Weak Witness – actions led Israel into sin and brought God's judgment (1 Kings 14:7, 16).

Result: Spiritual Decline & Weak Witness – Compromise leads to a sleeping church, spiritually powerless in a dark world.

Missed Opportunity – Jeroboam could have trusted God and led Israel in faithfulness.

Missed Opportunity – Today's church can still wake up, trust God's promises, and lead the world to Christ in these last days.

Lesson: Fear makes leaders turn to human strategies; faith leads them to obey God's Word no matter the cost.

Chapter 25 The Cross Was Enough – A Message to Every Nation, Religion, and Heart

I was broken, lost, and guilty, with chains of sin wrapped tight around my soul. Yet on a hill called Calvary, the blood of Jesus was spilled to make me whole. To the world, it looked like defeat. But to heaven, it was victory. Every nail that pierced His hands did not weaken Him—it drove love deeper. Every thorn pressed into His brow was not humiliating; it was a hidden crown declaring Him King.

The crowd mocked. The rulers scoffed. The soldiers gambled for His clothes. But in their foolishness, they fulfilled prophecy, unaware that their cruelty was playing into God's eternal plan. The cross was enough. The grave could not win. His mercy reached further than sin and stretched wider than shame. Love poured out when He breathed His last, and eternity shook when He declared, "It is finished."

On that hill, a thief hung beside Him, guilty beyond doubt. The world saw a criminal worthy of death. But the eyes of Jesus saw a soul worth saving. In his last moments, the thief looked to Christ and said, "Lord, remember me when You come into Your kingdom" (Luke 23:42) . To men, it was foolishness to think a dying man could inherit eternal life. But to Jesus, it was faith—the kind of faith that confounds the wise.

Jesus replied, "Today you will be with Me in paradise" (Luke 23:43). A condemned man, unbaptized, untrained, and broken by sin, became the first to enter eternal life with Christ. That alone confused the wisdom of religion, law, and tradition. The Roman soldiers thought they were conducting justice by crucifying Jesus.

In truth, they were fulfilling God's plan of redemption. Their swords could pierce His flesh, but not His promise.

When they saw the darkness cover the land at midday, their courage wavered. The sun refused to shine, and creation itself mourned. The soldiers stood confused, realizing something far greater was unfolding. One centurion, hardened by war and cruelty, looked up at the cross and declared, "Truly this man was the Son of God" (Mark 15:39). What the wise and powerful rejected, a pagan soldier recognized in awe.

Herod the king mocked Jesus, dressing Him in a robe as a cruel joke. To him, Jesus was a foolish distraction, a powerless prisoner. Yet, Herod's mockery only revealed his blindness to the true King standing before him. The High Priest tore his garments and accused Jesus of blasphemy. He believed the law stood on his side. But in truth, the very Scriptures he claimed to protect pointed directly to Christ. The wisdom of religion stumbled over the simplicity of the cross.

The crowd gathered, shouting, "Crucify Him! Crucify Him!" They thought they were defending truth, yet they condemned the Truth Himself. The wisdom of the majority proved to be the foolishness of the blind. When Jesus cried out, "Father, into Your hands I commit My spirit"? (Luke 23:46), The earth quaked, rocks split, and graves were opened. The natural world testified louder than the priests, rulers, or kings.

Imagine the confusion that swept through Jerusalem as the temple veil tore in two. For generations, only the High Priest could enter the Holy of Holies. Yet in that moment, God declared access open for all who believe. The "wise" leaders could not comprehend it. They believed they had silenced a troublemaker. Instead, they had opened the door of salvation to the entire world.

The thief's last-minute salvation shames the religious elite. The Roman centurion's confession silences the philosophers. The empty tomb humiliates the politicians who thought they had secured the body. This is how God works—using what seems weak to topple the mighty, and what appears foolish to reveal His wisdom.

At Calvary, kings failed, soldiers trembled, priests faltered, and the crowd scattered. But the Son of God, in His "weakness," triumphed. The cross was not only enough for the thief, but for the entire world. It was enough to bring down walls of separation, destroy the power of death, and silence the boast of sin.

When Jesus said, "It is finished," the wisdom of men was undone. The philosophers could not explain it. The rulers could not stop it. The priests could not control it. The message of the cross remains the greatest paradox: weakness is strength, death is life, and shame becomes glory. Paul captured it best: "The message of the cross is foolishness to those who are perishing, but to us who are being saved, it is the power of God" (1 Corinthians 1:18).

To the Greeks, wisdom was philosophy. To the Jews, wisdom was law. But to God, wisdom was a crucified Christ who rose again. The thief on the cross did not attend synagogue, memorize Torah, or live a holy life. Yet one plea of faith gave him eternity. That confuses the wise and humbles the pride. The Roman centurion had no theology degree, yet he proclaimed the truth that scholars denied. That shames the learned who rejected Jesus.

Herod had a throne but no wisdom. The High Priest had tradition but no truth. The crowd had zeal but no discernment. Yet the "foolish" cross proved all of them wrong. The cross is the greatest sermon ever preached—not with eloquence, but with blood. Not with philosophy, but with sacrifice. Not with power, but with love.

The empty tomb is God's exclamation mark that the world's wisdom is folly. Kings and rulers pass away, but the crucified and risen Christ remains forever. So, I will keep singing: Jesus is risen. He is the way. The cross was enough, the grave could not win, and the wisdom of men still falls silent before the foolishness of God.

The suffering of Jesus was not meaningless pain—it was substitution. He took our place. His stripes brought our healing. His crown of thorns lifted the curse from our minds. His cross carried the weight of sin that crushes humanity to this day. When we look at our world now—leaders who exploit their people, politicians who thrive on lies, and nations consumed with greed—we see the evidence of sin still raging. But Christ's suffering exposes the root of it all and promises an eternal solution. While political leaders argue for power, Jesus surrendered His power. While rulers today send thousands into war, He laid down His own life to bring peace.

Many church leaders have become like the High Priests of old—concerned with status, wealth, and image. Yet Christ was stripped naked, mocked, and despised, proving that true leadership is not control but sacrifice. As economies crumble, jobs disappear, and families struggle to make ends meet, the words of Jesus still echo: "Man shall not live on bread alone, but on every word that comes from the mouth of God." The Bread of Life Himself satisfies what the world cannot provide.

Homelessness floods our cities. Men, women, and children sleep in the cold with no place to call home. Yet the Son of Man Himself declared, "Foxes have holes, and birds have nests, but the Son of

Man has nowhere to lay His head." He bore that same rejection so that we might inherit an eternal home. Violence now stalks our schools, and innocent children and teachers suffer. Yet on the cross, the Innocent One bore the violence of the world so that the guilty might be saved. His blood cries louder than the bullets of this generation.

Natural disasters rise—storms, earthquakes, floods, and fires shaking our fragile sense of security. But at Calvary, creation itself quaked, the sky grew dark, and the earth mourned as its Creator suffered. Even nature testifies that the cross still speaks louder than disaster. The suffering of Jesus was not distant history—it is the lens through which we interpret our present pain. His agony reveals the seriousness of sin, but also the depth of His mercy.

When rulers use war to prove strength, the cross whispers a different message: "Power is perfected in weakness." Nations fight for dominance, but Christ conquered through surrender. While the cost of living rises and inflation crushes the poor, the cross declares that our worth is not measured in wealth but in the priceless blood of the Lamb.

When families are torn apart by violence, addiction, and despair, we remember that Jesus cried out, "My God, My God, why have You forsaken Me?" He entered into our abandonment so we would never be abandoned. While church scandals shake the faith of many, the cross reminds us that our hope was never in men, but in the Son of God who cannot fail.

As we hear reports of children suffering from war, famine, and abuse, the cross reminds us that Jesus welcomed the little ones, declaring that the Kingdom of God belongs to them. His arms, stretched wide on Calvary, are still open to every broken child. The politicians of Jesus' day— Herod, Pilate, the Sanhedrin—believed they held power over Him. Yet they were pawns in God's plan. Today's leaders may boast, but the cross still declares that Christ reigns above every throne and nation.

The thief on the cross is a message for this generation. Even in his dying breath, hope was possible. Even in his hopeless situation, grace broke through. That is the message we need in a world filled with despair. Christ's suffering shows us that no injustice, no corruption, and no disaster can erase the hope that flows from the cross. Our leaders may fail us, but Jesus did not.

Our systems may crumble, but His kingdom cannot be shaken. Our world may fall into chaos, but His cross has already secured the final victory.

We look at the rising tide of evil, and it seems overwhelming. Yet the darkness that covered the earth at Calvary was broken by resurrection light. So too will our present darkness give way to His return. The cross is not just a relic of the past—it is the compass of the present and the anchor of the future. It explains why suffering exists and shows us how suffering can be redeemed.

Every drop of blood He shed speaks louder than the cries of the oppressed, louder than the boasts of tyrants, and louder than the thunder of storms. To the wise of this world, the cross still seems foolish. They ask, "How can a crucified man save anyone?" But to us who believe, the cross is the power of God that confounds governments, rulers, and nations.

The suffering of Jesus reaches into every corner of today's broken world. It answers homelessness with a home in eternity. It answers injustice with the Judge of all the earth. It answers war with the

Prince of Peace. The message of Calvary is this: no suffering today is beyond the reach of His suffering then. He bore it all, so that in Him, we might have hope.

And when He returns, every corrupt leader will bow, every false prophet will be silenced, every war will cease, every tear will be wiped away, and every wound will be healed.

The Cross of Jesus Christ is not just a Christian story—it is the story of humanity. It speaks to the atheist, the skeptic, the believer, and the seeker alike. When Jesus declared, 'It is finished,' He was not merely ending His suffering, but opening a door for every soul under heaven to find peace with God.

To the atheist who denies God's existence, the Cross remains a paradox that history cannot erase. How could one Man's execution alter the course of nations, calendars, and civilizations? Even in denial, the testimony of Christ's suffering and resurrection continues to shape the world in ways human logic cannot contain.

To the Muslim reader, who honors Jesus as a prophet but not as the Son of God, the Cross is the place where prophecy and divine purpose converge. Jesus did not merely speak of God—He revealed Him in love, mercy, and sacrifice. The Cross is not defeat but the ultimate act of surrender to the will of God.

To the Jewish reader, the Cross fulfills what the prophets declared. Isaiah foresaw a suffering Servant, despised and rejected, who would carry the iniquities of many. The Messiah was not to come first as a political ruler, but as the Lamb led to slaughter, providing atonement not with the blood of goats or bulls, but with His own blood.

To the Hindu and the Nepali seeker, who search for light among many gods and paths, the Cross stands as the singular demonstration of love that cannot be matched. Here is not one god among many, but the One true God who entered human suffering to rescue all people, from every tribe and tongue.

To the Mormon who believes in additional revelations, the Cross is God's eternal declaration that nothing further is required for salvation. Christ's sacrifice is complete, sufficient, and final—no temple rituals or added scriptures can surpass what was accomplished finally on Calvary.

To the Jehovah's Witness, who diminishes the deity of Christ, the Cross proclaims that only God Himself could bear the full weight of sin for humanity. No mere angel, no created being, but the eternal Word made flesh was able to redeem mankind through His death and resurrection.

The Cross is God's wisdom hidden in plain sight. What kings, rulers, priests, and philosophers could not understand, the simplicity of a dying Savior reveals. The Roman soldiers, Herod,

Pilate and the religious leaders of Israel thought they were silencing a voice. Instead, they were amplifying the greatest message ever spoken.

Atheists argue that suffering disproves God. But the Cross flips this argument on its head: it shows that God Himself entered into suffering, not as a distant observer, but as one who bore the deepest agony for the sake of humanity. The problem of pain is answered at Calvary, where divine love meets human brokenness.

To Muslims who believe God is too great to humble Himself, the Cross is a shocking yet beautiful display that true greatness is not in power but in self-giving love. God did not remain untouchable in the heavens—He came down, bore the shame, and embraced suffering so that no one would be lost.

To Jews who long for the Messiah's kingdom, the Cross reminds us that the crown of glory must be preceded by the crown of thorns. Messiah came first to redeem hearts, and He will return to establish His eternal reign. The Cross is the foundation of that kingdom, purchased with His own blood.

To Hindus and Nepali people searching for karma's release, the Cross is the ultimate release.

Jesus bore the punishment we could never repay. His sacrifice breaks the endless cycle of striving and offers freedom not through countless lifetimes, but through one decisive act of love.

To Mormons and Jehovah's Witnesses and Seventh Day Adventists who are told that salvation requires works, rituals, Saturday's worship, or allegiance to an institution, the Cross declares that salvation is by grace alone. No church, no organization, no leader can replace the finished work of Jesus Christ.

The suffering of Jesus transcends culture and religion. Political leaders rise and fall, wars shake nations, economies collapse, natural disasters strike fear, and violence invades schools and homes. Yet the Cross speaks louder than every tragedy, declaring: 'God is with us in our suffering, and He has made a way of hope.'

When darkness covered the earth at Jesus' death, it was a sign not only to Israel but to the entire world. The atheist was silenced, the soldier trembled, the priest stood bewildered, and even creation groaned. Heaven and earth bore witness that this was no ordinary death—it was the turning point of history.

Every political leader today, whether righteous or corrupt, should tremble at the Cross. For it is the reminder that all power is temporary, and true authority belongs to the One who conquered death. Nations will bow, rulers will fall, but the Cross endures as the everlasting sign of God's kingdom.

Every religious leader today, whether sincere or deceived, must reckon with the Cross. Preaching without the Cross is powerless, worship without the Cross is empty, and religion without the Cross is dead. The Cross remains the dividing line between truth and error, life, and death.

The atheist may mock, the Muslim may question, the Jew may wait, the Hindu may search, the Mormon may add, the Jehovah's Witness may deny, Catholics may Hail Mary and Rosery, Seventh Day Adventist may legally hold Saturday worship and denies Sunday worship, Evangelical and Conservative groups may fight against each other for who denomination is better, —but the Cross stands immovable, confronting every heart with the question: 'What will you do with Jesus who was crucified?'

This chapter, this truth, is not meant to condemn but to call. The Cross calls us all—every nation, every tongue, every religion—to lay down pride, abandon false hopes, and receive the gift of eternal life. It is foolishness to the wise, weakness to the powerful, but to those who believe, it is the power of God unto salvation.

The chapter reminds readers that life and death are under God's authority: "It is appointed unto men once to die, and

And so, beloved reader, wherever you stand today, the Cross speaks directly to you. Your suffering, your questions, your doubts, your sins—they all meet their answer in Jesus Christ, crucified and risen. The Cross was enough, is enough, and will always be enough—for you, for me, and for the whole world.

Reflection Questions

1. Why do you think God chose the "foolishness" of the cross to display His greatest wisdom?
2. How does the thief on the cross encourage you when you feel unworthy of God's love?
3. In what ways does Jesus' suffering shed light on the struggles we face in today's world?
4. What areas of your life still need to come under the truth of "It is finished"?
5. How can you share the message of the cross with someone who sees it as weakness or foolishness?

Self-Assessment Activity

On a scale of 1–10, how much do you truly believe the cross is *enough* for your salvation and your struggles?

- If under 5 → Pray and reflect on Scriptures like John 19:30, Romans 5:8, and 1 Corinthians 1:18.
- If 6–8 → Ask God to deepen your faith in His finished work.
- If 9–10 → Write a testimony to encourage someone else that the cross is enough.

To my Readers:

Christ's suffering exceeds all human pain, proving His sacrifice is sufficient to save and restore every soul. The cross reaches across cultures, religions, and ideologies, offering hope, forgiveness, and eternal life to all who believe. It also shows that God can use the simplest of things—what the world may see as foolish—to confound those who see themselves as wiser than Him, even those who doubt His existence after this judgment," yet through the cross, God's wisdom and mercy are revealed beyond human understanding.

Prayer of Confession and Acceptance

Heavenly Father, I come before You in humility, acknowledging my sin, my doubts, and my failings. I confess that too often I have relied on my own wisdom, sought comfort in the opinions of the world, and ignored Your voice. I have been blinded to Your truth and deaf to Your call.

Lord Jesus, I thank You for the cross, where You bore my shame, my guilt, and the

weight of my sin. Though the world called Your sacrifice foolishness, I recognize it as the ultimate act of love. I accept that You took my place, that You bore my punishment, and that through Your resurrection, I am made new.

I surrender my heart, my mind, and my life to You today. Forgive me for trusting in the ways of man instead of Your eternal wisdom. Help me to follow You faithfully, to walk in Your light, and to proclaim Your truth boldly, even when the world considers it foolish.

Your Spirit that guides me into all truth. I receive You as my Savior, my Redeemer, and my Lord. In Jesus' name, Amen.

We are living in an hour where the signs of the times shout louder than the voices of politicians, media commentators, and world leaders. Everywhere we look, creation itself seems to groan, pointing to the reality that something greater is on the horizon. The world is unsettled, and the hearts of people are trembling. We live in a world trembling under uncertainty— nations divided, economies shaken, violence erupting, voices silenced, freedoms questioned.

Racism still poisons hearts, injustice cries out from the streets, equality is debated, and truth itself seems lost in a sea of lies. Fear grips many, and confusion fills the earth.

From wars and rumors of wars to earthquakes, fires, floods, and pestilence, Scripture is being fulfilled before our very eyes. What Jesus spoke in Matthew 24 is no longer distant prophecy—it is breaking news on our screens, headlines on our phones, and conversations in our homes. But none of this should surprise us. Scripture told us long ago that in the last days there would be wars and rumors of wars, lawlessness, deception, and hearts growing cold (Matthew 24:6-12).

What we are seeing is not random; it is prophetic. It is the shaking before the return of the King.

Racism, inequality, injustice, and corruption have left many disillusioned. Nations are rising against nations, but within nations, people are rising against one another. The love of many has grown cold, and trust in leadership has been shattered. These are not just cultural crises; they are prophetic signs. Culture tells us: *truth is relative.* But the Word of God declares: *Truth is a person—Jesus Christ* (John 14:6).

Governments promise peace but cannot deliver. Technology offers connection but deepens loneliness. Movements claim justice yet often fuel division. Many are blinded, accepting lies for truth and darkness for light (Isaiah 5:20).

The shaking is not random. It is Heaven's alarm clock, ringing louder and louder. God is calling the world to wake up from its slumber before the trumpet of eternity sounds. Yet, despite the evidence all around us, many continue to live as though tomorrow is promised and eternity is far away. But Scripture reminds us, "The night is far spent, the day is at hand: let us therefore cast off the works of darkness and let us put on the armour of light" (Romans 13:12).

This chapter is a trumpet blast, a prophetic call for Christians and non-Christians alike to prepare their hearts. The days of pretending, playing church, or ignoring the warnings are over. The hour is late. Injustice abounds in our world. We cry out for equality and fairness, yet the systems of men continue to crumble under the weight of sin. But what is hidden behind the curtain of politics, movements, and agendas is a spiritual battle raging for the souls of humanity.

Freedom of speech is under attack, and the truth of the gospel is being silenced in many places. Yet Jesus declared that this gospel of the kingdom will be preached in all the world before the end comes. No government, no platform, and no censorship can stop God's Word from reaching the nations. We cannot ignore the reality that deception is at an all-time high. Lies are being dressed as truth, and truth is being dismissed as hate. The prophet Isaiah warned of a day when people would call evil good and good evil— and that day is now upon us.

To the believer, this is not the time to retreat into fear but to rise in faith. To the unbeliever, this is not the time to harden your heart but to hear the voice of God calling you to repentance. Fear grips nations, but fear should not grip the Church. We are the people of hope, for our redemption is drawing near. Yet hope without preparation is empty. Christ will return for a bride without spot or wrinkle—are we ready? The question is not **if** Christ will return—it is **when.** And Scripture says He will come suddenly, like a thief in the night (1 Thessalonians 5:2). The tragedy will not be that the world is shocked, but that the *church* is caught sleeping.

Believers, do not be lulled by comfort or deceived by culture. Be rooted in the Word, filled with the Spirit, and watchful in prayer. Live as if Christ could return today—because He can. To the Unbeliever, you may not understand all the signs, but deep down, you know the world is not as it should be. That unease you feel is a call from God to turn to Him before it is too late. Salvation is a gift—but it must be received now. Tomorrow is not promised.

Jesus warned of lukewarm believers (Revelation 3:16), lamps without oil (Matthew 25:8), and servants distracted by the world (Luke 21:34). This is the hour to shake off spiritual slumber, to trim our lamps, to live holy and alert. But the discerning know: these are signs. The stage is being set. The world is groaning in labor pains (Romans 8:22), preparing for the appearing of the Son of Man.

Ready does not mean perfect by human standards; it means covered by the blood of Jesus, walking in His righteousness, and living with expectation. Too many have fallen asleep spiritually, distracted by entertainment, consumed by the pursuit of wealth, or lulled into complacency by comfort. But the hour has come to wake up. Jesus compared His return to the days of Noah. People were eating, drinking, marrying, and going about life as usual until the flood came suddenly. In the same way, the Son of Man will come at an hour when many least expect it.

The flood is a reminder of judgment but also of mercy. For 120 years, Noah built the ark while preaching repentance. He sounded the alarm, but the people laughed. Today, the ark is Jesus Christ— and the door is still open. Racism and division have blinded many, but at the cross, every wall of separation comes down. In Christ, there is neither Jew nor Greek, slave nor free, male nor female—we are all one in Him. Heaven's call is unity in Christ, while Hell's scheme is division through hate. Nations fight for power, but one day every knee will bow, and every tongue will confess that Jesus Christ is Lord. The kingdoms of this world will crumble, but the kingdom of God will remain forever.

Injustice cries out from the ground. From bloodshed in the streets to corruption in high places, the world is weary of oppression. But the Judge of all the earth will do right. He will expose every hidden thing, and His justice will prevail. Many ask, "Where is God in all of this?" The answer is clear: God is speaking, warning, and calling—but are we listening?

The shaking we see in the world is a preview of the final shaking when everything not built on Christ will fall. Only those whose lives are found on the Rock will remain standing. Believers, this is not the time to play religion. It is the time to pursue holiness, walk in truth, and proclaim the gospel with boldness. The world does not need a lukewarm church; it needs a church on fire.

Non-believers, this is not the time to gamble with eternity. Tomorrow is not promised, and death is not the end—it is the beginning of forever. Where will you spend eternity? Every sign point to the fact that the return of Christ is near. Wars, disasters, rebellion, persecution and deception are not random events—they are pieces of a divine puzzle that Scripture already outlined.

The danger is not in being unaware of the signs but in ignoring them. The Pharisees could interpret the weather but missed the Messiah standing before them. Will we make the same mistake? To the skeptic who doubts, I say this: Look at the evidence. No other book in history has so accurately predicted world events as the Bible. No other man in history has conquered death but Jesus Christ.

To the weary believer who feels overwhelmed, I say this: lift your head. Your Redeemer lives, and He is coming with power and great glory. The cry of Heaven is, "Repent, for the kingdom of God is at hand!" Repentance is not merely saying sorry; it is turning from sin and surrendering to Christ.

The cry of Hell is, "Delay, delay, delay." Hell whispers, "You have time." But the truth is, you don't know if you have tomorrow. This chapter is not written to scare you but to prepare you. Fear without faith leads to despair, but faith in Christ leads to hope and eternal life.

Today, we must choose whom we will serve. Neutral ground does not exist. To reject Christ is to choose against Him. The trumpet will sound, and the dead in Christ will rise first. Then we who are alive and remain shall be caught up together with them to meet the Lord in the air. This is not fantasy—it is a promise. But for those who reject Him, the return of Christ will not be joy but terror. For them, it will be too late.

The spirit of Antichrist is already at work, deceiving and preparing the world for the final rebellion against God. Yet greater is He that is in us than he that is in the world. Christian, do not hide your light.

The world is growing darker, but the darker it gets, the brighter the true light shines.

To every reader, believer, or unbeliever, I say this: Do not ignore the alarm. The alarm is ringing because the hour is late. God is not willing that any should perish but that all should come to repentance. That is why He delays His coming—not because He is slow, but because He is merciful. But mercy does not erase judgment. The same God, who is patient, is also holy. He will not overlook sin forever.

Are you ready? That is the question echoing in Heaven. Ready hearts are watching, praying, and living for Christ daily. If you are not ready, today is the day of salvation. Harden not your heart. The invitation is open. The ark is Christ, and the door is still unlocked— but it will not stay open forever.

Beloved reader, this chapter is Heaven's trumpet blast. It is not just information but an invitation.

Come while there is still time. Choose Christ and be ready for His glorious appearing.

The Wisdom of God vs. the Wisdom of Man

In these closing days, when the world is spinning in confusion and fear, the message of this book— *God Uses the Foolish to Confuse the Wise*— rings louder than ever before. Politicians promise peace while stirring division. News reporters speak as though they hold the keys to truth, yet their stories shift with each cycle. Professors, philosophers, and scientists assure us that human reason can solve every problem, yet their theories collapse under the weight of reality.

Even within the church, too many preachers have become silent on the subjects of heaven and hell, trading the eternal Word of God for motivational speeches, prosperity promises, and watered-down religion that comforts but never convicts. But the Bible tells us plainly that what the world calls wisdom is often foolishness to God, and what God calls wisdom appears foolish to the world. Paul declared in 1 Corinthians 1:27, *"But God hath chosen the foolish things of the world to confound the wise; and God hath chosen the weak things of the world to confound the things which are mighty."* That verse is not merely ancient history—it is a living truth for this very hour.

Solomon, the wisest man who ever lived, reached the end of his journey and declared in Ecclesiastes 12:13, *"Let us hear the conclusion of the whole matter: Fear God, and keep his commandments: for this is the whole duty of man."* Notice that after all his knowledge, riches, experiences, and endless searching, he returned to the simplicity that many today dismiss as foolishness— reverence God, obey His Word, and prepare to meet Him. Yet, we live in a generation that scoffs at this very foundation. Kings and presidents issue decrees as if their words are higher than Scripture. Lawyers, judges, and legislators attempt to redefine morality, marriage, and truth. Doctors and scientists deny the Creator while dissecting His creation.

University professors fill young minds with philosophies that erase God from the equation of life. Even clergymen, sworn to uphold the gospel, now twist it to fit cultural convenience. But the Word of God has not changed and will not change, no matter how wise a man believes himself to be. The heavens will pass away, nations will fall, and voices of worldly wisdom will fade into silence—but God's Word will stand forever.

Right now, the Spirit of God is sounding the alarm through what seems foolish in the eyes of the world. Street preachers mocked on corners, mothers teaching their children Scriptures at the kitchen table, faithful pastors in small congregations who refuse to compromise, and even the testimonies of ordinary believers who dare to live holy lives—these are the voices God is raising. The media ignores them. The culture ridicules them. Politicians dismiss them. False teachers try to drown them out. Yet heaven applauds them, because they are declaring the unchanging truth: Christ is coming soon, and the only safe place is in Him. The world says, "Do not be alarmed, things will improve." But God says, "Be watchful, be ready, for in such an hour as you think not, the Son of Man comes" (Matthew 24:44). To many, the preaching of repentance and holiness sounds outdated, irrelevant, or foolish— but it is God's wisdom for saving souls from eternal destruction.

Therefore, we must decide whose voice we will follow. Will we listen to the kings, presidents, lawyers, doctors, professors, clergymen, and news reporters who believe they are wiser than God? Or will we humble ourselves and cling to the Word that has stood the test of time? The message of this book has been clear: God uses what the world despises, mocks, and calls weak or foolish to reveal His wisdom and His power. And in these final days, He is still doing it. The systems of man are crumbling. Nations are trembling. Lies are being exposed. And through it all, God is preparing a people who will not bow to the wisdom of the world but will stand firm on the foundation of Christ. To the world, it looks foolish. To heaven, it is the greatest.

When Wisdom Fails and God's Word Prevails
In these last days, when the world appears to be unraveling, God is once again showing His sovereignty by using what seems foolish

to the world to confound the so-called wise. Many people trust politicians, professors, and news anchors more than the living Word of God. Yet, God reminds us that He chooses the weak things of this world to shame the strong, and the foolish things to shame the wise.

Politicians stand behind podiums promising peace, unity, and prosperity, but history has proven that no earthly leader can bring true and lasting peace. The kingdoms of this world rise and fall, yet the Kingdom of God endures forever. To trust the words of man above the words of God is to build one's house on shifting sand.

False teachers abound, twisting Scripture to fit cultural trends and personal gain. Many avoid preaching about hell, judgment, or Christ's return because they fear offending people. But the gospel without repentance, without warning, and without truth is no gospel at all. God is raising a remnant who will boldly declare His Word even when it seems foolish in the eyes of the world.

Preachers who water down the truth are celebrated by crowds, but prophets who call for repentance are often ridiculed. Yet throughout history, the voices that seemed foolish were the very ones God used to bring revival, correction, and salvation. Noah, mocked for building an ark, became the vessel of salvation for his family. The same pattern continues today.

Many pastors and teachers are afraid to preach about heaven and hell, though Jesus Himself spoke more about hell than anyone else in Scripture. To deny or ignore the reality of eternity is to leave souls unprepared for what is to come. Silence in the pulpit has left a generation confused, entertained, but unequipped for the return of Christ.

The news media shape opinions and stir fears daily. Reporters speak with authority, yet their words are often filled with deception, speculation, and half-truths. Sadly, millions believe their narratives more than they believe the Bible. The wisdom of news anchors may trend for a moment, but the eternal truth of God's Word outlasts every headline.

Universities are filled with professors who dismiss God, mock faith, and exalt human reason. Degrees and titles are respected, but knowledge without God leads only to pride and destruction. Paul declared that professing themselves to be wise, many became fools (Romans 1:22). This same spirit of arrogance pervades our generation.

Doctors, lawyers, and scholars are esteemed as voices of authority, and while their contributions may benefit society, they are still fallible men and women. Science and medicine change with time, but the Word of God does not change. When their words contradict God's truth, we must remember: "Let God be true, and every man a liar" (Romans 3:4).

Presidents, kings, and rulers rise to power, but none of them can override God's plan. Many nations today are shaken by leadership crises, corruption, and division. God allows such shakings to remind us that salvation does not come from the White House, the palace, or the government, but from the throne of heaven.

The great deception of our day is that man's wisdom is sufficient. People boast in technology, wealth, education, and progress, but without God, these things become empty idols. True wisdom begins with the fear of the Lord, not the exaltation of man.

Solomon, the wisest man who ever lived, pursued knowledge, wealth, pleasure, and power. Yet, at the end of his life, he concluded that all was vanity except this: "Fear God and keep His commandments, for this is the whole duty of man" (Ecclesiastes 12:13). His final words destroy the arrogance of human wisdom and remind us where true purpose lies.

In our culture, many laugh at the Bible, calling it outdated or irrelevant. Yet, it remains the most read, most translated, and most transformative book in human history. While scholars debate its authority, lives continue to be changed by its truth. What the world calls foolish, God calls power.

Hell is mocked, denied, or ignored, yet Jesus warned repeatedly of its reality. To reject the message of hell may sound intelligent to modern ears, but it is a deadly deception. Hell is not a metaphor but an eternal destiny for those who reject Christ. Warning people that it may sound foolish, but silence is cruelty.

Heaven, too, is dismissed as a fantasy by the so-called wise. Yet believers know it is the eternal home prepared for those who trust in Christ. To preach about heaven is not escapism but truth. The reality of heaven fuels our endurance and gives hope in a hopeless world.

Many people prefer to hear soothing words from leaders rather than the convicting truth of God's Word. Paul warned Timothy that in the last days people would gather teachers to say what their itching ears wanted to hear (2 Timothy 4:3). This prophecy is fulfilled in our time, as entertainment replaces doctrine.

The church must rise above the noise of politicians, false teachers, and worldly wisdom. God is calling for voices that will sound the alarm, declare truth without compromise, and prepare people.

for the return of Christ. The gospel is not a suggestion; it is a divine mandate.

Every sign around us points to the soon return of Christ. Wars and rumors of wars, earthquakes, lawlessness, apostasy, and moral decay are increasing. While many dismiss these signs as coincidences, Jesus told us to watch and be ready. Only the foolish ignore the signs of the times.

The pursuit of equality, diversity, and freedom of speech has its place, but without Christ at the center, these ideals collapse into chaos. True justice flows from the throne of God, not from human systems. To fight for rights without submitting to righteousness is to miss the heart of God.

Racism, injustice, and oppression are factual issues, but the solution is not found in politics or human wisdom. The solution is the transforming power of the gospel, which tears down walls and unites people under the banner of Christ. What the world cannot solve, God has already accomplished in Christ.

The Spirit of Antichrist is at work in our generation, deceiving many with lies that sound wise but are rooted in rebellion against God. Christians must discern the times and resist being swayed by every new philosophy or political agenda. Our allegiance belongs to Christ alone.

The cross itself looked like foolishness to the world. A crucified Messiah made no sense to philosophers or rulers. Yet, through the cross, God displayed His greatest wisdom, defeating sin, death, and hell. What appeared to be a weakness was the ultimate victory. In the same way today, the message of repentance, holiness, and Christ's return may seem foolish to many. Yet this message carries eternal weight. To ignore it is to perish. To embrace it is to gain eternal life.

God is shaking the nations to wake people up. Natural disasters, political upheavals, and moral confusion are not random events but divine alarms calling humanity to repentance. Will we listen, or will we dismiss them as a coincidence? The days of neutrality are over. Every person must choose between the wisdom of the world and the wisdom of God. To delay is dangerous; to reject is deadly. Eternity is at stake, and silence is no longer an option.

The so-called wise of this world will be silenced when Christ returns. Every knee will bow, and every tongue will confess that Jesus Christ is Lord. Professors, presidents, preachers, and politicians will stand before the throne, stripped of titles, and judged by the truth they once rejected.

Christians cannot afford to be distracted or deceived. The call to readiness is urgent. We must live holy, bold, and faithful lives, knowing that our labor in the Lord is not in vain. The church must stop fearing man and start fearing God again. A reverent fear of the Lord produces wisdom, boldness, and power. Without it, we become powerless and compromised, unable to stand in these evil days. To the unbeliever, the time for excuses is over. God is patient, but His patience has limits. The day of the Lord will come like a thief in the night. Now is the day of salvation; tomorrow is not promised.

To the believer, the command is clear: stay awake, stay ready, and stay faithful. The world may laugh at your devotion, but when Christ returns, it will be the faithful who are vindicated.

In the end, Solomon was right. The whole duty of man is to fear God and keep His commandments. This wisdom will never fade, and this truth will never fail. While the world exalts its intellect, God is raising a people who will sound foolish to men but will shine with eternal wisdom. The choice is clear: cling to the wisdom of men and perish, or cling to the Word of God and live forever.

Closing Prophetic Prayer

"Lord, open the eyes of Your people in this hour. Shake us from complacency, awaken us from deception, and fill us with holy fire to stand in these last days. Let no lie of the enemy blind us and let no fear paralyze us. We declare that Your truth is greater than the lies of nations, and Your light is stronger than the darkness around us. Prepare us as a bride without spot or wrinkle, watching and waiting for Your return. May every reader of this message hear the trumpet call and be found ready when You come. In Jesus' mighty name—Amen."

Chapter 27: When Heaven Shocks and Hell Surprises

Heaven will be a place of joy, but also of great surprise. And hell, tragically, it will shock many who never imagined they would end up there. These are not scary tactics or clever sermon titles. These are the unfiltered words of Jesus Christ Himself, who warned that *not everyone who says to Me, 'Lord, Lord,' will enter the kingdom of heaven, but only the one who does the will of My Father who is in heaven* (Matthew 7:21). It is a terrifying and sobering truth that many professing believers will find themselves outside the gates of heaven, not because they were not religious, but because Christ never truly knew them.

This is the wake-up call we dare not ignore. Too many take Jesus' words lightly, as if His warnings are only for the worst of sinners and not for those sitting in pews, serving in ministries, or quoting Scriptures daily. But Jesus was speaking to the religious crowd—to those who thought they were safe because they appeared righteous on the outside. Think deeply about this: not everyone who worships in a sanctuary, attends a mosque, reads the Bible, or even preaches from a pulpit will enter the Kingdom of God.

The harsh reality is this—murderers and thieves will not just populate hell, but by preachers, politicians, professionals, skilled workers, evangelists, and worshippers who looked the part but never lived in true submission to Jesus. They were praised by people, admired for their religious works, but unknown to heaven. Their names were on church rosters, denominational rolls, and charitable giving lists, but never found in the Lamb's Book of Life.

So here is the question I ask every reader: **Are you trembling-sure that the Jesus you claim to follow knows you?** Not whether you know about Him, but whether *He knows you.* Are your intentions pure? Are your prayers rooted in surrender or performance? Jesus said, *"I will say to them plainly, 'I never knew you. Away from Me, you evildoers!'"* (Matthew 7:23). That warning was not for outsiders—it was directed at those who assumed they were already in.

This is not about being a "good" person or a "bad" person. It is not about your past mistakes or present status. It is not about religious titles, outward behaviors, or your place in society. What matters is whether your heart has been reborn—whether you have truly repented and surrendered your life to the authority of Jesus Christ. You can feed the poor, give generously, and serve with excellence—but if your motives are rooted in pride, recognition, or self-salvation, you are building a fragile house on sand.

Hell will be filled with people who imitate Christianity—those who mimicked the sound of worship, carried the look of devotion, and learned the language of church culture, but never had a genuine relationship with Christ. They performed righteousness without transformation. They praised God loudly but never bowed their hearts low. Their worship was elevated, but their hearts were far from Him.

God doesn't want your perfection—He desires your repentance. He's not impressed by how loudly you preach, how well you sing, or how many people follow you. He is after your surrendered heart. You cannot buy your way into heaven with tithes or offerings, nor can you fake your weight in with emotional worship and empty declarations. You must choose— willingly, not out of fear or force—to turn from sin and follow Jesus with everything you are.

Many grew up in the sanctuary. They were raised in Christian homes, surrounded by faithful parents who never missed a Sunday service. They attended youth group meetings, served worship teams in churches and on college campuses, memorized entire passages of Scripture, and could quote verses fluently. Yet, despite this rich spiritual environment, their hearts remained untouched. They knew *of* God but never truly surrendered *to* Him. They treated salvation as though it were a family heirloom, something to be passed down like a spiritual inheritance. But salvation does not come by proximity; it is not absorbed through osmosis. It must be personally embraced through rebirth and repentance.

You do not inherit the Kingdom of God because of your denomination, your parents' faith, or the time you have spent inside a church building. Regeneration—not tradition—is what saves the soul. Sadly, many who call themselves believers live polished, respectable lives on the outside, but on the inside, they are like whitewashed tombs—clean in appearance, but spiritually dead. They avoid the sins that look scandalous or shameful but harbor the more "socially acceptable" sins— pride, envy, gossip, jealousy, bitterness, and unforgiveness. They do not drink, smoke, or curse, but they refuse to crucify the flesh and deny themselves daily.

Far too many have confused morality with salvation. They believe that being better than the next person qualifies them for heaven. They compare themselves to the fallen, the immoral, or the irreligious, and conclude they're safe. But one day, when death comes knocking— when the appointment no one can reschedule arrives—they will stand before a holy God, not with the excuses they rehearsed for the world, but with hearts exposed and souls trembling.

And in that moment, many will cry out, *"Lord, I served You! I led worship! I went to Bible study! I gave to the poor! I did all these things in Your name!"* But God will not be moved by activities that lack intimacy. He will not be swayed by performances void of repentance. Jesus will reply with the most terrifying words ever spoken: *"I never knew you. Depart from Me, you worker of iniquity."*

So much has been done "in His name," but heaven is not impressed by empty religious works. God does not grade on a curve. He does not compare you to others to see if you did "well enough." He judges according to truth, righteousness, and the inward condition of the heart. Many will wake up in hell, not because they didn't do good things, but because they trusted in those good things rather than in Christ alone. Hell will echo with the sound of weeping, grinding teeth, and unbearable regret. It will be filled with the haunting voices of those who lived deceived, who convinced themselves they were safe while ignoring the warnings.

As you read this chapter, the enemy may whisper lies to your heart. He may tempt you to label these words harshly, judgmental, or unnecessary. But I assure you, this is not condemnation; it is mercy. Mercy that calls out before it is too late. Mercy urges you to examine your life now, while you still have breath in your body. God is allowing you to hear this message because He wants to spare you from an eternity of separation. He does not want you to face that final day with horror and guilt, crying out in regret when there is no more time to repent.

God's payday is coming, and each of us will be compensated based on the life we truly lived, not the image we projected. You will receive the wages for what you have sown, and if you have sown to the flesh, you will reap destruction. If you have sown to the Spirit, you will reap life. These truths may be hard to hear, but they are deadly to ignore. I would rather offend you now than remain silent while you perish later. This chapter was not written to comfort your flesh but to awaken your spirit.

Far too many preachers today avoid these truths. They won't speak about hell or repentance, fearing people will stop giving, stop attending, or stop supporting their ministries. But the gospel is not a business, and the sanctuary is not a marketplace. Jesus did not die to make us comfortable in sin—He died to deliver us from it completely. The road to eternal life is narrow, and Jesus did not say few people *want* to find it—He said few *do* (Matthew 7:14). Many choose the broad road because it feels easier. It is filled with blessings, false assurances, soft preaching, and casual Christianity. But it leads to destruction.

The gospel is not an accessory you can wear when convenient. You cannot add Jesus to your life like a spiritual upgrade. The gospel demands your death—the death of your old self. It is the crucifixion of your flesh and the burial of your selfish will. Following Jesus means laying down your pride, your comfort, your preferences, and your sin.

It is impossible to cling to Jesus with one hand while grasping sin with the other. You cannot stand with one foot in His sanctuary and the other in the world. God will not share His throne with idols. He will not dwell in a divided heart. Jesus is not one of many options or a backup plan. He is either Lord of *all* or not Lord *at all.*

What has become truly frightening in today's world is how many have settled for religion, denomination, and doctrine—yet never sought a real relationship with Jesus Christ. They have become comfortable performing rituals, singing worship songs they don't mean, and praying prayers that never touch their lifestyle. They sit through sermon after sermon, but the words never penetrate their hearts. The Word of God, which is supposed to guide, convict, and transform, simply bounces off like raindrops hitting a metal roof.

My dear reader, don't allow yourself to become numb to the voice of God. His Word is your compass, your sword, your protection. Put yourself in a posture of sensitivity, where conviction matters more than comfort. Do not just feel bad when your sin causes inconvenience or consequences—run toward holiness because it honors your Savior. Do not flirt with rebellion when no one is watching. Character is revealed not in public worship but in private obedience.

Today's Christianity, especially in the modern age of digital religion, is often about *image* over *intimacy*. People wear shirts with Scripture on them, share daily verses on their Facebook or Instagram, and attend every conference and church event—but privately, they are filled with bitterness, jealousy, pride, and spiritual neglect. They have abandoned the challenging work of sincere heart cleansing and replaced it with polished appearances. They crave applause more than they crave truth.

Reputation has become more valuable than repentance. Many would rather protect their image than purify their soul. When temptation comes, when trials shake the foundation, they fall— because there is no real root. Their faith was not anchored in a living Savior but in lifeless routines. Quietly and steadily, they drift away from intimacy with God. The fire dies out, the passion fades, and worship becomes mechanical. Their prayer life dries up, and before they know it, they are only going through the motions, spiritually hollow.

And then—when death comes knocking and eternity begins— they come to the shocking realization that all they ever had was a performance. What they needed was living faith. What they settled for was religion. And what they rejected was the Savior who loved them enough to die in their place. At that moment, many will wake up in hell, not because God did not try to reach them, but because they never truly responded.

Jesus Himself warned of a coming separation—the wheat from the chaff, the sheep from the goats, the true from the false. This is not symbolic language or spiritual poetry; it is a prophetic declaration of divine judgment. There will be a great divide between those who truly belonged to Him and those who only looked at the part. So, I ask you again, has your heart truly been changed by the Holy Spirit? Has He led you into truth, broken your pride, and convicted you of sin? Do you genuinely hate the sin that grieves God, or do you simply sweep it under the rug, saving it for moments when no one is watching? Are you hiding iniquity in places of convenience, ready to retrieve it when it suits you? Do you love the truth, even when it cuts deeply through the core of your heart and forces change? Or do you resist it, preferring comfort over conviction?

Are you walking in the light daily, or merely visiting it once a week, on Saturday for Sabbath worship, or on Sunday to honor resurrection day? Your faith cannot be confined to a calendar. God is not interested in part-time devotion. The time for playing spiritual games is over. Eternity is not a subject for debate—it is a reality that demands preparation. One day, you will stand before Jesus Christ, and there will be no time left for negotiation, no second chance, and no appeal.

You will not be able to rely on the memory of a prayer you once said if your life never bore fruit afterward. You won't be saved by someone else's intercession if you refuse to walk in personal obedience. The decision about your eternity is not made in that moment; it is already being made now. Your actions, your surrender, and your relationship with Christ today determine your destiny. If you put it off until later, it may already be too late.

Salvation is not a religious badge you wear—it is a rebirth you experience. It is not something you display on the outside, but something that transforms you from the inside out. The Bible makes it clear: *"Examine yourselves, to see whether you are in the faith. Test yourselves."* (2 Corinthians 13:5). That is not a casual suggestion—it is a command. Your eternity hinges on whether you are truly in Christ.

Remember this: there is no safety in assumptions, and no peace in presumption. Many are living with a false sense of security, thinking they are saved simply because they prayed for prayer, walked in an aisle, or grew up in a church culture. But assumptions about salvation can be eternally dangerous. Presumption can blind you until it is too late.

The enemy does not care if you *think* you are saved; he just does not want you to *be* saved. He is not concerned with your attendance at the sanctuary, the mosque, the temple, or whatever religious space you visit. He is content as long as your heart never changes. He is fine with you reading the Bible because he knows it too. He can quote it better than many believers. His goal is not to keep you away from religion, but to keep you from repentance.

Satan does not fight against empty religion; he thrives in it. He is not threatened by people who appear godly but lack true power. What he hates is a heart broken over sin, a soul surrendered at the feet of Jesus, and a life laid down in obedience to God's Word. That is why he fights repentance so fiercely, because repentance leads to transformation, and transformation leads to true freedom in Christ.

I beg you, do not let hell rejoice over your spiritual confidence while heaven grieves your lack of surrender. Some of the most moral, respectable, and successful people will be eternally lost, not because they were evil in the eyes of man, but because they never bowed to Jesus Christ. They bowed instead to idols of wealth, careers, popularity, pride, and possessions. They worshiped their image more than their Creator.

And yet, some of the most broken, weeping sinners—those who were crushed by the weight of their sin—will enter into glory. Not because they were perfect, but because they threw themselves at the mercy of God. They did not rely on reputation or religion—they trusted wholly in the blood of Jesus Christ. Heaven is not reserved for the proud or the polished. It is promised to the poor in spirit— those who know with absolute certainty that they are nothing apart from Christ.

Jesus is the Lamb of God, sacrificed for our sins. He was pierced for our transgressions and crushed for our iniquities. His blood is not a symbol—it is a payment. It is not a decoration, it's our only hope. And those who are truly saved understand that nothing they own, nothing they've done, and nothing they have earned could ever replace what Jesus did for them on the cross.

The ones who will enter heaven are not those who lived perfectly, but those who fell to their knees, cried out in repentance, and pleaded, *"God, be merciful to me, a sinner."* They came not as polished saints, but as broken people clinging to the cross. They were not offering God a résumé—they offered Him a heart of surrender. They did not ask Him to simply fix their lives— they asked Him to reign in their hearts forever.

So again, I ask you: **Is Jesus Christ truly your Lord, or just your inspiration?** Is he your greatest treasure, or simply a tradition you follow? When you speak His name, does your voice tremble with awe and joy, or is it just part of your religious routine? Do you truly rejoice in Him, or merely recite truths without transformation?

The gospel is not about making bad people better—it is about making dead people come alive. Yet tragically, there are terrifying numbers of people filling sanctuaries today who have never been made alive in Christ. They sit through service after service, but their hearts remain stone cold. Why? Because many preachers have traded the fear of God for the favor of men. They preach what congregations want to hear instead of what the Holy Spirit commands them to proclaim.

And so, people walk into church empty—and leave just as empty. Spiritually dead. Emotionally numb. Religiously active. If you were to ask many attendees what they took away from the sermon, you'd likely hear answers about giving or general encouragement, but rarely about repentance, obedience, or life transformation. The true invitation of Jesus is not just *"come give,"* but *"Come to Me, all you who are weary and burdened, and I will give you rest... for My yoke is easy and My burden is light"* (Matthew 11:28-30).

Today, many are little more than religious corpses—walking through rituals, doctrines, and denominational labels, but still dead in sin and trespasses. But if that is you, don't live in despair, and don't harden your heart. There is hope. The same Jesus who warned of hell is the One who opened heaven. He came for the lost, died for the rebellious, rose for the guilty, and still stands ready to forgive—even the worst of sinners.

But He requires your surrender—**not someday, not halfway, but now.** He calls you to die to yourself, to confess your desperate need for Him, and to turn not only from your visible sins, but from the hidden poisons of pride, lust, bitterness, greed, and secret rebellion. Come to the crossroads as a tourist taking pictures, but as a beggar in need of mercy. Only the humble will enter. Only the surrendered will be saved. And only those truly born again will escape the flames of hell and walk into the joy of eternal life.

The world will tell you to follow your heart, but Jesus calls you to *deny it*. The world says, "You're a good person," but Jesus reminds us that only God is good, and that the heart of man is deceitful above all things and desperately wicked (Jeremiah 17:9). The world celebrates compromise and calls it love. But Jesus demands a cross—and the narrow road that few are willing to travel.

You will not drift into heaven by accident. You must *strive* to enter through the narrow gate. That means deliberate surrender, deep repentance, and an ongoing decision to count the cost. This kind of gospel will not fill stadiums, but it *will* fill heaven. It won't entertain the flesh, but it will awaken dead souls to eternal life.

I plead with you, don't be deceived by the mask of religion. Don't assume that just because you once prayed for a prayer or had an emotional moment, you are now exempt from examination.

Salvation is not proven by a single decision made long ago—a miracle of transformation reveals it. A changed heart. A new nature. A growing hunger for holiness. A sorrow over sin. And no, not perfection—but *direction*. The question is not "Were you once sincere?" but rather, "Are you walking toward Christ *now*?"

Are you pressing into Jesus, or drifting from Him? Are you feeding your flesh or cultivating your faith? Because the shocking truth is this: many who claimed the name of Christ—many who thought they were saved—will wake up in hell. And in that moment of eternal awakening, they will ask themselves, *How did I get here?* And they will hear the most terrifying words ever spoken: *"I never knew you. Depart from Me into the lake of fire."* (Matthew 7:23)

Yes, heaven is real. But so is hell. And you are choosing even now where your soul will spend eternity. Not with words alone, but with your heart, your obedience, your direction, and your surrender. Choose the day whom you will serve. As for me and my house, **we will serve the Lord.** We will reject empty religion, flee from cultural Christianity, and follow the risen Savior—because our destination is heaven, and we refuse to make peace with hell.

Choose Heaven, Reject Hell

The deception of our day is subtle yet deadly: that as long as we feel spiritual, attend services, and do good, we are safe. But Jesus did not die to make us feel religious—He died to make us reborn. His call has never changed: *"If anyone wants to be My disciple, let him deny himself, take up his cross, and follow Me."* (Luke 9:23)

This chapter is not an attack on your faith—it is a plea for your soul. Examine yourself. Do not assume your eternity is secure because of past prayer or a religious label. The evidence of salvation is not found in your emotions, experiences, or habits, but in your transformation. True faith leaves evidence—hunger for God, hatred of sin, growing holiness, and a heart that follows Jesus more deeply every day.

Don't wait for a more convenient moment. The narrow gate is open now. The call is urgent. Hell is real, but so is heaven—and you must choose. Come to Jesus, not casually or culturally, but completely. Do not be among the many who are surprised in eternity. Be among the few who are found faithful.

When Heaven Shocks and Hell Surprises deeply tie into the central theme of this book—*God uses the foolish to confuse the wise.* In the story of the rich man and Lazarus (Luke 16:19–31), we see a striking reversal of earthly wisdom and status. The rich man, who appeared wise by worldly standards, lived in luxury but was.

ultimately condemned. Meanwhile, Lazarus, whom society might have seen as "foolish" or insignificant—ailing and ignored—was comforted by God in eternity.

This chapter reminds readers that the true measure of wisdom is not wealth, status, or outward religiosity, but the condition of the heart before God. Many who seem wise in the eyes of world leaders, professionals, and religious elites may be spiritually blind, deceived by their pride and self-reliance. On the other hand, those who appear foolish, poor, or broken by the world's standards may be rich in faith and heirs of God's kingdom.

God confounds the wisdom of the world by choosing the humble and the contrite to reveal His glory. This chapter calls readers to reject false confidence and superficial faith and to embrace genuine repentance and surrender—the way of the "foolish" who are wise in God's sight. It challenges the assumption that a life of religious appearances or material success guarantees salvation, pointing instead to the eternal truth that only a transformed heart secures a place in heaven.

I therefore challenge my readers who may rely on status, religion, or outward appearances as proof of salvation. It reveals how God often confounds human wisdom by choosing the humble and broken— those the world might label as foolish—to inherit His kingdom. True wisdom and salvation come from a heart transformed by repentance and surrender, not by wealth, reputation, or empty rituals.

In calling on them to examine their hearts deeply, this chapter aligns with the biblical truth that many who seem wise in the world's eyes will be surprised in eternity, while those deemed foolish will enter into eternal joy. It is a call to embrace the humble path that leads to life, turning away from false confidence and toward the Savior who truly knows and saves.

Reflection Questions:

1. Have you ever mistaken religious activity or emotion for true salvation?
2. What does your current life direction reveal—are you moving toward Christ or away from Him?
3. Are there areas of sin, pride, or compromise you've hidden or excused?
4. When you think of standing before Jesus, does your heart tremble in surrender, or rely on past works?
5. What needs to change today so your life reflects a truly transformed, born-again believer?

Devotional Prayer:

Father God,

I come before You with honesty and humility. I don't want a counterfeit faith. I don't want to be one of the many who are surprised in eternity. Search for my heart. Show me where I've relied on religion, appearances, or past experiences instead of full surrender.

Jesus, I confess I have sinned. I repent—not just of the obvious sins, but of the pride, lukewarmness, and compromise I've excused for too long. I ask You to reign in my heart completely—not just as my Savior, but as my Lord.

Holy Spirit, help me walk in truth. Guide me into holiness. Let my life bear the fruit of real salvation, and may I never trade the cross for comfort. I chose heaven. I chose to surrender. And I choose You.

In Jesus' name, Amen.

Salvation is not memorizing; it is a miracle. It does not come from emotions, religion, or assumptions. It is proven by a transformed heart, surrendered will, and a life that follows Jesus daily. Hell is real, but so is heaven—and the choice is now, not later.

Conclusion:

A Final Call to the Foolish, the Faithful, and the Forgotten

Throughout the pages of this book, a consistent truth unfolds: God does not operate according to the world's logic. He has always chosen the least expected, the weak, the broken, the overlooked, the unqualified—to carry His message and accomplish His will. From Noah's ark to David's

sling, from Rahab's redemption to the stammering lips of Moses, God has moved through what the world called foolish to reveal His eternal wisdom.

Now, in this present hour of global confusion, immorality, and spiritual apathy, God is once again stirring the earth. He is using even the confusion within national leadership, beginning in places.

like the United States, to signal a shift. A shaking is happening in government, in the church, in the culture, and God is not absent in the chaos. He is allowing the pride of man to collide with the sovereignty of heaven so that His people might awaken.

This book is not merely a collection of stories or theological reflections—it is a prophetic call to repentance and readiness. The foolishness of God is wiser than the wisdom of men (1

Corinthians 1:25), and those who humble themselves under His mighty hand will rise with power in these last days. God is calling a remnant—young and old—to remember who He is, to return to their first love, and to walk in radical obedience.

This is not the time for passive religion or cultural Christianity. The days ahead will demand a bold faith, a holy separation, and an unwavering loyalty to Jesus Christ. Many will be pressured to compromise, to bow to the systems of the beast, and to forget their Creator. But God is marking those who will remain faithful. He is raising worshipers in spirit and truth who will not be silenced by fear, flattery, or persecution.

To you, the reader, perhaps you have felt like your voice did not matter. Perhaps you have been.

laughed at, left out, or labeled a fool for your faith. But take heart: you are exactly who God delights in using. You were born for such a time as this. This is your hour to rise.

Let the church awaken. Let the youth arise. Let the prophets speak. Let the faithful endure. And let the foolish, those fully surrendered to God, confuse the wise of this world until every knee bow and every tongue confesses that Jesus Christ is Lord.

We are living in prophetic times. The signs are all around us— political division, natural disasters, moral confusion, and spiritual apathy. Yet even in the chaos, God is speaking. The question is not whether God is sending a warning. The question is: **are we listening?**

This book has traced the footprints of a God who moves through the margins, who raises voices that the world mocks, and who accomplishes His will through people society deems unqualified. From Noah to Paul, from Rahab to Mary, we have seen that God has never needed the approval of man to carry out His purpose. Now, the mantle passes to us.

We are the generation called to stand in the gap, to prepare the way for Christ's return, to be set apart in a culture that celebrates compromise. We cannot afford to remain lukewarm or distracted. The hour is urgent, and the harvest is ripe.

But here's the good news: God is still using the foolish. He is still using the broken, the rejected, the repentant, and the surrendered. He is raising a remnant—not with earthly credentials, but with spiritual authority. Not with polished platforms, but with purified hearts.

As you close this book, do not walk away the same. Let this be a **turning point** in your life. Examine your heart. Repent of apathy. Return to your first love. And if God is calling you, answer. Even if you feel unworthy, unprepared, or too far gone, remember: He delights in using the unlikely.

The stage is set. The King is coming. And God is preparing His Bride. May you be found ready, burning, and bold?

Let the foolish rise up in faith. Let the Church awaken.
Let the world be warned.
Let glory be His alone.

Amen. Come, Lord Jesus.

The time is short. The King is coming. What a Day That Will Be

To close this message, we remember the hope that sustains the faithful—the promised return of Jesus Christ. This hope is beautifully expressed in the classic gospel song:

"What a day that will be.
When my Jesus I shall see,
When I look upon His face,
The One who saved me by His grace…"

This song is not just sentimental, it's prophetic. It reminds us that the struggle, rejection, and foolishness we endure in this life for Christ's sake are not in vain. One day soon, the trumpet will sound, the sky will split, and the One we've preached, served, and trusted in the darkness will appear in glory.

Until that day, we pressed on not in fear, but in faith. Not in retreat, but in boldness. We fight the good fight, finish the race, and keep the faith… because what a day that will be, when our Jesus we shall see.

Bibliography & Scripture References

Scriptural References by Chapter

The following Scripture passages form the spiritual foundation for this book's message. They are.

listed by Testament and associated with the chapters where they are most prominently referenced.

Old Testament

- Genesis 6–9 – The Days of Noah | Chapter 13
- Genesis 12:1–3
- Genesis 19 – Sodom and Gomorrah | Chapter 11
- Exodus 3:7-9 – God hears the cries of the oppressed | Chapter 9
- Exodus 7–12 – Plagues and Pharaoh's hard heart | Chapter 2
- Leviticus 9:24 – Fire falls on consecrated altar | Chapter 12
- Leviticus 10 – Strange fire defiles the temple | Chapter 4
- Numbers 13 – Fear of giants in the land | Chapter 8
- Deuteronomy 6:6-7 (NIV)
- Deuteronomy 18:22 – Testing prophetic words.
- Deuteronomy 30:3
- Joshua 24:15 (NIV)
- 1 Samuel 3:1-10 – God calls Samuel as a youth | Chapter 19
- 1 Samuel 8 – Israel demands a king | Chapter 7
- 1 Samuel 17 – David and Goliath | Chapter 19 (reference)
- 1 Kings 18 – Elijah rebuilds the altar and calls down fire | Chapters 12 & 19
- 2 Kings 22–23 – Josiah restores worship | Chapter 12 (reference)

- 1 Chronicles 12:32 – Sons of Issachar discern the times | Chapter 13 (implied)
- 2 Chronicles 7:14 – Humble, pray, seek, and turn | Chapters 4&13
- Nehemiah 5 – Social injustice and righteous reform | Chapter 9
- Psalm 34:18 – God is near to the brokenhearted | Chapter 10
- Psalm 121:4
- Psalm 146:3 – Don't trust in princes | Chapter 7
- Isaiah 1:17 – Defend the oppressed | Chapters 10 & 11
- Isaiah 5:20 – Woe to those who call evil good | Chapter 11
- Isaiah 43:6, 19 – Behold, I am doing a new thing | Chapter 19
- Jeremiah 1:6–7 – God calls the youth | Chapter 19
- Jeremiah 3:15 – Shepherds after God's heart | Chapter 4
- Jeremiah 6:14 – False peace declared | Chapter 5
- Jeremiah 30:7
- Ezekiel 3:17 – Watchmen to warn | Chapter 13
- Ezekiel 36:24
- Daniel 2:44 – God's kingdom outlasts all | Chapter 7
- Daniel 3:17 18 – Shadrach, Meshach, Abednego | Chapter 19
- Daniel 4 – Nebuchadnezzar humbled | Chapters 1 & 7
- Daniel 9:27
- Daniel 10:12 – God honors humble pursuit | Chapter 6
- Amos 5:24 – Let justice roll like a river | Chapter 9
- Amos 7:14 15 – God calls the unlikely | Chapter 3
- Ecclesiastes 12:1 – Remember your Creator in youth | Chapter 19
- Zechariah 12:10

New Testament

- Matthew 4:8-10 (NIV)
- Matthew 5:13-16 – Salt and light | Chapter 11
- Matthew 10:34 – Not peace, but a sword | Chapter 5

271

- Matthew 21:12 13 – Jesus cleanses the temple | Chapters 4 & 9
- Matthew 24:6–14, 37–39 – Signs of the end; Days of Noah | Chapters 6 & 13
- Matthew 25:1–13 – Ten virgins and readiness | Chapter 13
- Luke 17:32 – Remember Lot's wife | Chapter 19
- Luke 21:25-36 – Signs in the heavens | Chapter 13
- John 4:29 (NIV)
- John 10:10, 27 (NIV)
- John 15:19 – The world will hate you | Chapter 11 (reference)
- Acts 2:17 21 – I will pour out My Spirit | Chapter 13
- Romans 1:21-32 – Cultural decline | Chapter 11
- Romans 13:1 – God ordains authority | Chapter 19
- 1 Corinthians 1:25-29 – God chooses the foolish | Chapter 1 & throughout.
- 1 Corinthians 1:27 (KJV)
- Galatians 1:10 – Seeking God's approval | Chapter 4
- Philippians 3:20 – Our citizenship is in Heaven | Chapter 7
- 2 Timothy 1:7 – Spirit of fear vs. power and sound mind | Chapter 8
- 2 Timothy 3:15 – Perilous times in the last days | Chapter 11
- 2 Peter 3:9 – The Lord delays judgment out of mercy | Chapter 13
- Hebrews 12:2 (KJV/NIV)
- Revelation 3:4 – The faithful in Sardis | Chapter 14
- Revelation 12:7–12 – War in Heaven | Chapter 6
- Revelation 13:16-17 – The mark of the beast | Chapter 19
- Revelation 14:15 – The Lamb and the faithful remnant | Chapter 19
- Revelation 22:12-13 – Christ is coming soon | Chapter 13

Historical and Theological Sources

Booth, William. *Prophetic Warnings on the Coming Century.* Compiled from sermons and addresses. The Salvation Army Historical Archives, early 20th century. A sobering statement on the dangers of superficial religion: "Religion without the Holy Ghost, Christianity without Christ, forgiveness without repentance, salvation without regeneration, politics without God, and heaven without hell."

Lindsey, Hal. *The Late Great Planet Earth.* Grand Rapids: Zondervan, 1970.

A foundational work on end-times prophecy and Israel's modern-day significance.

Reagan, David. *Israel in Bible Prophecy: Past, Present, & Future.* McKinney, TX: Lamb & Lion Ministries, 2017.

Examines Israel's prophetic role across Scripture and modern times.

Walvoord, John F. *Armageddon, Oil, and the Middle East Crisis: What the Bible Says About the Future of the Middle East and the End of Western Civilization.* Grand Rapids: Zondervan, 2007. A deep dive into Israel's geopolitical tensions and prophetic implications.

Tsarfati, Amir. *The Day Approaching: An Israeli's Message of Warning and Hope for the Last*

Days. Eugene, OR: Harvest House Publishers, 2020.

Written by a Messianic Jew, providing real-time insights into Israel and prophecy.

Prophetic and Adventist Reference

White, Ellen G. *Early Writings / A Word to the Little Flock.* Various printings. Key insights on time-setting and prophetic warnings from the Adventist tradition.

Cultural & Current Event Sources

The Jerusalem Post – www.jpost.com
News source for up-to-date coverage on political and military events in Israel.

The Times of Israel – www.timesofisrael.com
Comprehensive news platform tracking Israel's spiritual and geopolitical landscape.

The Family Dinner Project. "Benefits of Family Dinners."
Harvard Graduate School of Education. Accessed July 2025. https://thefamilydinnerproject.org/about-us/benefits-of-family-dinners

Worship Songs & Media Credits

Hill, Jim. "What a Day That Will Be." 1955.
A timeless hymn of hope about the return of Christ.

Maverick City Music. *Refiner.* Featuring Chandler Moore and Steffany Gretzinger. A contemporary worship song about spiritual purification and surrender.

Invitation to Know Christ

No matter what your past. No matter what your pain. No matter how foolish, broken, or forgotten you may feel, **God sees you**. He knows your name, your story, and your destiny.

The message of this book has shown that God uses the unexpected, the overlooked, and even the despised to reveal His glory. But the greatest revelation of all is the love of Jesus Christ, who came not for the perfect, but for the lost.

Jesus is calling you.

He is not asking for your performance. He is asking for your heart.

"For God so loved the world, that He gave His one and only Son, that whoever believes in Him shall not perish but have eternal life." —John 3:16

Salvation is not about religion or ritual. It's about a real relationship with a living Savior. Jesus died on the cross to take the penalty for your sins—and rose again so that you could live with Him forever.

If you're ready to accept Him as Lord and Savior, pray a prayer like this from your heart:

Prayer of Salvation
Lord Jesus, I believe You are the Son of God. I believe you died for my sins and rose again with all power. I confess that I have sinned, and I ask You to forgive me. I turn away from my old life, and I surrender my heart to You. Be my Lord, my Savior, and my King. Fill me with Your Spirit and teach me to follow You every day. In Jesus' name, Amen.

If you prayed that prayer in faith, **you are saved** (Romans 10:9-10). Welcome to the family of God!

I encourage you to:

- Get connected to a Bible-believing, Spirit-led church.
- Begin reading the Word of God daily, starting with the Gospel of John.
- Surround yourself with believers who will walk with you in faith.
- Stay rooted in prayer and praise.

The journey ahead may not be easy, but **you will never walk alone.**

What a day that will be—when we see our Savior face to face.

God Uses the Foolish to Confuse the Wise

What if the world's confusion is part of God's divine strategy? God Uses the Foolish to Confuse the Wise is a prophetic and biblically grounded journey through Scripture, world events, and spiritual awakening. Reverend Dr. Eugene Edwards examines how God works through unexpected people, political leaders, and shaking events to reveal His will, awaken the Church, and expose what's hidden in the heart of nations and individuals.

This timely and relevant book explores:

- How God uses flawed leaders to accomplish His purposes
- Why political turmoil and global fear can be divine wake-up calls.
- How spiritual discernment is needed more than ever in the last days.
- What the Church must do to remain faithful, united, and ready
- Why God is still speaking through the foolish, the broken, and the unexpected

With bold clarity and a call to repentance, this book challenges readers to see today's shaking world not with fear, but with faith, recognizing that God is not silent, and He is not finished.

God Uses the Foolish to Confuse the Wise –
Workbook Study Guides

Introduction and Chapters 1– 27 with Devotional Workbook Sections Author: Reverend Dr. Eugene C. Edwards

Introduction: When God Shouts Instead of Whispers There comes a moment in history when God ceases to whisper. He moves mountains, shakes thrones, and speaks so loudly that the entire world stands still—and listens. Today, we find ourselves in such a moment. This introduction reminds us that no ruler rises or falls outside of God's sovereign plan. It calls the Church to discern divine purpose behind political shifts and cultural upheaval, awakening believers to hear Heaven's voice.

Workbook Study Guide – Introduction Reflection
Chapter Summary:
God uses leadership, crises, and world events as His megaphone to awaken hearts to His sovereignty and call to repentance.

Key Scriptures:
Daniel 2:21; 1 Corinthians 1:27–29; Romans 13:1;
Proverbs 21:1

Reflection Quotes:
"God does not react—He reigns."
"What appears as chaos on earth is often divine order in Heaven."

Reflection Questions:
1. What current event has made you question God's control?
2. How can you grow in trust when leadership disappoints?

3. In what ways might God be using today's turmoil to reach His people?

Group Discussion Prompts:
• How can the Church reflect faith in God's sovereignty during national tension?
• What hinders believers from discerning God's voice in political or social upheaval?

Action Step / Weekly Challenge:
Spend this week praying daily for world leaders and ask God to help you see His hand in current events.

Challenge Verse:
Daniel 2:21 – 'He changes times and seasons; He removes kings and sets up kings.'

Biblical Character Connection:
Daniel – A prophet who trusted God's sovereignty under corrupt regimes.

Key Quote / Takeaway:
"When the world panics, Heaven is at peace."

Worship Song Suggestion:
"Sovereign Over Us" – Aaron Keyes

Creative Response Option:
Write a journal entry titled 'God's Hand in the Headlines,' reflecting on how His sovereignty is visible in today's news.

Self-Assessment Questions:

I trust God even when I can't see His plan.

I respond to political shifts with prayer, not panic. I

look for God's purpose before forming opinions.

Devotional Prayer:

Lord, You rule overall. When the world trembles, remind me that Your throne is unshaken. Give me faith to see Your hand in every season. Amen.

Chapter 1: Sovereignty Over Thrones
God speaks through the rise and fall of leaders. Nations may be shaken, but His throne remains firm. This chapter teaches that political changes are not random— they are reflections of divine orchestration.

Workbook Study Guide – Chapter 1
Reflection Chapter Summary:
Leadership rises and falls by God's command; He rules over every earthly throne.

Key Scriptures:
Daniel 2:21; Romans 13:1; Proverbs 21:1; Isaiah 45:7

Reflection Quotes:
"Kings may reign, but God rules."
"Heaven's government never faces elections."

Reflection Questions:
1.What recent leadership change has assessed your faith?
2.How can recognizing God's sovereignty bring you peace?
3. How might this truth impact how you pray for your nation?

Group Discussion Prompts:
• How can believers respond biblically to leadership failures?
• What does it mean to intercede rather than criticize?

Action Step / Weekly Challenge:
Choose one leader (local or national) and pray daily for their wisdom and humility.

Challenge Verse:
Psalm 47:8 – 'God reigns over the nations; God sits on His holy throne.'

Biblical Character Connection:
Nebuchadnezzar – Humbled by God to reveal Heaven's authority.

Key Quote / Takeaway:
"God does not lose control of what He allows."

Worship Song Suggestion:
"How Great Is Our God" – Chris Tomlin

Creative Response Option:
Sketch or write a list of leaders and pray over each name, declaring God's sovereignty.

Self-Assessment Questions:
I pray for leaders instead of complaining.
I view leadership through the lens of God's control. I trust God even when rulers fail.

Devotional Prayer:
Sovereign Lord, You reign above every ruler and system. Help me to live with confidence that You alone are in control. Amen.

Chapter 2: The Foolish Vessel, the Divine Message God often chooses what the world deems unqualified to deliver His greatest truths. This chapter explores how God's wisdom is revealed through unlikely messengers and humble hearts.

Workbook Study Guide – Chapter 2
Reflection Chapter Summary:
God uses ordinary and flawed people to carry extraordinary messages of truth and redemption.

Key Scriptures:
1 Corinthians 1:27-29; Judges 13–16; Numbers 22–24.
1 Samuel 16:7

Reflection Quotes:
"When the vessel is weak, the message is strong." "God's glory shines brightest through cracked clay."

Reflection Questions:
1. Have you ever felt too weak or flawed for God to use?
2. What lessons can we learn from Samson or Balaam?
3. How can you be a willing vessel this week?

Group Discussion Prompts:
• Why does God often choose the least likely?
• How can we avoid rejecting messages because of the messenger?

Action Step / Weekly Challenge:
Identify one area of weakness and surrender it to God for His glory.

Challenge Verse:
1 Corinthians 1:27 – 'But God chose the foolish things of the world to shame the wise.'

Biblical Character Connection:
Samson – A flawed yet chosen instrument of deliverance.

Key Quote / Takeaway:
"God's choice often offends human logic."

Worship Song Suggestion:
"Broken Vessels (Amazing Grace)" – Hillsong Worship

Creative Response Option:
Write a poem or short story about how God can use weakness for His strength.

Self-Assessment Questions:
    I see my weaknesses as opportunities for God's glory. I listen to the truth even from unexpected voices.
I trust God's choice more than my comfort.

Devotional Prayer:
Father, thank You for choosing the weak and the willing. Use me despite my flaws to reveal Your glory. Amen.

Chapter 3: Pharaoh's Hardened Heart and Heaven's Glory
Even resistance cannot stop God's plan. Pharaoh's hardened heart became the stage for God's glory. This chapter reminds believers that defiance and delay are sometimes divine tools to magnify Heaven's power.

Workbook Study Guide – Chapter 3
Reflection Chapter Summary:
God can use even hardened hearts and opposition to reveal His glory and bring deliverance.

Key Scriptures:
Exodus 5–14; Romans 9:17; Psalm 2:1–4; Isaiah 14:27

Reflection Quotes:
"Resistance is the soil where revelation grows." "God raised Pharaoh to display His power."

Reflection Questions:
1. How have you seen God use resistance to strengthen your faith?
2. What can Pharaoh teach us about pride and submission?
3. How can hardship prepare you for greater obedience?

Group Discussion Prompts:
• How should believers respond to ungodly authority?
• Why does God allow certain leaders to rise and harden?

Action Step / Weekly Challenge:
When facing resistance, choose to respond with faith and patience instead of frustration.

Challenge Verse:
Exodus 9:16 – 'I have raised you… that my name might be proclaimed in all the earth.'

Biblical Character Connection:
Moses – A humble leader who faced resistance with obedience.

Key Quote / Takeaway:
"God allows defiance to display deliverance."

Worship Song Suggestion:
"Way Maker" – Sinach

Creative Response Option:
Create a short reflection titled 'When Resistance Reveals Glory' about how trials have strengthened your trust in God.

Self-Assessment Questions:
    I trust God's timing when facing opposition. I
    see resistance as a chance to grow.
I remain faithful even when outcomes are uncertain.

Devotional Prayer:
Lord, thank You for working through every obstacle. When hearts harden around me, soften mine. Let Your glory be revealed through my obedience. Amen.

Chapter 4: Cyrus the Persian and Divine Rebuilding

Main Chapter Message:
God can and does use outsiders to accomplish His purposes. Cyrus — a pagan king — was raised by God to restore Israel and rebuild the Temple. His story reminds us that God's sovereignty reaches beyond religious labels; He directs hearts and nations to fulfill His redemptive plan.

Workbook Study Guide – Chapter 4 Reflection Chapter Summary:

God sometimes appoints those who do not know Him to execute His will. Cyrus illustrates that God's plans can move through unexpected people and political seasons to bring restoration.

Key Scriptures:

Isaiah 45:1–4; Ezra 1:1–4; 2 Chronicles 36:22–23; Proverbs 21:1

Reflection Quotes:
- "God uses unexpected hands to rebuild what was broken."
- "Anointing is not always visible, but Heaven knows whom to choose."

Reflection Questions:
6. Where have you seen God use an unlikely person for His purposes?
7. How does Cyrus's story expand your view of God's sovereignty?
8. What walls in your life or ministry does God want to rebuild?

Group Discussion Prompts:

• Discuss why God might use an unbeliever to accomplish a godly task.
• How should the Church respond when God moves?
through secular authorities?

Action Step / Weekly Challenge:
Pray this week for one unexpected leader or public figure — ask
God to work through them for blessing and restoration.

Challenge Verse:
Isaiah 45:4 – "I will go before you and level the mountains... that
you may know that I am the Lord."

Biblical Character Connection:
Cyrus — A Gentile used to fulfill God's promise to restore His people.

Key Quote / Takeaway:
"God's plan is bigger than our categories of 'acceptable' vessels."

Worship Song Suggestion:
"Build My Life" – Pat Barrett / Housefires

Creative Response Option:
Write a short reflection or prayer titled *"God Rebuilds Through
the Unexpected,"* noting areas needing restoration.

Self-Assessment Questions:
    I believe God can use anyone for His purposes. I
    look for God's hand even in secular events.
I receive restoration when God begins to rebuild. Devotional Prayer:

Lord, open my eyes to Your sovereign work in every place and person. Use the unexpected to restore what is broken and lead me to participate in Your rebuilding. Amen.

Chapter 5: Nebuchadnezzar and the Humbling of Nations

Main Chapter Message:
God humbles proud hearts to teach that all authority is His. Nebuchadnezzar's fall and restoration demonstrate that divine correction is intended to return rulers and nations to reverent dependence on God.

Workbook Study Guide – Chapter 5 Reflection

Chapter Summary:
Pride invites correction; God's humbling of the mighty is both a warning and a path to restoration. Nebuchadnezzar's testimony shows God's mercy in discipline and the glory of a humbled heart.

Key Scriptures:
Daniel 4:28–37; Daniel 4:34–37; Proverbs 16:18; James 4:6–10

Reflection Quotes:
- "When kings forget God, God remembers kings."
- "Humbling is not punishment alone—it is a doorway back to worship."

Reflection Questions:
1. In what ways does pride show up in your life or community?
2. How can you respond when God humbles you or someone you know?
3. What restoration looks like after humility in your context?

Group Discussion Prompts:
• Why is humility essential for leaders and nations?

• How can communities cultivate environments that encourage repentance and restoration?

Action Step / Weekly Challenge:
Practice an act of humility this week — apologize, seek reconciliation, or serve unnoticed.

Challenge Verse:
Daniel 4:37 – "He does as he pleases with the powers of heaven and the peoples of the earth. No one can hold back his hand…"

Biblical Character Connection:
Nebuchadnezzar — A proud ruler humbled and returned to praise God.

Key Quote / Takeaway:
"God humbles so we may worship."

Worship Song Suggestion:
"Humble King" – Brenton Brown / Bethel Music

Creative Response Option:
Sketch or write a short testimony of a time humility led to spiritual growth or restoration.

Self-Assessment Questions:
I welcome God's correction as an act of love.
I practice humility in my relationships and leadership.
I turn quickly to worship when convicted. Devotional Prayer:

Most High God, strip away my pride and teach me to bow. Let humility led me to worship and restoration, that Your name alone may be exalted. Amen.

Chapter 6: When God Exposes Through Elevation

Main Chapter Message:
Elevation reveals the heart. God sometimes promotes leaders so hidden motives and character are exposed— either for purification or correction. Promotion is a test; how we respond reveals whether we will be instruments of God or instruments of self.

Workbook Study Guide – Chapter 6 Reflection

Chapter Summary:
Promotion can be purification. God allows elevation to surface the true condition of hearts so that He may refine, correct, or use leaders more transparently for His purposes.

Key Scriptures:
1 Samuel 16:7; Luke 12:2–3; Matthew 23:12; Proverbs 16:18

Reflection Quotes:
- "Promotion uncovers; humility sustains."
- "God exposes what elevation hides so He might heal what pride breaks."

Reflection Questions:
1. Has success revealed something in you that needed change?
2. How do you guard your heart when honored or promoted?
3. What disciplines keep leaders pure during seasons of rise?

Group Discussion Prompts:
• How should the church hold its leaders
accountable during seasons of success?

• What spiritual practices help preserve humility
in elevated positions?

Action Step / Weekly Challenge:
This week, serve someone in your ministry or community
anonymously to practice humility in success.

Challenge Verse:
Luke 12:3 – "What you have said in the dark will be heard in the
daylight."

Biblical Character Connection:
David and Saul — Contrasting responses to elevation and exposure.

Key Quote / Takeaway:
"Elevation reveals whether your foundation is faith or fame."

Worship Song Suggestion:
"Give Me Faith" – Elevation Worship

Creative Response Option:
Journal about a time you were elevated and write what God
revealed and how you responded.

Self-Assessment Questions:
    I evaluate my motives when praised or promoted. I
    seek accountability when opportunities increase. I
    prioritize character over position. Devotional Prayer:

Father, guard my heart in seasons of honor. Let every rise be an opportunity to serve You more faithfully, not to exalt myself. Keep me humble and true to Your call. Amen.

Chapter 7: Divisive Leaders and Divided Hearts

Main Chapter Message:
Division has always been one of the enemy's most effective weapons. Yet even through divisive leaders and turbulent seasons, God reveals the true condition of our hearts. He allows division to expose loyalty, to separate light from darkness, and to call His people back to unity rooted in truth.

Workbook Study Guide – Chapter 7 Reflection

Chapter Summary:
God sometimes allows division to reveal devotion. He exposes the motives of both leaders and followers, calling His people to walk in spiritual unity, not political conformity.

Key Scriptures:
1 Corinthians 1:10–13; Matthew 12:25; John 17:21; James 3:16

Reflection Quotes:
"Division reveals what devotion hides."

"True unity is built on truth, not popularity."

Reflection Questions:
When has division revealed what was truly in your heart?
How can we guard our unity without compromising?
God's truth?
What steps can you take to promote reconciliation in your sphere of influence?

Group Discussion Prompts:
• Why do you think God allows division in the Church or government?

• How can believers model unity in times of societal conflict?

Action Step / Weekly Challenge:
Choose one relationship or group affected by division and pray intentionally for unity and understanding this week.

Challenge Verse:
Matthew 12:25 – "Every kingdom divided against itself is brought to desolation."

Biblical Character Connection:
Rehoboam – His pride divided a nation, but his story teaches the cost of ignoring wise counsel.

Key Quote / Takeaway:
"Division exposes hearts, but unity heals nations."

Worship Song Suggestion:
"Make Us One" – Jesus Culture

Creative Response Option:
Write a personal declaration titled *"My Commitment to Unity"* describing how you will pursue peace and truth in relationships.

Self-Assessment Questions:
I seek unity rooted in God's truth.
    I refuse to let offense divide my relationships. I

    pray more than I argue. Devotional Prayer:

Lord, when division surrounds me, gives me a heart of peace. Help me to walk in unity without compromising Your Word. Use me to be a bridge of reconciliation in a divided world. Amen.

Chapter 8: God's Warning Through Unlikely Messengers

Main Chapter Message:
God often sends warnings through the voices we least expect.
Whether it's a child, an enemy, or a broken soul, His message can
come wrapped in humility or imperfection. When we dismiss the
messenger, we risk ignoring Heaven's call to repent and return.

Workbook Study Guide – Chapter 8 Reflection

Chapter Summary:
God's warnings are not always delivered by the qualified but by
the obedient. His choice of unlikely messengers humbles the
proud and awakens the sleeping.

Key Scriptures:
Numbers 22:28–32; 1 Kings 13:1–5; Amos 3:7; Luke 19:40

Reflection Quotes:
"Sometimes the voice you ignore carries the warning you need."
"Heaven's alarms often sound from unlikely mouths."

Reflection Questions:
Have you ever ignored a message because you didn't like
messenger?
What prevents you from hearing God through unexpected people?

How can humility make you more receptive to God's voice?

Group Discussion Prompts:
• Discuss a time when God used someone unlikely to reveal truth to you.
• Why is spiritual discernment essential in this generation?

Action Step / Weekly Challenge:
Be intentional this week to listen with humility. Ask God to open your ears to His voice—even through unexpected people.

Challenge Verse:
Amos 3:7 – "Surely the Sovereign Lord does nothing without revealing His plan to His servants the prophets."

Biblical Character Connection:

Balaam's Donkey – A simple creature chosen by God to stop a prophet from destruction.

Key Quote / Takeaway:
"When pride deafens us, God speaks through humility."

Worship Song Suggestion:
"Speak to Me" – Kari Jobe

Creative Response Option:
Write a short paragraph or prayer titled *"Lord, Let Me Hear You"* expressing your desire to discern God's voice clearly.

Self-Assessment Questions:
    I am open to God speaking through
    anyone. I test every message by Scripture.
I respond with humility to correction.

Devotional Prayer:

Father, open my ears to hear You—even when Your voice comes through unexpected sources. Keep me humble and obedient to Your Word. Amen.

Chapter 9: The Call to Repentance Before the Return

Main Chapter Message:
Before Christ's return, God issues one urgent call: repentance. The Church must awaken from complacency, turning from compromise and returning to holiness. Repentance is not condemnation—it's restoration. It prepares the Bride for the coming Bridegroom.

Workbook Study Guide – Chapter 9 Reflection

Chapter Summary:
Repentance is Heaven's invitation to restoration. God calls His people to cleanse their hearts and realign with His will before the return of Christ.

Key Scriptures:
2 Chronicles 7:14; Acts 3:19; Revelation 2:5; Joel 2:12–13

Reflection Quotes:
"Repentance is not shame; it's a doorway to
renewal." "Before revival comes repentance."

Reflection Questions:
What areas of your life need realignment with God's will?
How does repentance lead to revival in individuals and nations?
What does true repentance look like beyond words?

Group Discussion Prompts:
• Why do we resist repentance, even knowing it brings healing?
• How can the modern Church model repentance to the world?

Action Step / Weekly Challenge:

Take time this week for honest self-examination. Confess anything God reveals and ask for a renewed spirit.

Challenge Verse:
Acts 3:19 – "Repent, then, and turn to God, so that your sins may be wiped out, that times of refreshing may come from the Lord."

Biblical Character Connection:
Jonah – Called to deliver repentance yet needed repentance himself.

Key Quote / Takeaway:
"Repentance opens the floodgates of revival."

Worship Song Suggestion:
"Refiner" – Maverick City Music

Creative Response Option:
Write a private prayer journal titled *"Lord, Renew My Heart"* and reflect on how repentance has restored you.

Self-Assessment Questions:
    I see repentance as a gift, not punishment. I
    confess and correct when God convicts me.
I long to live with a pure heart before Christ's return.

Devotional Prayer:

Lord, cleanse me from anything that separates me from You. Let repentance be my daily rhythm and holiness my desire. Prepare me for Your glorious return. Amen.

Chapter 10: God's Sovereignty in Political Shifts

Main Chapter Message:
Every election, uprising, and regime change unfolds under the eye of a sovereign God. Though nations rage and people debate, Heaven's throne remains unmoved. Political shifts do not surprise God; they serve His ultimate redemptive plan.

Workbook Study Guide – Chapter 10 Reflection

Chapter Summary:
God rules over all political transitions. Human decisions do not shake their sovereignty, but it works through them to accomplish its divine purpose.

Key Scriptures:
Daniel 2:21; Romans 13:1–2; Psalm 33:10–11; Isaiah 40:23–24

Reflection Quotes:
"The ballots of man cannot override the decrees of Heaven."
"God's sovereignty never changes with administrations."

Reflection Questions:
How can we find peace during political uncertainty? What does it mean to trust God beyond your political preference?
How can believers influence politics without idolizing power?

Group Discussion Prompts:
• Why is it important for the Church to stay focused on God's kingdom rather than earthly governments?
• How does prayer change how we view authority?

Action Step / Weekly Challenge:
Pray for your nation's leaders and seek opportunities to be a light of peace amid division.

Challenge Verse:
Psalm 22:28 – "For dominion belongs to the Lord and He rules over the nations."

Biblical Character Connection:
Joseph – Elevated to political power to preserve a nation.

Key Quote / Takeaway:
"God governs governments."

Worship Song Suggestion:
"God of the City" – Chris Tomlin

Creative Response Option:
Write a personal prayer for your nation, asking God to direct its leaders and heal division.

Self-Assessment Questions:
I trust God's sovereignty more than human authority. I pray for leaders regularly.
I respond with faith, not fear, to national changes.

Devotional Prayer:

Lord, remind me that Your throne is above every nation. Help me to trust You through every change and to be a peacemaker wherever You've placed me. Amen.

Chapter 11: Political Idolatry and Kingdom Identity

Main Chapter Message:
Many have traded the cross for a political banner. When loyalty to leaders outweighs devotion to Christ, idolatry is born. God calls His people to return to their true citizenship—the Kingdom of Heaven.

Workbook Study Guide – Chapter 11 Reflection

Chapter Summary:
True followers of Christ must not let politics define their identity. Our allegiance belongs to the King of kings, not earthly kings.

Key Scriptures:
Philippians 3:20; Matthew 6:33; Exodus 20:3; 1 John 5:21

Reflection Quotes:
- "Idolatry begins where identity ends."
- "The Church must wave the banner of the cross, not the colors of division."

Reflection Questions:
1. Have you ever placed more trust in political systems than in God?
2. How can believers balance civic responsibility and spiritual loyalty?
3. What does Kingdom identity mean to you personally?

Group Discussion Prompts:
• What are modern forms of political idolatry?
• How can the Church maintain a prophetic

voice without becoming partisan?

Action Step / Weekly Challenge:
Examine your conversations and media habits. Replace one political discussion with a Christ- centered one this week.

Challenge Verse:
Philippians 3:20 – "Our citizenship is in heaven."

Biblical Character Connection:
Daniel – A faithful servant who never compromised his allegiance to God while serving in government.

Key Quote / Takeaway:
"When Christ defines you, politics can't divide you."

Worship Song Suggestion:
"Jesus at the Center" – Israel & New Breed

Creative Response Option:
Write a reflection titled *"My True Allegiance"* affirming your loyalty to Christ's Kingdom.

Self-Assessment Questions:
I keep Christ above all political opinions. I influence culture without idolizing leaders.
My conversations reflect Heaven's priorities.

Devotional Prayer:

King Jesus, forgive me when I have placed anything before You. Restore my heart to honor You alone as Lord. Make my life a reflection of Your Kingdom. Amen.

Chapter 12: The Church's Role in the Last Days

Main Chapter Message:
The Church was born for such a time as this. In the last days, God is raising a remnant that stands for truth, loves without fear, and prepares the world for Christ's return. The Church is not a building but a battalion of believers advancing light in darkness.

Workbook Study Guide – Chapter 12 Reflection

Chapter Summary:
The end-time Church is called to holiness, boldness, and compassion. It must awaken from slumber and carry the gospel to the ends of the earth.

Key Scriptures:

Matthew 24:14; Acts 2:17–21; Revelation 3:15–20; Ephesians 5:25–27

Reflection Quotes:
- "The Church's silence gives darkness permission to speak."
- "Revival begins when the Church remembers who she is."

Reflection Questions:

1. What distractions keep the Church from fulfilling its mission?
2. How can believers live as light in a dark world?
3. In what ways is God calling you to take a stand in this generation?

Group Discussion Prompts:

• What does it mean to be a "last-days Church"?
• How can we balance truth and grace in a hostile culture?

Action Step / Weekly Challenge:
Commit to sharing your testimony or inviting someone to church this week.

Challenge Verse:
Matthew 24:14 – "And this gospel of the kingdom will be preached in the whole world as a testimony to all nations, and then the end will come."

Biblical Character Connection:
Esther – Chosen and positioned for a crucial moment in history.

Key Quote/Takeaway:
"The last day's Church must be both watchful and working."

Worship Song Suggestion:
"Build Your Church" – Elevation Worship

Creative Response Option:
Create a short vision for how you can personally help strengthen the Church in your community.

Self-Assessment Questions:
 I am active in building God's Kingdom. I
 live ready for Christ's return.
I support and strengthen my local church.

Devotional Prayer:
Lord, awaken Your Church. Revive Your people and prepare us for Your coming. Let us shine with love, truth, and power until the day You return. Amen.

Chapter 13: God's Judgment and Mercy in the Last

Days

Main Chapter Message:
God's judgment is not meant to destroy but to draw His people back to righteousness. Even as He shakes the earth, His mercy offers redemption. In these last days, both judgment and mercy reveal His holiness and His heart.

Workbook Study Guide – Chapter 13 Reflection

Chapter Summary:
Judgment and mercy walk hand in hand in God's plan. His correction leads to repentance, and His mercy gives us another chance to return to Him.

Key Scriptures:
Habakkuk 3:2; Joel 2:12–13; Romans 2:4–6;
Revelation 14:6–7

Reflection Quotes:
- "God's judgment without mercy would crush us; His mercy without judgment would corrupt us."
- "Every warning is an invitation to grace."

Reflection Questions:

1. How have you experienced both God's discipline and His mercy in your life?
2. Why is understanding God's holiness essential to receiving His mercy?

3. What should be the Church's response to divine judgment in the world today?

Group Discussion Prompts:
- How can we share the truth about judgment while still reflecting love?
- What happens when mercy is preached without repentance?

Action Step / Weekly Challenge:
Ask God to search your heart this week and reveal any area where He is calling you to repentance or renewal.

Challenge Verse:
Habakkuk 3:2 – "In wrath remember mercy."

Biblical Character Connection:
Noah – Found grace in a generation facing judgment.

Key Quote / Takeaway:
"Mercy opens the door that judgment knocks on."

Worship Song Suggestion:
"Mercy" – Elevation Worship

Creative Response Option:
Write a brief reflection titled *"Mercy in the Midst of Judgment"* describing how you've seen God's grace even in hard seasons.

Self-Assessment Questions:
I understand that correction is love in action. I repent quickly when convicted.
I extend mercy to others as God has shown me mercy.

Devotional Prayer:

Father, thank You for mercy that meets me even in Your correction. Help me to turn from anything that grieves Your Spirit and walk humbly in Your grace. Amen.

Chapter 14: Preparing for Christ's Return – Living with Eternity in View

Main Chapter Message:

Every believer must live with eternity in focus. Christ's return is not a myth or metaphor—it is a coming reality. This chapter challenges us to live with urgency, purity, and purpose, making our days count for His Kingdom.

Workbook Study Guide – Chapter 14 Reflection

Chapter Summary:
Living with eternity in view means aligning every choice, thought, and dream with the reality of Christ's soon return.

Key Scriptures:
Matthew 24:42–44; 2 Peter 3:10–14; 1
Thessalonians 5:1–6; Revelation 22:12

Reflection Quotes:
- "Heaven is not a destination for the distant future—it's the motivation for daily living."
- "Those who await His coming live differently."

Reflection Questions:
1. What does living with eternity in view look like in your life right now?
2. How can we prepare our hearts for Christ's return?
3. Why does focusing on eternity bring peace in a troubled world?

Group Discussion Prompts:

• How can believers encourage one another in expectation of Christ's return?
• What does "watch and pray" mean for us today?

Action Step / Weekly Challenge:
Spend time each morning this week meditating on heaven and praying, "Lord, make me ready."

Challenge Verse:
Revelation 22:12 – "Behold, I am coming soon; my reward is with me."

Biblical Character Connection:
The Wise Virgins – Prepared and watchful for the Bridegroom.

Key Quote / Takeaway:
"Eternal focus produces earthly faithfulness."

Worship Song Suggestion:
"Even So Come" – Passion Worship

Creative Response Option:
Create a "Heaven Journal" and write how you envision living faithfully until Christ's return.

Self-Assessment Questions:
    I live daily as if Christ could return
    today. I seek purity and readiness.
I long more for Heaven than for the world.

Devotional Prayer:

Lord Jesus, awaken my heart to eternity. Help me to live ready, watchful, and faithful until You return.

Amen.

Chapter 15: God's Foolishness is Wiser Than Men

Main Chapter Message:
The wisdom of God often appears foolish to the world. From the cross to the resurrection, His ways defy human understanding. This chapter reveals that true wisdom comes from surrender, not intellect, and that God's foolishness is our greatest hope.

Workbook Study Guide – Chapter 15 Reflection

Chapter Summary:
What the world calls foolish, Heaven calls divine wisdom. God's ways are higher, and His plans often contradict human logic to display His glory.

Key Scriptures:
1 Corinthians 1:18–25; Isaiah 55:8–9; Proverbs 3:5– 6; Romans 11:33

Reflection Quotes:
- "God's foolishness confounds the proud but comforts the humble."
- "The cross was Heaven's paradox—the place where wisdom and weakness met."

Reflection Questions:
1. When has obedience to God seemed foolish to others but proved wise in the end?
2. How can believers walk confidently in God's wisdom despite criticism?
3. What does this truth teach us about humility before God?

Group Discussion Prompts:

• Why does God delight in using the weak and simple to reveal His power?
• How can we discern between human reasoning and divine wisdom?

Action Step / Weekly Challenge:
This week, choose to obey one instruction from God even if it doesn't make sense to others.

Challenge Verse:
1 Corinthians 1:25 – "For the foolishness of God is wiser than men, and the weakness of God is stronger than men."

Biblical Character Connection:
Gideon – His small army became God's victory strategy.

Key Quote / Takeaway:
"What confuses man often confirms God."

Worship Song Suggestion:
"Trust In You" – Lauren Daigle

Creative Response Option:
Draw or write a reflection titled *"God's Wisdom in My Weakness."*

Self-Assessment Questions:
I trust God's plan even when I don't understand it. I see weakness as an opportunity for God's strength. I value divine wisdom over human approval.

Devotional Prayer:

Father, thank You for showing Your wisdom through what the world calls foolish. Teach me to trust You completely and follow wherever You lead. Amen.

Chapter 16: Called, Commissioned, and Sent

Main Chapter Message:
Every believer has a divine assignment. God calls us, equips us, and sends us into a world in need of light. This chapter reminds us that our calling isn't about being perfectionists about obedience to the One who sends.

Workbook Study Guide – Chapter 16 Reflection

Chapter Summary:
God doesn't just call the qualified; He qualifies the called. When we respond to His commission, He supplies everything needed to fulfill His mission.

Key Scriptures:
Matthew 28:19–20; Isaiah 6:8; Jeremiah 1:4–10; John 20:21

Reflection Quotes:
- "Your call is not a suggestion—it's a command with a promise."
- "When God calls, obedience becomes the evidence of faith."

Reflection Questions:
1. What has God called you to do in this season?
2. How can you overcome fear or inadequacy in fulfilling your calling?
3. What happens when we delay obedience?

Group Discussion Prompts:
- How can the Church better equip believers to live out their callings?
- What role does prayer play in staying faithful to your commission?

Action Step / Weekly Challenge:
Take one practical step toward your calling this week—make a phone call, write a plan, or serve in a new area.

Challenge Verse:
Isaiah 6:8 – "Here am I; send me."

Biblical Character Connection:
Moses – Called despite weakness, sent with divine authority.

Key Quote / Takeaway:
"God never sends you where His grace won't sustain you."

Worship Song Suggestion:
"Send Me" – Jenn Johnson

Creative Response Option:
Write a short letter to God expressing your willingness to be used for His purpose.

Self-Assessment Questions:
    I recognize God's call on my
    life. I obey even when uncertain.
I trust God to equip what He commands. Devotional Prayer:

Lord, thank You for calling me. Give me courage to go where You send and faith to trust Your plan. Amen.

Chapter 17: God's Warning Through Leadership – A Wake-Up Call from Heaven

Main Chapter Message:
God often uses leadership—both good and bad—to reveal spiritual conditions in the land. When leaders rise or fall, Heaven sends a wake-up call for repentance and discernment. This chapter urges believers to watch, pray, and respond rightly to divine warnings.

Workbook Study Guide – Chapter 17 Reflection

Chapter Summary:
Leadership shifts often carry prophetic meaning. God uses authority as a mirror to reflect the heart of a nation and the readiness of His people.

Key Scriptures:
Daniel 4:17; Proverbs 29:2; Hosea 8:4; Isaiah 3:4–5

Reflection Quotes:
- "When God changes leadership, He's changing direction."
- "Leaders reveal the spiritual climate of the people they govern."

Reflection Questions:
1. How can believers discern God's message during leadership changes?
2. What is our responsibility when God exposes corruption or pride in leaders?
3. How does prayer influence political or spiritual renewal?

Group Discussion Prompts:

• What biblical examples show God's hand in leadership transitions?
• How can we intercede rather than criticize in seasons of political turmoil?

Action Step / Weekly Challenge:
Dedicate time this week to pray for local and national leaders to hear and obey God's voice.

Challenge Verse:
Proverbs 21:1 – "The king's heart is in the hand of the Lord."

Biblical Character Connection:
Saul and David – A story of transition, testing, and God's timing.

Key Quote / Takeaway:
"When leaders fall, it's a signal—not the end."

Worship Song Suggestion:
"God of This City" – Chris Tomlin

Creative Response Option:
Write a short reflection titled *"When God Sends Warnings"* describing a time He awakened your discernment through leadership shifts.

Self-Assessment Questions:
    I seek God's perspective on leadership
    changes. I pray for my leaders regularly.
I remain humble when God exposes hidden things.

Devotional Prayer:

Father, give me discernment to recognize Your hand in leadership.
Help me to pray faithfully and walk humbly as You guide nations.
and hearts.
Amen.

Chapter 18: Reclaiming True Discipleship in a World Turned Upside Down

Main Chapter Message:
Modern Christianity often celebrates membership more than discipleship. Yet Jesus calls His followers to deny themselves, take up the cross, and follow Him wholeheartedly. This chapter invites believers to return to authentic discipleship—rooted in obedience, love, and sacrifice.

Workbook Study Guide – Chapter 18 Reflection

Chapter Summary:
True discipleship is not about attendance but allegiance. Following Christ means surrendering comfort for conviction and choosing obedience over convenience.

Key Scriptures:
Luke 9:23; Matthew 28:19–20; John 8:31–32; James 1:22

Reflection Quotes:
- "Discipleship is costly, but so is disobedience."
- "Following Christ means saying 'yes' even when the crowd says 'no.'"

Reflection Questions:
1. What's the difference between being a believer and a disciple?
2. How does true discipleship require daily surrender?
3. What hinders modern Christians from living as disciples?

Group Discussion Prompts:
- Why is the Church called to make disciples, not just converts?
- What does it mean to "count the cost" today?

Action Step / Weekly Challenge:
Commit to one new spiritual discipline this week— consistent prayer, fasting, or deeper Bible study.

Challenge Verse:
Luke 9:23 – "If anyone would come after Me, let him deny himself and take up his cross daily and follow Me."

Biblical Character Connection:
Peter – A disciple restored and refined through failure.

Key Quote / Takeaway:
"Discipleship is not a label—it's a lifestyle."

Worship Song Suggestion:
"Follow You Anywhere" – Passion

Creative Response Option:
Write a declaration titled *"My Discipleship Commitment"* listing three ways you will intentionally follow Christ more closely.

Self-Assessment Questions:
I live out my faith daily.
I pursue growth, not comfort.
I follow Jesus even when it costs me.

Devotional Prayer:

Jesus, make me a true disciple. Teach me to follow You in word and deed and help me to live out Your truth boldly in a confused world. Amen.

Main Chapter Message:

In every generation, God raises unexpected voices— young, passionate, and unpolished—to proclaim His truth. The rising generation is not to be dismissed but discipled. Their boldness may seem reckless to some, but it carries the spark of revival that the Church desperately needs.

Workbook Study Guide – Chapter 19 Reflection Chapter Summary:

God is awakening a new generation to carry His Word with purity and power. Though often misunderstood, these young messengers are vessels of divine purpose.

Key Scriptures:

1 Samuel 3:1–10; Joel 2:28–29; Acts 2:17; Jeremiah 1:6–8

Reflection Quotes:
- "God often hides His next move in the mouths of the young."
- "The next revival will not come from platforms but from pure hearts."

Reflection Questions:
1. How can the Church empower the next generation without controlling them?
2. What does it mean to disciple rather than dismiss young believers?
3. Have you ever seen God use someone younger or less experienced to teach you something?

Group Discussion Prompts:

• Why does God often choose youth to lead movements of change?
• What are some practical ways older generations can support younger ones in ministry?

Action Step / Weekly Challenge:
Encourage or mentor a young believer this week—pray with them or affirm their spiritual gifts.

Challenge Verse:
1 Timothy 4:12 – "Let no one despise your youth, but set the believers an example…"

Biblical Character Connection:
Samuel – A child who heard God's voice when seasoned priests could not.

Key Quote / Takeaway:
"God's next move may come from a voice you least expect."

Worship Song Suggestion:
"Fresh Wind" – Hillsong Worship

Creative Response Option:
Write a prayer titled *"Revive a Generation"* asking God to awaken young hearts for His glory.

Self-Assessment Questions:
I honor and invest in the next generation.
I listen when God speaks through unlikely people. I pray for revival among youth and young adults.

Devotional Prayer:

Lord, thank You for raising a new generation to carry Your truth. Give me eyes to see their purpose and a heart to support their calling. Let revival flow through every age. Amen.

Chapter 20: When Leaders Fail and Lampstands Fall

Main Chapter Message:
Spiritual and moral failures among leaders can shake faith communities—but they also reveal God's call for holiness and accountability. When a lampstand falls, God's light still shines through those who remain faithful. This chapter reminds us that failure is a warning, not the end.

Workbook Study Guide – Chapter 20 Reflection

Chapter Summary:
When leaders stumble, it's not to destroy the Church but to purify it. God's glory cannot dwell where compromise reigns. His exposure is both justice and mercy.

Key Scriptures:
Revelation 2:5; Luke 12:2–3; 1 Peter 4:17; Galatians 6:1

Reflection Quotes:
- "Exposure is not cruelty—it's God's mercy calling His Church back to holiness."
- "Even when the lampstand falls, the Light of the world remains."

Reflection Questions:
1. How should believers respond when a leader falls from grace?
2. What safeguards can we put in place to maintain integrity in leadership?
3. How can the Church rebuild trust after failure?

Group Discussion Prompts:
• Why does God sometimes expose sin publicly?
• How can humility and accountability preserve the Church's witness?

Action Step / Weekly Challenge:
Pray for a pastor, leader, or ministry this week. Ask God to strengthen them with integrity and grace.

Challenge Verse:
1 Peter 4:17 – "For it is time for judgment to begin with the household of God."

Biblical Character Connection:
King Saul – A leader whose pride led to his downfall.

Key Quote / Takeaway:
"Exposure purifies what excuses have polluted."

Worship Song Suggestion:
"Clean Hands" – Chris Tomlin

Creative Response Option:
Journal about a time God used failure—your own or another's—to bring healing or humility.

Self-Assessment Questions:
I pray for my leaders faithfully.
I value integrity more than influence.
I respond to others' failures with grace and truth.

Devotional Prayer:

Father, keep me humble and pure in heart. Let me be a vessel that reflects Your holiness. When others fall, teach me to restore with compassion and courage. Amen.

Chapter 21: Screens and Shadows – When the Enemy Enters Through Devices

Main Chapter Message:
Technology is a powerful tool—but also a doorway. The enemy uses screens to sow distraction, addiction, and deception. This chapter calls believers to guard their hearts, redeem their time, and use technology for God's glory rather than spiritual decline.

Workbook Study Guide – Chapter 21 Reflection

Chapter Summary:
Every screen carries influence. We must choose whether it shapes us into the image of Christ or the image of the world.

Key Scriptures:
Psalm 101:3; Ephesians 5:15–16; Matthew 6:22–23; Romans 12:2

Reflection Quotes:
- "Screens can be windows of light—or mirrors of temptation."
- "What we scroll shapes what we see."

Reflection Questions:
1. How has technology affected your spiritual focus or peace?
2. What steps can you take to guard your mind and eyes daily?
3. How can you use social media or media platforms for God's purposes?

Group Discussion Prompts:
• How can believers set healthy boundaries with technology?

• What are ways to replace screen time with soul time?

Action Step / Weekly Challenge:
Take one "digital Sabbath" this week—unplug from screens and spend intentional time with God.

Challenge Verse:
Psalm 101:3 – "I will set no wicked thing before mine eyes."

Biblical Character Connection:
David – Learned the importance of guarding his eyes and heart.

Key Quote / Takeaway:
"What you consume eventually consumes you."

Worship Song Suggestion:
"Turn Your Eyes Upon Jesus" – Helen H. Lemmel

Creative Response Option:
Write a personal pledge titled *"Eyes for Eternity"* outlining your commitment to purity and focus.

Self-Assessment Questions:
      I monitor what enters through my eyes and
      ears. I use technology to glorify God.
I prioritize presence over entertainment.

Devotional Prayer:

Lord, cleanse my eyes and mind from every distraction. Help me to use technology wisely and guard my soul from the enemy's devices. Amen.

Chapter 22: Recognizing the People God Sends Into Our Lives

Main Chapter Message:
God places people in our lives for a reason—some to bless, some to refine, and some to teach us discernment. Recognizing divine connections is key to walking in wisdom and avoiding distractions disguised as opportunities.

Workbook Study Guide – Chapter 22 Reflection

Chapter Summary:
Every relationship has a purpose. God ordains some for partnership, others for pruning, and all for spiritual growth.

Key Scriptures:
Proverbs 27:17; Ruth 1:16–17; 1 Samuel 18:1–4; Ecclesiastes 4:9–10

Reflection Quotes:
- "Not everyone who enters your life is sent by God, but everyone can be used by Him."
- "Discernment reveals divine design in human connections."

Reflection Questions:
1. Who has God used in your life to shape your faith?
2. How do you discern between a God-sent connection and a distraction?
3. What relationships require boundaries or deeper prayer?

Group Discussion Prompts:
• What are the signs of a divine connection versus a draining one?
• How can believers honor every person God allows into their lives?

Action Step / Weekly Challenge:
Pray over your current relationships and ask God to strengthen divine connections and remove unhealthy ones.

Challenge Verse:
Proverbs 27:17 – "As iron sharpens iron, so one person sharpens another."

Biblical Character Connection:
Ruth and Naomi – A bond of divine destiny that changed generations.

Key Quote / Takeaway:
"Discernment in relationships preserves destiny."

Worship Song Suggestion:
"For Every Mountain" – Kurt Carr

Creative Response Option:
Make a "Relationship Map" showing people who have impacted your walk with God and thank Him for each.

Self-Assessment Questions:
  I pray for wisdom in relationships. I
  recognize divine connections.
I honor those God places in my path. Devotional Prayer:

Lord, open my eyes to see the people You've placed in my life for Your purpose. Help me to walk in love, wisdom, and gratitude for every divine connection.
Amen.

Chapter 23: When God Speaks Through the Foolish —Listen Beyond the Noise

Main Chapter Message:
Throughout history, God has used unlikely voices to wake His people—prophets, children, and even enemies. These days, He is sounding the alarm again. The sleeping Church must awaken to His voice, repent, and return before the trumpet sounds from Heaven.

Workbook Study Guide – Chapter 23 Reflection

Chapter Summary:
God uses what the world considers foolish to awaken His people. His prophetic alarm shakes the comfort zone to prepare hearts for revival and repentance.

Key Scriptures:
Ezekiel 33:6–7; Amos 3:7–8; Romans 10:14–15; Revelation 3:1–3

Reflection Quotes:
- "When the wise stay silent, God raises the foolish to speak."
- "Prophetic alarms are Heaven's mercy, not man's madness."

Reflection Questions:
1. How can believers discern when God is sending a warning?
2. Why does God use unlikely messengers to reach His people?
3. What alarms are God sounding in our nation or Church today?

Group Discussion Prompts:
• What role does the prophetic voice play in the modern Church?
• How can we respond to warnings without fear but with faith?

Action Step / Weekly Challenge:
Spend time in prayer asking God to reveal what He is saying to the Church in this hour and how you can respond.

Challenge Verse:
Ezekiel 33:7 – "Son of man, I have made you a watchman for the people of Israel."

Biblical Character Connection:
Jonah – The reluctant prophet who became a warning and a witness of mercy.

Key Quote / Takeaway:
"God shouts to wake what slumber has silenced."

Worship Song Suggestion:
"Awake My Soul" – Hillsong Worship

Creative Response Option:
Write a reflection titled *"The Alarm of Heaven"* describing how God has called you to spiritual awareness.

Self-Assessment Questions:
    I respond when God warns me. I
    stay spiritually alert and prayerful.
I help awaken others through truth and love.

Devotional Prayer:

Father, awaken Your people. Help me to hear Your alarms and respond with obedience. Let me be a voice that points others back to You before the day of Your return. Amen.

Chapter 24: When God Speaks Through the Foolish

— Israel, the Sleeping Church, and the Sound of Prophetic Alarm

Main Chapter Message:
God has always used what the world considers foolish to awaken His people. From prophets rejected in their time to modern voices ignored by the complacent, His message remains the same: *Wake up, Church!* Before Christ's return, Israel and the global Church must hear the prophetic alarm and prepare for His glory.

Workbook Study Guide – Chapter 24 Reflection

Chapter Summary:
Throughout Scripture, God's warnings come.
through unexpected messengers. The same is true today. Israel's history mirrors the Church's condition—blessed yet often asleep. God is calling His people to spiritual alertness before the trumpet sounds.

Key Scriptures:
Ezekiel 33:6–7; Amos 3:7–8; Joel 2:1; Revelation 3:1–3; Romans 11:25–26

Reflection Quotes:
- "When the Church sleeps, the enemy sows."
- "Prophetic warnings are invitations to repentance, not reasons for fear."

Reflection Questions:
1. How has God used unexpected people to get your attention?

2. Why does the Church struggle to discern or receive prophetic corrections?
3. What are the signs that a believer or community has fallen spiritually asleep?

Group Discussion Prompts:
• How do we know when God is sounding a prophetic alarm to His people?
• What practical ways can we stay spiritually alert and discerning in this generation?

Action Step / Weekly Challenge:
Dedicate specific time this week to pray for the awakening of the global Church and for discernment in hearing God's voice.

Challenge Verse:
Ephesians 5:14 – "Wake up, sleeper, rise from the dead, and Christ will shine on you."

Biblical Character Connection:
Jonah – A reluctant messenger whose warning led to a nation's repentance.

Key Quote / Takeaway:
"When the foolish speak what Heaven declares, the wise must listen."

Worship Song Suggestion:
"Awake My Soul" – Hillsong Worship

Creative Response Option:
Write a journal entry titled *"If God Is Speaking, Am I Listening?"* Reflect on any current warnings or spiritual nudges He has placed in your heart.

Self-Assessment Questions:

    I respond quickly when God convicts me. I

    stay alert to the Holy Spirit's leading. I

    help others awaken to truth with love.

Devotional Prayer:

Lord, awaken me. Let Your voice shakes me out of complacency and stir a holy fire within. May Your Church rise with purity and boldness as we prepare for Your return. Amen.

Your sacrifice lightly. Let my life reflect the power of redemption and the love that conquered all. Amen.

Chapter 25: The Cross Was Enough – A Message to Every Nation, Religion, and Heart

Main Chapter Message:
The cross of Jesus Christ is the center of redemption and the power of God revealed to the world. No system, religion, or nation can add to what Christ finished at Calvary. His sacrifice is the eternal answer to sin, division, and every human attempt at self-salvation.

Workbook Study Guide – Chapter 25 Reflection

Chapter Summary:
Every generation must return to the simplicity of the cross. It is not a symbol of weakness, but the victory of God's love and justice. The blood of Christ tears down walls of separation and unites all people under one banner — *the banner of the Lamb.*

Key Scriptures:
John 3:16–17; 1 Corinthians 1:18; Colossians 2:14– 15; Galatians 6:14; Romans 5:8

Reflection Quotes:
- "The cross is not a monument to death, but a gateway to eternal life."
- "Religion strives to earn what grace has already given."

Reflection Questions:
1. What does "the cross was enough" mean to you personally?
2. Why is it important to keep the message of the cross central in every sermon, song, and mission?

3. How does the power of the cross-break barriers between nations, races, and denominations?

Group Discussion Prompts:
• How does the Church sometimes complicate or dilute the simple message of the cross?
• What happens when believers focus more on religious identity than on Christ's sacrifice?

Action Step / Weekly Challenge:
Share the message of the cross with at least one person this week. — whether through your testimony, an act of kindness, or a written message of encouragement.

Challenge Verse:
1 Corinthians 1:18 – "For the message of the cross is foolishness to those who are perishing, but to us who are being saved it is the power of God."

Biblical Character Connection:
The Thief on the Cross – A sinner saved in the final hour by simple faith in Jesus.

Key Quote / Takeaway:
"What Christ finished at Calvary cannot be improved, only received."

Worship Song Suggestion:
"The Old Rugged Cross" – Traditional Hymn (Alan Jackson / Gaither Version)

Creative Response Option:
Write a reflection titled *"The Cross and Me"* describing how Christ's sacrifice has changed your identity and purpose.

Self-Assessment Questions:

I rest in Christ's finished work, not my own
performance. I share the message of the cross boldly.
I remember daily that grace is greater than work.

Devotional Prayer:

Jesus, thank You for the cross. Help me to live in awe of Your sacrifice and to carry this message wherever I go. May my words and actions always point back to the power of Your blood. Amen.

Chapter 26: Sounding the Alarm – Preparing for Christ's Return

Main Chapter Message:
The final trumpet is nearby. God's people are called to awaken, warn, and prepare others for the soon return of Jesus Christ. This chapter reminds us that sounding the alarm is not fear-based—it's love in action for a world asleep to eternity.

Workbook Study Guide – Chapter 25 Reflection

Chapter Summary:
Heaven's alarm is sounding, calling the Church to purity, prayer, and proclamation. Time is short, and the message is urgent: *Prepare the way of the Lord!*

Key Scriptures:
Joel 2:1; Matthew 24:42–44; Romans 13:11–12; Revelation 16:15

Reflection Quotes:
- "The alarm of God's mercy always rings before His judgment."
- "To stay silent when eternity is at stake is the greatest unkindness."

Reflection Questions:
1. What does it mean to "sound the alarm" in your sphere of influence?
2. How can urgency coexist with peace in a believer's heart?
3. What practical steps can the Church take to prepare for Christ's return?

Group Discussion Prompts:
- Why do many Christians avoid talking about Christ's return?
- How can the message of the end of times bring hope rather than fear?

Action Step / Weekly Challenge:
Share one conversation of hope about Christ's return with a friend, coworker, or family member.

Challenge Verse:
Romans 13:11 – "The hour has already come for you to wake up from your slumber."

Biblical Character Connection:
John the Baptist – A voice crying in the wilderness, preparing the way for the Lord.

Key Quote / Takeaway:
"Warning is mercy in motion."

Worship Song Suggestion:
"People Get Ready, Jesus Is Coming" – Crystal Lewis

Creative Response Option:
Create a short written or spoken message titled *"If He Returned Today"* and reflect on readiness.

Self-Assessment Questions:
I live with spiritual urgency.
I share the message of Christ's return.
I help awaken others through prayer and love.

Devotional Prayer:

Lord, make me a faithful watchman. Help me to sound Your alarm with courage and compassion. Keep my heart pure and my lamp burning brightly until You come. Amen.

Chapter 27: When Heaven Shocks and Hell Surprises

Main Chapter Message:
Heaven's justice and hell's reality are not myths—they are divine truths. This chapter reveals how God's justice can shock the proud while His grace surprises the humble. Hell is real, but so is redemption. Heaven's gates are open to those who surrender while there's still time.

Workbook Study Guide – Chapter 26 Reflection

Chapter Summary:
Heaven and hell are eternal realities that demand our attention. God's mercy delays judgment, but it never denies truth. The gospel is both a warning and a rescue.

Key Scriptures:
Luke 16:19–31; Matthew 25:31–46; Revelation 20:11– 15; John 14:1–3

Reflection Quotes:
"Heaven will shock many who thought they wouldn't make it; hell will surprise many who thought they would." "Grace is free—but never cheap."

Reflection Questions:
How does understanding eternity change the way you live daily? What does this chapter teach about the balance of grace and accountability? How can we lovingly warn others about eternal realities?

Group Discussion Prompts:
• Why does modern culture reject the idea of hell?

• What does the reality of heaven inspire in your heart?

Action Step / Weekly Challenge:
Meditate on eternity each morning this week. Ask God to align your priorities with eternal purpose.

Challenge Verse:
Matthew 25:46 – "Then they will go away to eternal punishment, but the righteous to eternal life."

Biblical Character Connection:
The Rich Man and Lazarus – A contrast between worldly comfort and eternal consequence.

Key Quote / Takeaway:
"Eternity is too long to live unprepared."

Worship Song Suggestion:
"I Can Only Imagine" – MercyMe

Creative Response Option:
Write a reflection titled *"Heaven's Hope and Hell's Warning."*

Self-Assessment Questions:
I am aware of eternal realities.
   I value souls more than possessions.
   I share the gospel with compassion.

Devotional Prayer:

Father, thank You for Heaven's hope and the warning of Your justice. Help me to live ready and to lead others toward eternal life through Jesus Christ. Amen.

When God Uses the Foolish — A Final Call to Faith and Fire

Main Chapter Message:

The theme of God's wisdom through foolishness reaches its climax here: He is still using ordinary, imperfect, and underestimated people to accomplish extraordinary purposes. This final chapter is a call to surrender, courage, and revival before Christ's return.

Workbook Study Guide – Chapter 27 Reflection

Chapter Summary:
God's wisdom confounds the proud and uplifts the humble. The foolish things of this world still carry Heaven's fire, awakening nations to repentance and faith.

Key Scriptures:
1 Corinthians 1:27–29; Acts 4:13; Zechariah 4:6; James 2:5

Reflection Quotes:
- "The world calls them foolish; Heaven calls them chosen."
- "Weakness in God's hands becomes a weapon of revival."

Reflection Questions:
1. What "foolish" thing has God called you to do that requires faith?
2. How can humility position you for divine power?
3. What does it mean to be a vessel God can use in these last days?

Group Discussion Prompts:
- Why does God choose ordinary people to carry extraordinary messages?
- How can the Church embrace divine foolishness in a prideful world?

Action Step / Weekly Challenge:
Say "yes" to one act of obedience that seems small or strange, but that God has placed on your heart.

Challenge Verse:
1 Corinthians 1:27 – "But God chose the foolish things of the world to shame the wise."

Biblical Character Connection:
Gideon – The least in his family yet chosen to lead with 300 men and great faith.

Key Quote / Takeaway:
"When you yield your weakness, God releases His wisdom."

Worship Song Suggestion:
"Spirit Lead Me" – Influence Music & Michael Ketterer

Creative Response Option:
Write a declaration titled *"Use Me, Lord"* as a personal dedication to serve God's purpose fully.

Self-Assessment Questions:
> I see my weakness as an invitation for God's power. I am willing to be used even when misunderstood. I walk in obedience, not fear.

Devotional Prayer:

Lord, I surrender my pride, my plans, and my limitations. Use me, even in my weakness, to display Your glory. Let my life be a living testimony that confuses the wise and glorifies the King. Amen.

www.ingramcontent.com/pod-product-compliance
Lightning Source LLC
Chambersburg PA
CBHW051131120626
46547CB00012B/764